The Wars Between Greeks and Carthaginians

About the Author

Sotirios F. Drokalos holds three Master's degrees, in International Relations, Military History, and International Anti-terrorism, from the University of Bologna and the Niccolò Cusano University of Rome. He is the author of several books and articles published in Italian, Greek and English, including contributions to peer-reviewed journals such as the British Journal for Military History.

See more at www.drokalos.com

The Wars Between Greeks and Carthaginians

Sotirios F. Drokalos

Pen & Sword
MILITARY

First published in Great Britain in 2025 by
Pen & Sword Military
An imprint of Pen & Sword Books Limited
Yorkshire – Philadelphia

Copyright © Sotirios F. Drokalos 2025

ISBN 978 1 03611 640 8

The right of Sotirios F. Drokalos to be identified as
Author of this Work has been asserted by him in accordance
with the Copyright, Designs and Patents Act 1988.

A CIP catalogue record for this book is
available from the British Library.

All rights reserved. No part of this book may be reproduced,
transmitted, downloaded, decompiled or reverse engineered in
any form or by any means, electronic or mechanical including
photocopying, recording or by any information storage and retrieval
system, without permission from the Publisher in writing. No part of
this book may be used or reproduced in any manner for the purpose
of training artificial intelligence technologies or systems.

Typeset by Mac Style
Printed in the UK by CPI Group (UK) Ltd, Croydon, CR0 4YY.

The Publisher's authorised representative in the EU for product
safety is Authorised Rep Compliance Ltd., Ground Floor,
71 Lower Baggot Street, Dublin D02 P593, Ireland.
www.arccompliance.com

For a complete list of Pen & Sword titles please contact

PEN & SWORD BOOKS LIMITED
47 Church Street, Barnsley, South Yorkshire, S70 2AS, England
E-mail: enquiries@pen-and-sword.co.uk
Website: www.pen-and-sword.co.uk
or
PEN AND SWORD BOOKS
1950 Lawrence Road, Havertown, PA 19083, USA
E-mail: uspen-and-sword@casematepublishers.com
Website: www.penandswordbooks.com

Dedication

This book is dedicated to my wonderful kittens, who make everything more beautiful (and fierce!). Those who have been with me since I was still writing the book's initial Greek version in 2017: Asproula, Meloukos, Mavroukos, Zina and Clio. Those whom we lost along the way: Melis and Julietta. And those who joined the family while I was writing this new English version: Riko and Tiko.

Contents

List of Illustrations	viii
Maps	ix
Preface	xiii
Introduction	xv
Chapter 1 The Phoenician Colonisation and the Rise of Carthage	1
Chapter 2 The Greek Colonisation and the First Conflicts	11
Chapter 3 The Rise of Syracuse and the Battle of Himera	24
Chapter 4 The Second Major Carthaginian Attack in Sicily	37
Chapter 5 Dionysius I of Syracuse against Carthage	61
Chapter 6 Liberator Timoleon and the Battle of the Crimissus	91
Chapter 7 Agathocles and the Greek Attack on Carthage	103
Chapter 8 The Campaign of Pyrrhus	131
Chapter 9 The Rise of Rome	141
Chapter 10 Hannibal and the Greeks	148
Epilogue	164
Notes	167
Bibliography	179
Index	185

List of Illustrations

1. Relief depiction of what is thought to be an ancient Phoenician-Carthaginian ship from a sarcophagus of the second century CE. (*World History Encyclopedia; Wikimedia Commons*)
2. Ceramic representing the Phoenician deity Tanit, found in a necropolis of Ebusus, present-day Ibiza, fifth–third century BC. (*Archaeological Museum of Catalonia, Barcelona*)
3. Carthaginian amulets made of glass, fourth-third century BCE. (*National Archaeological Museum, Cagliari*)
4. Odysseus and the Sirens, on an Attic red-figure vase, made about 480–470 BCE.
5. Scene from an ancient Greek red-figure vase, 490–480 BCE. (*Museum of Fine Arts, Boston*)
6. The temple of Zeus in Cyrene (Libya) as it is today. (*Adobe Stock*)
7. Corinthian bronze helmet, sixth–fifth century BCE. (*Archaeological Museum of Olympia*)
8. The head of the Charioteer of Delphi, a statue donated to the Oracle by Polyzalos, tyrant of Gela and brother of Gelon and Hieron of Syracuse, around 470 BCE.
9. Modern reconstruction of the ancient port of Carthage.
10. Phoenician mask used to exorcise evil, found in Sardinia, fourth century BCE. (*National Archaeological Museum, Cagliari*)
11. Greek hoplites in battle, from the Nereid Monument in the city of Xanthos, Lycia, 390–380 BCE. (*British Museum, London*)
12. Effigy of Dionysius I of Syracuse, sculpted by the American sculptor and historian George Stewart, 1929.
13. Greek tragedy mask, fourth century BCE. (*Archaeological Museum of Piraeus*)
14. Two Phoenician glass vases, fifth–third century BCE. (*Museum Kunstpalast, Düsseldorf*)
15. Apollo of Belvedere. Roman copy of a bronze statue made by the famous Athenian sculptor Leochares, around 350 BCE. It is considered a model of aesthetic perfection. (*Vatican Museums*)
16. The Temple of Omonia in the Valley of Temples, at Akragas.
17. The Riace Bronzes. Two Greek statues of naked warriors, from 460–450 BCE. (*Museo Nazionale della Magna Grecia, Reggio Calabria*)
18. The ancient theatre of Syracuse as it is today. It had capacity for 16,000–20,000 spectators.

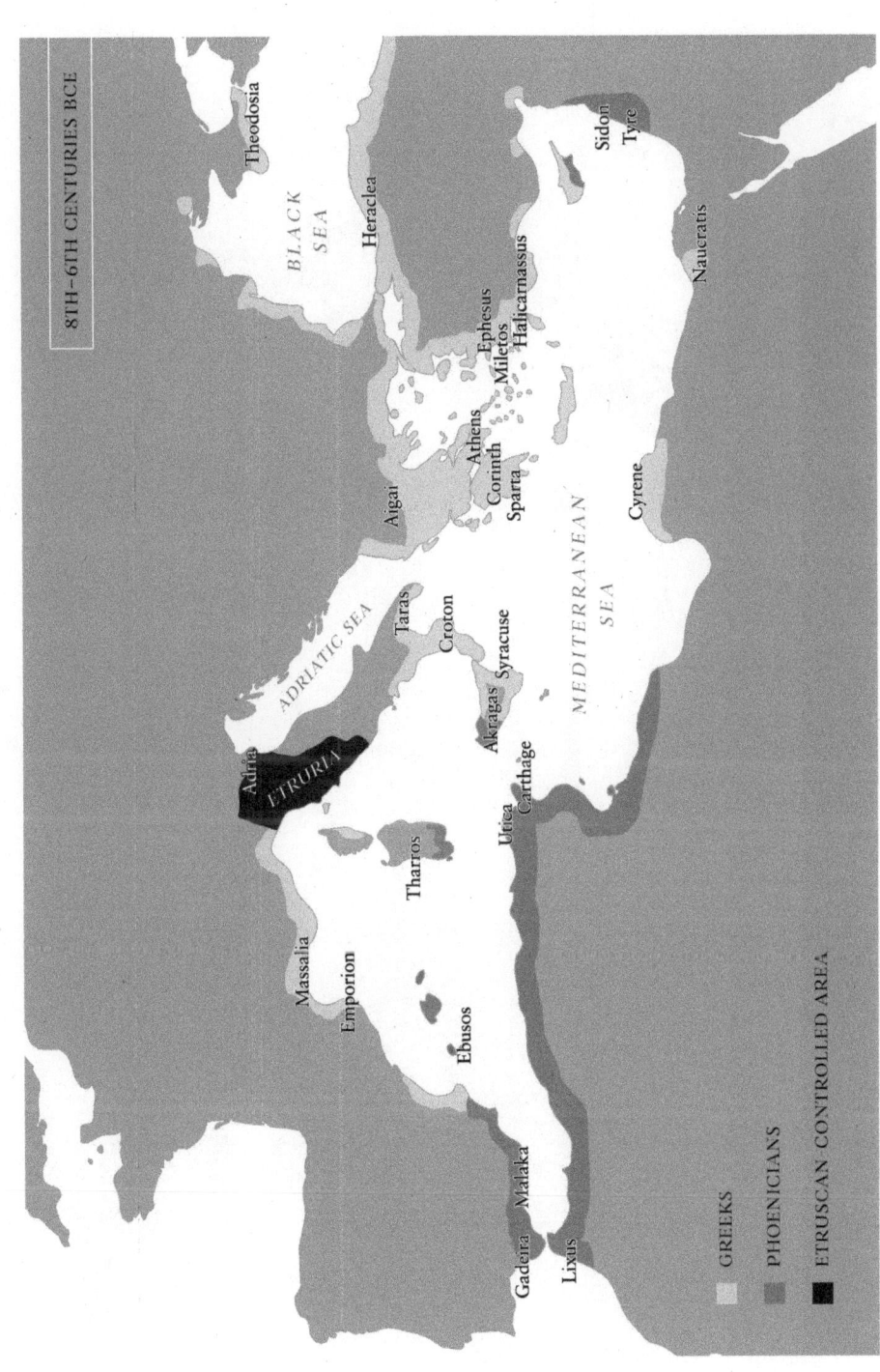

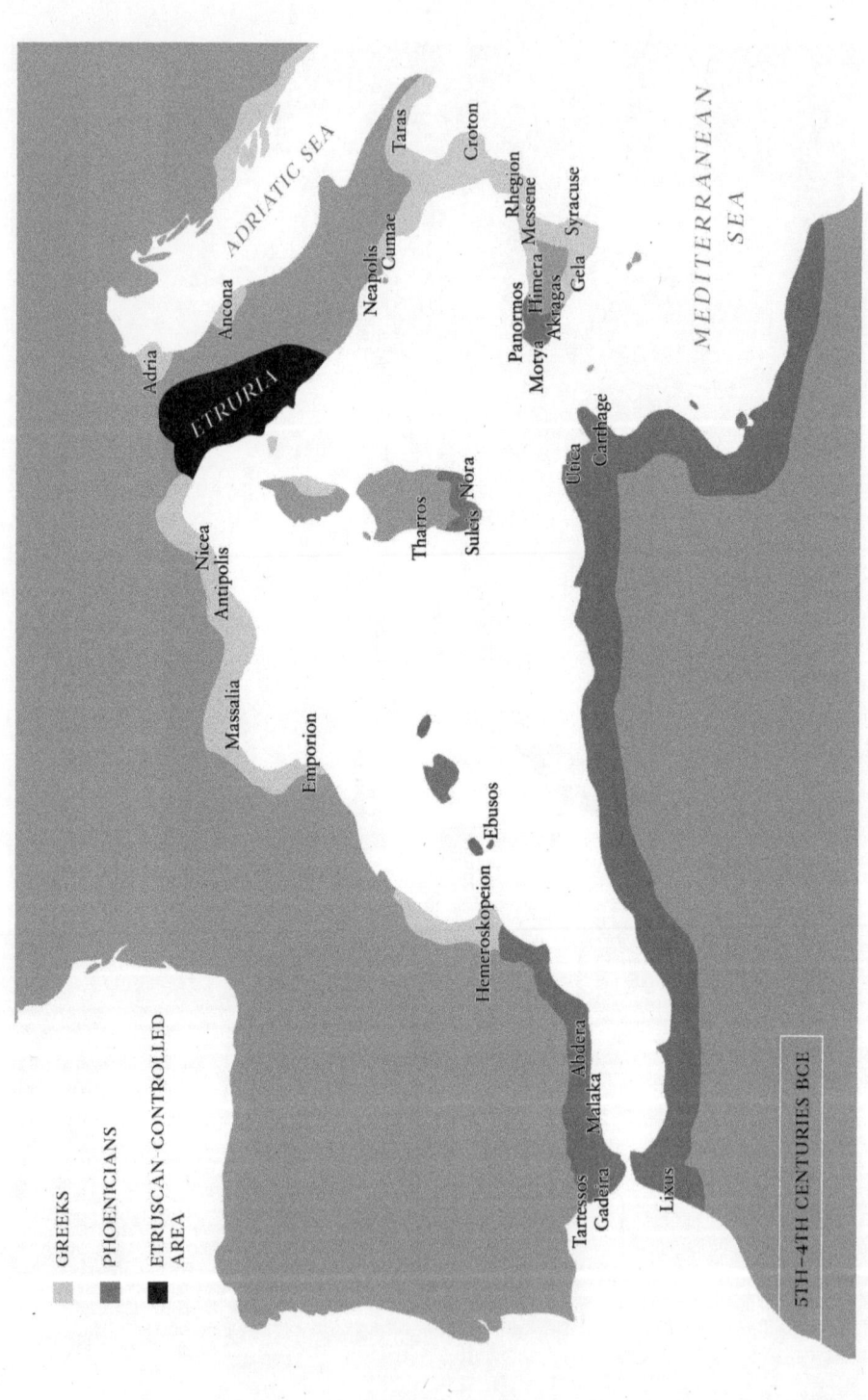

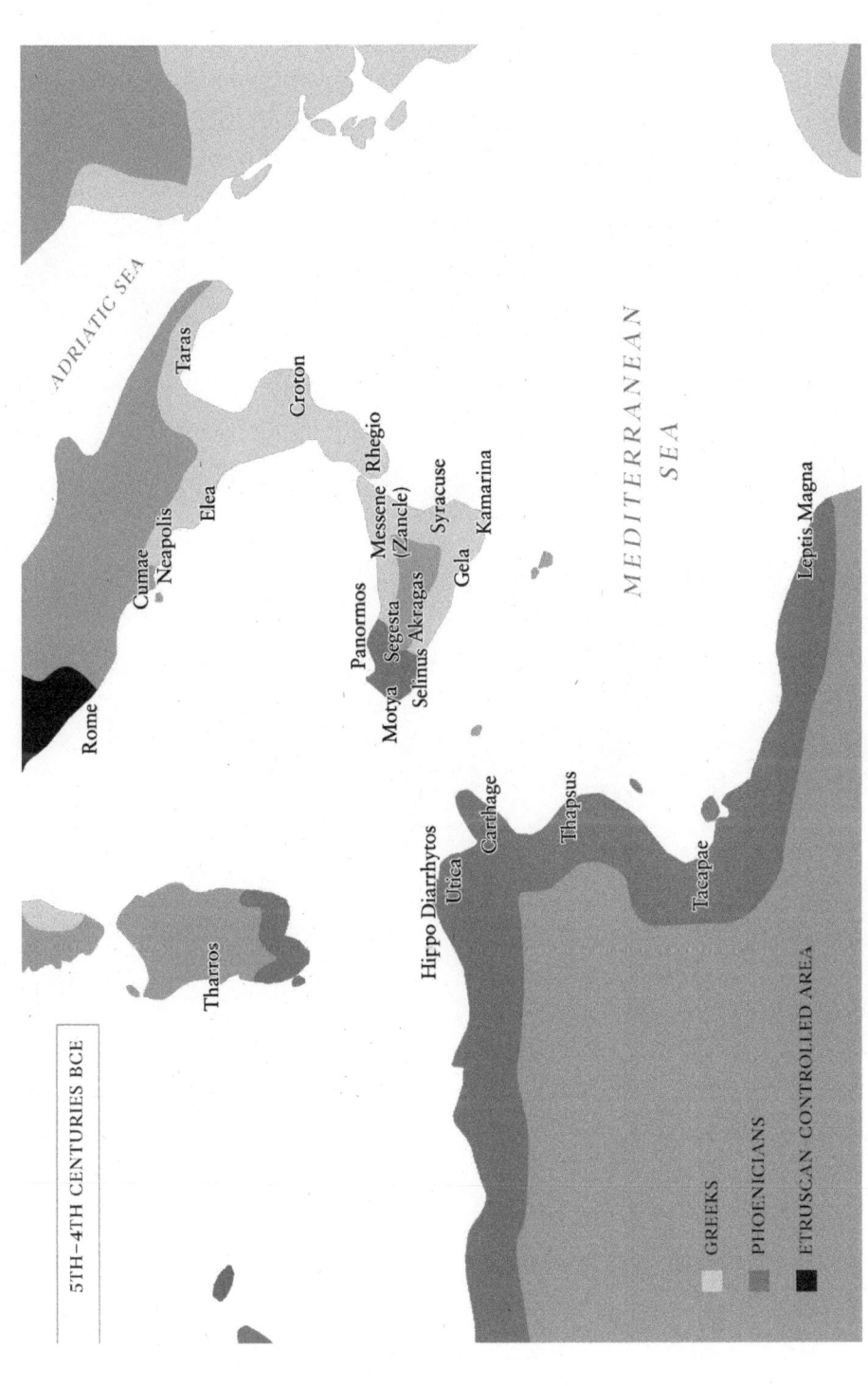

Preface

This book about the Western Greeks and the Carthaginians and the bloody wars between them, one of the most fascinating and less studied topics of ancient military history, is much more than a simple translation in English of the previous text, published in Greek in 2017. I added new parts, chapters and citations to present a much more complete and enhanced revised edition, intended for history lovers, experts of war and politics, and international scholars.

Sotirios Fotios Drokalos
Acharnes, Athens, March 2025

Introduction

Competition and conflict between Greeks and Phoenicians played a central role in the historical development of the ancient Mediterranean Sea. In the Eastern Mediterranean, the interaction and competition between the two predominantly maritime and commercial nations primarily manifested itself in the context of the conflicts between the Greeks and the Persian Empire, of which Phoenicia was a part. In the Western Mediterranean, however, the colonies of the two metropolitan areas formed the two great and competing poles of the region. The wars between them were numerous; some were undoubtedly among the bloodiest and most dramatic in ancient history.

However, modern literature on this subject is surprisingly scarce. Therefore, a focused account of the prolonged Greco-Carthaginian conflict is vital. Sparse attention to the subject is probably because the Greco-Carthaginian wars, unlike the Greco-Persian and Roman–Carthaginian wars, were not ultimately decisive, although they were just as bloody and more prolonged.

The Greeks of the West and the Carthaginians engaged in an endless conflict, yielding no decisive outcomes or lasting political shifts. The two ethnicities constituted a conflictual bipolar system in the Western Mediterranean, which remained stagnant throughout this period without either of the two poles being able to prevail over the other and without arriving at a harmonious coexistence.

It is precisely this element, though, in combination with the eventual sweeping victory of Rome, that makes the history of the Greco-Carthaginian wars worthy of much more in-depth study than that completed so far, as many interesting historical questions arise from this particular historical sequence, which in addition offer the opportunity to draw significant and valuable theoretical conclusions.

Apart from this, a concise presentation of the Greco-Carthaginian wars and books on the history of the Western Greeks and the Greek colonies, in general, are of great importance, as even the experts often are determined in their perspective of the ancient Greek world by the dimensions of modern Greece. It comes out that while Westerners, or modern Greeks, boast of ancient Greek cultural achievements, they practically ignore and reduce the true scope of the ancient Greek world, resulting in misunderstandings on the conditions of Greek culture's evolution and, consequently, of growth and progress as such. The almost exclusive focus on the Greek mainland area and the reduced interest in the equally powerful, wealthy, and culturally developed Greek colonies reflects a distorted perspective, which perceives the ancient Greeks as a relatively small nation from a geopolitical standpoint, which resisted giant empires.

The historical reality is very different from this picture, as the Greeks were one of the most widespread and populous ethnicities of the ancient world centuries before Alexander the Great's magnificent campaign and conquest of the East. The expansion of the Greeks was massive and dominant over a vast area, from Italy and Gaul to the Black Sea and the Danube, and from Asia Minor and North Africa to Spain. On their side, the Phoenicians represented the second most expanded ethnicity of the ancient Mediterranean, a rival and associate of the Greeks for centuries.

One of the main ambitions of this book is to contribute to a deeper understanding of the geopolitical and demographic dimensions of the ancient Greek and Mediterranean world, which were as broad as the cultural ones and represented the objective base on which the latter developed. It was a vivid sea with two great adventurous and exploratory ethnicities that formed a network of routes and settlements that connected the various peoples of this area of the planet, accelerating the cultural development that manifested and consolidated itself mainly through the ancient Greek culture.

Chapter 1

The Phoenician Colonisation and the Rise of Carthage

Carthage's name in Phoenician was 'Qart-Hadast', the equivalent of the Greek 'Neapolis', i.e. 'New City', which for the Phoenicians probably sounded also like 'New Tyre'. According to the ancient historian Timaeus, the foundation of Carthage occurred in 814 BCE.[1] So far, archaeological findings only roughly confirm this information, as they date slightly later. There are, therefore, different opinions on the exact date of the foundation of Carthage and, more generally, on the periods of Phoenician colonisation.

What is certain is that the city was one of the first Phoenician colonies in the West, as well as that the contacts and relationship of the Phoenician Carthaginians with Tyre and the other metropolitan Phoenician cities, such as Sidon, never ceased. It is also certain that Phoenician colonisation peaked in the mid-eighth century BCE, having begun mainly about a century earlier. It is probable that there was an earlier Phoenician presence in the Western Mediterranean, perhaps even earlier than the tenth century BCE, as well as that of the Mycenaean Greeks. However, the mass colonisations with lasting effects and critical historical significance are those that took place from the ninth to the eighth centuries BCE onwards.[2]

The tendency of the Phoenicians to establish colonies at that period can be interpreted from two complementary perspectives. On the one hand, it represented the natural expansion of a predominantly commercial and maritime culture such as the Phoenician. On the other hand, it was accelerated by the developments in the Middle East at the time, with the expansion of the Assyrian Empire and the imposition of its suzerainty over Phoenicia.

Phoenician colonisation was a quite centrally organised and guided process, not a set of relatively loose processes like the later Greek one.

Therefore, Phoenician colonies, and later Carthaginian colonies, unlike the Greek ones, did not have political independence and their own foreign policy. They were somewhat autonomous within themselves but belonged to a kind of 'federation' or 'empire', which initially had its centre in Phoenicia, especially in Tyre, and later in Carthage.

The Phoenicians' choice to proceed with intensive and organised colonisation of the Western Mediterranean was probably reinforced by the Assyrians, who used Tyre as a centre for the commercial expansion of their empire to the West. More generally, the powerful aristocracies of the East had given impetus to discovering and exploiting precious metals in places increasingly remote from the metropolitan Phoenician area and Asia. However, from the end of the eighth century BCE, during the reign of Sennacherib, the position of Tyre probably began to decline, and in 573 BCE, the Babylonians occupied the Phoenician metropolis.

The decline of Tyre was one of the main reasons for the parallel strategic rise of wealthy Carthage, which, as is evident from historiography and archaeology, emerged as a leading power of the Phoenicians, especially those of the West, at exactly the same period. It is clear from archaeological research that the Phoenician colonies showed signs of decline in the first half of the sixth century BCE and that the flourishing and thriving Carthage took over their leadership at that time in place of Tyre, as well as the establishment of new colonies of its own. Indeed, the archaeological finds of the Phoenician colonies in the West reflect the transition from an initial 'Phoenician' to a 'Carthaginian' period from the mid-sixth century BCE onwards, as the Carthaginian culture undoubtedly contains its origins, but is distinct and separate from the metropolitan Phoenician culture.

By the middle of the sixth century BCE, Carthage had therefore fully asserted its dominance over the broader area surrounding it. Its expansion included the parts of the African coast that the Phoenicians had occupied at the time of the original colonisation, and it had taken control of the existing Phoenician cities, also establishing new colonies of its own. Beyond the coast, the Carthaginians extended their dominance inland, building cities and forts and occupying territories, as Carthage's new status as a major power in the international arena of the entire Mediterranean required extended control in the interior of the African continent. In the East, the Carthaginians had occupied all the territories up to the present-day Cape Bon, where they built forts.[3]

However, the Carthaginian possessions and colonies became more numerous as one moved away from Carthage to the West, as the Phoenician ones had already done in the past. That happened because the centre of gravity of Carthaginian trade and general Carthaginian foreign policy was at the western end of the Mediterranean. The control of Sardinia, Corsica, the Balearic Islands, and the Iberian coast was strategically fundamental for Carthage in its attempt to control the Mediterranean trade and the connection between Europe and Africa, emerging as the dominant power of the Western Mediterranean.[4]

The Iberian Peninsula was of primary importance to the Phoenicians from very early on. Therefore, their Iberian colonies were already consolidated by the eighth century BCE, as Iberia was the extreme point of expansion of Phoenician trade. However, the peninsula also had an additional particular value derived from its large reserves of mainly silver, gold, and tin. The Phoenicians extracted or bought significant quantities of precious metals cheaply, then processed them and made jewellery, which they sold much more expensively throughout the Mediterranean.

The expansion of the Carthaginian presence and dominance also took place on the western side of the African coast. The important Phoenician city of Lixus already existed, which, together with Gadeira (present-day Cádiz) in southern Spain, Utica, and Carthage itself, constituted the largest Phoenician colonies in the West. Lixus and Gadeira effectively controlled the Pillars of Hercules, present-day Gibraltar, the shortest passage between Africa and Europe.[5]

Until the middle of the sixth century BCE, Carthage was not directly involved in Iberian affairs. The dynamic establishment of its control over the region at that time followed an evident upheaval that had intervened in the Phoenician colonies of Spain, during which some of them had been abandoned and others had been reorganised. We can trace the cause of this upheaval back to a second historical development that caused severe problems for the Phoenician colonial structure and brought about the need to reorganise it, in addition to the fall of Tyre to the Babylonians. That was the Greek colonisation.

The Greeks, in turn, established colonies in the Western Mediterranean in general some decades later than the Phoenicians, and after they consolidated, Greek trade developed rapidly, ending up seriously damaging the respective commercial activities of the Phoenician cities. The findings from Spain, for example, show a gradual decline in Phoenician trade in the Iberian Peninsula and a weakening of Gadeira, due to the dynamic Greek entry into the region.[6]

In the sixth century BCE, the appeal of Greek tradable products, initially especially ceramics, was enormous, to the point of being bought and promoted by Carthage itself, resulting in a crisis in Phoenician production of similar products. There was therefore a decline in the Phoenician towns, and the Phoenicians abandoned some of their mines in Spain. The relative weakness of the Phoenicians also enabled Iberian tribes to carry out attacks and raids against Phoenician settlements, including Gadeira. In the face of the great difficulties of the Phoenicians of the Iberian Peninsula, Carthage intervened decisively, taking over the governance and defence of their interests.

The pattern observed in Iberia is the same as that recorded earlier in Sicily and more widely. The initial Phoenician colonisation created a Phoenician commercial dominance in the Western Mediterranean in general. Yet, the Greek colonisation that followed gradually reversed this favourable condition for the Phoenicians, as the Greeks proved to be compelling competitors in the field of trade, and ready to use military force whenever necessary.

This new situation, combined with the fall of Tyre under Babylonian rule, created the need for the emergence of a new solid Phoenician centre. Carthage was the wealthiest and most potent Phoenician city in the West, and its position was strategically more favourable to perform such a role so that by the middle of the sixth century BCE, it had emerged as the undisputed leader and protector of all Phoenicians in the Western Mediterranean, as mentioned above, effectively establishing a Carthaginian empire.[7]

Carthage established its presence first in the Balearic Islands and specifically in Ebusus (present-day Ibiza), which it has since been used as a Carthaginian base at the western end of the Mediterranean. Also,

Gadeira ('Gdr' in Phoenician, meaning 'rock' or 'fortified city'), which was the most important Phoenician colony in Iberia and was founded in 770–760 BCE, was transformed from a primarily commercial hub into a strategic centre at the time of the spread of Carthaginian control over the Phoenician colonies. The same happened with other Phoenician colonies in Spain, such as Malaca (modern Malaga) and Abdera, which were incorporated into the Carthaginian federation and experienced significant growth in the following centuries.[8]

As a rule, Carthaginian politics required few concentrated urban centres rather than scattered polities, favouring the development of the Carthaginian – now – cities of Iberia and the rest of the Western Mediterranean. Trade continued to be the main activity, but the new conditions created by the Greek competition required the military element to become more powerful.[9]

Probably also some depletion of natural resources played a role in transforming the Phoenician cities from trading posts linked to Phoenicia to parts of a militarised Carthaginian empire.[10] The continuous mining of ores, as well as the use of timber, may have made certain areas unsuitable for habitation and created the need for centralised administration, with the formation of an essentially unitary state with Carthage as its capital and all the Phoenician towns clustered around it.

In Sicily, which was to be the main theatre of the Greco-Carthaginian conflicts, Phoenician colonisation also began in the first half of the eighth century BCE.[11] There, too, perhaps even more than in other cases, the original settlements were essentially commercial hubs linked to their mother cities, whose role was mainly to facilitate travel and the transport of goods from Phoenicia to the westernmost points of the Mediterranean. That enabled the Phoenicians, who lived all along the Sicilian coast, to develop often-friendly relations with the indigenous Sicilians, who occupied the mainland and had not developed navigation and trade. The three indigenous Sicilian peoples were the Elymians, who inhabited the western part of the island, the Sicani in the central part, and the Siculi in the eastern part.

Nonetheless, the situation was to change with the arrival of the Greeks, which took place from the middle of the eighth century BCE onwards. The Greeks established colonies on the coast of Sicily, mainly in the eastern and central parts. Consequently, the Phoenicians living in these areas also moved and settled in the Phoenician colonies located in the western part of Sicily since this was closest to Carthage and Utica, the largest Phoenician colonies in the Western Mediterranean. Consequently, Motya, Panormos (now Palermo), and Solus grew in population and expanded in territory, becoming the three Phoenician and later Carthaginian cities of Sicily. However, they never developed that much and remained decisively smaller than the most important Greek cities. Their population and size during the period in which most of the Greco-Carthaginian wars took place, i.e. between the fifth and third centuries BCE, were clearly smaller not only than those of the larger Greek cities, namely Syracuse and Akragas, modern Agrigento, but also than those of medium-sized cities like Gela and Messene, modern Messina.

Political Institutions and Military Organisation of Carthage

Carthage's constitution was one of the oligarchic regimes, as the dominant and almost exclusive role in the city's governance played an aristocratic class consisting of the wealthiest families. The supreme rulers of the state, with extensive jurisdiction and power, were the two 'shophets', which can be translated as 'elders', 'judges', or 'kings', who were elected exclusively from the aristocratic families and had an annual term of office. The institution of the shophets was, therefore, similar to that of the Roman councillors, except that the latter were elected by all the citizens of Rome rather than just by the nobles, and they were also the supreme commanders of the army. In contrast, the Carthaginian shophets exercised political control over the troops but were not their direct operational commanders.

Instead, among the duties of the shophets was to preside over the debates of the Senate, which consisted of about 300 members descended and elected from aristocratic families. The Senate was the legislative and judicial body of Carthage, but also the place for public debate and where decisions on foreign policy were made. The Senate heard the reports of colonial governments, received ambassadors, decided wars, and carried out legislative work through five-member committees dealing with specific areas of interest and regulation.[12]

Next to the Senate and in connection with it was a council with the role of guarantor of the constitution. It consisted of about a hundred members,[13] who were also elected from the aristocratic families and had the task of overseeing the functioning of the political and military leadership as well as ensuring that there was no danger of the constitution being overthrown, either by the nobles or by the masses.

The Carthaginian constitution also provided for the existence of a people's assembly, but this was convened only in the event that the shophets and the Senate failed to reach a decision on a matter and there were significant disagreements between them, in which case the participation and position of the citizen body became necessary. Convening a people's assembly was, therefore, not compulsory, even in the case of a declaration of war. Nevertheless, once the people's assembly was convened, citizens were not limited to voting among the various proposals but also had the right to submit their own proposals for discussion and voting, at least from the fourth century BCE onwards.[14] It is also sure that the popular assembly gradually acquired more significant political influence through the increasing wealth of the lower classes. However, at the same time, political life became more intense and confrontational as more diverse and rival factions and interest groups emerged. In any case, not all citizens indiscriminately participated in the people's assembly, but only those who exceeded a minimum threshold of property and income.

Aristotle refers to the Carthaginian constitution in the second book of his *Politics*, presenting it in comparison with the Spartan and Cretan constitutions, concluding that it was similar to them and maybe better. He notes that in his time, all three polities were rightly praised as being excellent.[15] Proof of how well organised and functional the Carthaginian polity was, he points out, was the fact that no tyranny had ever been established in the city, nor had any significant popular uprisings taken place.[16]

The history of Carthage is indeed characterised by political stability, as the masses were relatively contented thanks to the expansion of the city's sovereignty and the possibilities of prosperity offered to them in the places where Carthaginian domination and commercial activity were spreading. In addition, through enrichment a family could achieve elevation and acceptance into the aristocratic class and the Senate, so since there was economic growth and prosperity over time, much of the citizenry could hope that they or their descendants would be able to rise in terms of their ability to participate in political power.

On the other hand, the political stability of Carthage was also due to the fact that the ruling oligarchy took care to keep the army under control and to prevent the formation of movements and coups that would overthrow the constitution. As mentioned, the two shophets did not have direct command of the troops. They consequently could not mobilise the army against the other political and governmental institutions. In contrast, the generals, who were also elected exclusively from aristocratic families, had no executive political power and were under the watchful eye of the mechanism of control of the political leadership. The latter was particularly suspicious and harsh towards military commanders, whom it was customary to execute or force to commit suicide if they failed to comply with its orders or did not comply perfectly.

One can therefore say that the Carthaginian military organisation separated political and military leadership, unlike the Greek and Roman examples, where political leaders were also commanders of the armed forces. This fact reflects a broader difference between Carthaginian and Greek and Roman perceptions and mentality, since in Carthage there was no widespread conscription of citizens, but Carthaginian armies were composed mainly of mercenaries. Unlike what was the case in the Greek cities and Rome, for the Carthaginians, there was no equation of citizenship with that of the hoplite. On the contrary, they considered recruiting mercenaries more convenient than recruiting massive forces from their population by distracting them from their commercial and other financial activities.[17]

Carthage and the other Phoenician colonies were founded as trading cities, as overseas extensions of Phoenicia and the great Eastern empires. They were not independent cities of people struggling to survive and establish themselves in new and unknown lands, as was the case with the Greek colonies. Also, from very early on, as early as the eighth century BCE and definitely from the sixth century BCE onwards, the Phoenicians had been identified in the military field with the navy in the context of the Assyrian, Babylonian, and Persian empires.[18] Their social structure and their approach to the phenomenon of war were, therefore, radically different from that of the Greeks, who in their metropolitan area were divided into independent states, often at war with each other, within the changing and often mountainous and rugged Greek landscape.

Consequently, the Phoenicians and then the Carthaginians did not attach the same importance to military activity, nor was active participation in the armed forces a decisive factor in the prestige of aristocrats or ordinary citizens.

Yet, that professional structure of Carthaginian military leadership gave more powers to generals on their mainly mercenary armies, since they had almost nothing to do with the Senate and the political administration. According to great Athenian orator Isocrates, the Carthaginians were ruled by an oligarchy, but their army in the field was commanded by a 'king'.[19]

The advantage of Carthage was that because of its wealth and the large areas it controlled in many parts of the Western Mediterranean, it was able to spend large sums of money and build mighty armies with little involvement of its citizens. In contrast, the Greeks of the West, fragmented almost as much as the metropolitan Greeks, relied on the forces they could draw from their citizens.

Therefore, the Carthaginian armies were mainly composed of mercenary forces from many different geographical areas and peoples. Light cavalry, slingers and archers were recruited from vassal regions such as Numidia and the Balearic Islands. At the same time, tough foot soldiers were recruited from the mountainous Spanish tribes, as well as from the tribes of the Italian peninsula. Sometimes, Carthage also used a few Gauls, while it usually drew the bulk of its armies from the peoples of the immediate Carthaginian territory, namely Tunis and Libya, which provided heavy and light infantry.[20]

Carthaginian citizens participated in the Carthaginian armies when they did, with smaller numbers, not exceeding 10–15 per cent of the total force. In the process, of course, the Greeks and the Carthaginians, through their constant clashes, adopted more elements from one another.

10   The Wars Between Greeks and Carthaginians

The Greeks began to use mercenary corps on a permanent basis as early as the beginning of the fifth century BCE, long before the cities of metropolitan Greece adopted this practice. At the same time, the forces formed by Carthaginian citizens gradually adopted more and more of the Greek armament and way of fighting. The latter was particularly true of the Sacred Band, an elite unit composed of Carthaginian nobles, citizens distinguished for valour, reputation, and wealth, which numbered about 3,000 men, and after its establishment, the entire upper echelon of the Carthaginian army came from its ranks.[21]

The Carthaginian armies, being essentially mercenary, were usually more numerous than the Greek armies, at least according to our ancient sources, but they lacked cohesion, unity, and organisation. For this reason, the compact Greek armies were generally more robust and had an advantage in line-up battles. On the other hand, although the Greeks were excellent seafarers, the Carthaginians had relative superiority in terms of naval forces. Therefore, it could be said that the Carthaginians were more potent at sea and the Greeks more capable on land.

Chapter 2

The Greek Colonisation and the First Conflicts

The Greek colonisation of the Western Mediterranean differed from the Phoenician colonisation in terms of its causes and the way it took place. The Phoenicians spread westwards in order to promote their trade, and for the first few centuries, their colonies in the West functioned mainly as trading posts. For the Greeks, on the other hand, the establishment of colonies in the Western Mediterranean was not only a commercial operation but also a way out of the significant social problem of the Greek metropolitan area of that period. The problem was caused by the immense population growth and the resulting conflicts in a geographical area that, moreover, was not particularly fertile or not fertile enough, at least in some cases. Greek colonisation of the West began shortly after the Phoenician colonisation, the first Greek colony of Pithecusa, founded in 770 BCE on the present-day island of Ischia in the Bay of Naples.[1]

In the case of the Greeks, unlike that of the Phoenicians, the colonists, after their flight, were not an organic part of the cities from which they came but had to settle permanently in new areas and, as a rule, were not welcome back in their native city. The Greek colonies were therefore founded by people seeking a better future away from their mother city. They often left as immigrants or refugees, because either the economic situation made it impossible to maintain them or social unrest had broken out in which they had played a leading role.[2]

The Greek colonies were typically founded following the Oracle of Delphi's instructions, which considered two fundamental factors: the geographical location's suitability for cultivation and trade, and the extent of already settled populations in the region. The city founders, οικισταί, came from aristocratic families of the mother city and had with them groups of relatives, friends, and allies.³

The basis of the economy in that historical period was, of course, agricultural, and during the so-called Greek Dark Ages that followed the fall of the Bronze Age and especially of the advanced Mycenaean civilisation, the developed trade that had previously existed among kingdoms and societies of the Greek area and the Eastern empires almost disappeared. Therefore, Archaic Greek colonial expeditions consisted of people determined to conquer new, preferably uninhabited, fertile lands, always located along coastlines. This objective gave a dynamic and adventurous character to Greek colonisation, whereas Phoenician colonisation had, as we've seen, more qualities of an organised establishment of trading posts and hubs around the Mediterranean, as Phoenicia was an outpost and a passage of the Eastern empires to the Mediterranean.

Probably the earlier Greek colonisations were mostly private enterprises. Later, the cities began to organise the founding of new colonies.⁴ In any case, there was no central political planning and control of colonisation, and only the great religious centre of Delphi carried out its guidance and coordination.⁵ These are the reasons some scholars think the terms 'colonisation' and 'colonies' are inappropriate for the Greek settlements overseas.⁶

There is also a linguistic notion. The Latin term '*colonia*' is related to terms like '*colere*', that is, cultivation. On the contrary, the Greek term 'αποικία' means 'home away from home'. The emphasis of the Latin term was on the possession of land, while the Greek term was on separation and connection with the mother city.⁷ Greek 'colonies' created a network of connected independent cities and communities, an 'οικουμένη' (*ecuméne*), i.e. 'inhabited world'. In contrast, the Roman and modern colonies were regions and cities strictly controlled by Rome or the modern colonial powers as parts of their empires. The disparity had nothing to do with different morals or approaches but with objective and profound differences between the phenomena. The Greek and Phoenician colonisations were series of events that took place in an ever-changing archaic Mediterranean world, confused and disordered after the fall of the Bronze Age civilisations, sparsely populated and lacking established and extended states. The protagonists, the colonists, were a galaxy of independent cities, communities, or groups of renegades and adventurers, and they were not established and extended states themselves.

The Carthaginians, who had already emerged as the commercial rulers of the Western Mediterranean, were highly negative about Greek mobility and the prospect of establishing rival Greek cities in the Western Mediterranean. They tried to prevent the settlement of Greeks by using naval blockades and by trying to prevent Greek ships from accessing the places where new cities were to be established. Consequently, the first Greek attempts at colonisation by Euboean sailors probably failed to consolidate due to Phoenician control of the main sea routes and the strengthening of the already established Phoenician colonies. Nevertheless, there is also evidence to the contrary. According to a study, Greek and Phoenician mariners and settlers had generally good relations during the early stages of the colonisation of the Mediterranean,[8] something archaeologists have affirmed for example in the case of the island of Cyprus.[9]

Eventually, the Greeks managed to found their first western colonies in Italy in the first half of the eighth century BCE. Subsequently, they founded Cumae, Sybaris, Croton (708 BCE), Rhegio, Metapontium, Locris, Poseidonia, and in Sicily Syracuse (733 BCE), Zancle, Gela (688 BCE), Himera, Selinus and many other cities.[10] A few hundred thousand people lived in Italy when the Greek colonisation began.[11]

Unlike the Phoenicians, the Greeks did not use Sicily as a hub but as the main area for establishing their colonies, along with southern mainland Italy. As early as the seventh century BCE, the Greek colonies occupied most of the island, reaching, in the case of Selinus, a very short distance from the Phoenician territories. Moreover, in the early sixth century BCE, Akragas was founded on the southern Sicilian coast and, from the beginning, was one of the most important Greek cities in the West. From the seventh century BCE, colonies of colonies were being built, such as at Selinus, mentioned above. The latter was a colony of the city of Megara Hyblaea in eastern Sicily, which was, in turn, a colony of Megara.

In addition, at the end of the seventh century BCE and the beginning of the sixth century BCE, Greek colonisation continued with the establishment of cities in even more western parts of the Mediterranean. It was precisely during this period that the first recorded military conflicts between Greeks and Phoenicians in the Western Mediterranean occurred. Phocaeans from Ionia, the Greek coastal part of Asia Minor, intending to settle in the Gulf of Lion in southern Gaul, faced Phoenician forces in a series of naval battles, and succeeded in prevailing. This victory resulted in the establishment in 600 BCE of Massalia, now Marseilles, one of the most important naval and commercial centres in the Mediterranean to this day.

The strategic importance of Massalia was immense, as its existence was a direct link between the Greek world and central and northern Europe.[12] After an initial phase of conflicts with the local Gauls and the neighbouring Ligurians of northern Italy, the Greeks of Massalia, having succeeded in establishing their presence in the region, maintained good relations with the populations of the hinterland, thriving thanks to trade with them. Indeed, Massalia became very rich and grew prosperous. At the same time, it had an enormous impact on the populations of southern Gaul, promoting their acculturation. The Gaul Greeks introduced the oil tree and the vine in the south of modern France, i.e. the region of Provence. Pompeius Trogus wrote that the Greeks taught Gauls higher and more advanced ways of living, and by adopting them, the Gauls left behind their previous primitive ways. The Gauls began to cultivate and build fortresses for their towns. Moreover, they learned to live under laws instead of using arms force to resolve controversies. They began to cultivate olive trees and vines. Their progress was spectacular, and they became so rich that Gaul looked like a part of Greece instead of just a colony of the latter, Trogus and Justin wrote.[13]

In the same years, the city of Emporion was founded, the most important Greek city in the Iberian Peninsula, where other Greek colonies settled between the end of the sixth and the beginning of the fifth century BCE.[14] Probably during the same period, a settlement was also made at Olbia in Sardinia. In 562 BCE, Alalia was founded in Corsica, again by Phocaeans, and the city developed, remarkably, because many Ionians were transferred there due to the Persian invasion of Asia Minor during the reign of Cyrus II.[15] The latter development had a similar indirect beneficial effect on the Greek cities of Gaul and Spain.[16]

The Phoenicians, who until then had maintained control of the sea and trade routes in the Tyrrhenian Sea and the wider region, were not reconciled to the rising Greek presence, especially to the Greek bases in Corsica, Sardinia, and Iberia. The same was true of the peoples of central and northern Italy, especially the Etruscans, who resented the entry of Greek competition.

In particular, the founding of Massalia and Alalia and their growing influence in the surrounding area created significant problems for both the Carthaginians and the Etruscans. Thus, whereas until then, these two nations had been the main competitors in the Tyrrhenian Sea, they now had to face the common threat of the impetuous Greek entry into the Tyrrhenian.[17] Moreover, controlling the main Iberian trade route was now precarious for the Carthaginians. This combination led the Etruscans and Carthaginians to form an alliance against the Greeks.[18]

Nevertheless, I want to underline that those conflicts and rivalries do not indicate a total divergence between the Greeks and the Etruscans. On the contrary, Greeks and Etruscans had close cultural and economic ties. In fact, Etruscan cities housed entire quarters populated by Greek sailors and merchants, similar to what happened in Egypt with the Greek town Naucratis, which was the central trading post of the storied kingdom. The Greek quarters in Etruria were like semi-autonomous towns with a vivid commercial nature, albeit they had not territorial sovereignty and were under Etruscan administration and law.[19]

One of the best-known Greek quarters in Etruria was Gravisca. It was the port of Tarquinia and housed a rich and heterogeneous Greek trading district characterised, even urbanistically, by Greek cult buildings instead of Etruscan. Another prominent Greek settlement in Etruria was Agylla (Cere), a seat of Intermediterranean trade. Agylla was so successful and prosperous that it once offered to the Oracle of Delphi its own thesaurus, like a real city – a shrine with very rich volitional offerings to god Apollo. Finally, another important Greek town in Etruria was Spina, at the coast of the Adriatic Sea, in North Italy, which also boasted an equally opulent thesaurus at Delphi. Spina was an important commercial port and one of the bigger Etruscan cities in northern Italy along Felsina, modern Bologna. Greek tradition considered Spina *polis hellenìs*, Greek city.[20]

Moreover, according to a Greek myth, Odysseus ended up in Etruria after a series of adventures, and finally he died and was buried there. Similar legends often indicate realities lost in the fog of pre-history, and in this case, they enhance the notion that the Greek presence in Italy was in fact much older than the era of colonisation that recorded history informs us about. Archaeological evidence suggests that before the Archaic Greeks, Mycenaeans had already travelled to Italy and Sicily and settled, possibly contributing to the very formation of the Etruscan and Roman ethnicities. Maybe they went even beyond Italy: according to Strabo, Odysseus was also the founder of Lisbon at the western coast of the Iberian Peninsula, what is now Portugal.[21]

Returning to the recorded history, we know that Lucius Tarquinius Priscus, the fifth king of Rome and the first of the three Etruscan kings of Rome, was also Greek, as he was the son of Demaratus of Corinth.[22] Demaratus arrived in Etruria in 657 BCE and had two sons with an Etruscan noblewoman. His sons, Priscus and Arruns Tarquinius had Greek and Etruscan education. Demaratus also brought the Greek writing system to Etruria.[23]

Wars in Sicily, Africa and Corsica

By the time the Carthaginians allied with the Etruscans against the Greeks in the Tyrrhenian Sea, the situation had become extremely unstable in Sicily. In 580 BCE, Selinus came into conflict with the Elymians of Segesta, probably over control of fertile areas between the two cities. Segesta was the largest city of the Elymians, and its neighbouring Phoenicians, traditionally allied with them, rushed to its aid. The Selinunteans reinforced, in turn, Dorian colonists from Rhodes and Cnidus of Caria, again in Asia Minor, led by a Cnidian named Pentathlos. The latter advanced with the support of Selinus' troops to the western end of Sicily and attempted to found a new Greek city at the cape of Lilybaeum, near Motya. However, the allied forces of the Elymians and the Phoenicians repulsed them and drove them back after clashes in which Pentathlos was killed.[24]

Nevertheless, in the following decades, the Phoenician cities of Sicily faced many problems in their commercial activities due to the increasing Greek competition. They turned to the mighty Carthage for help. Consequently, around 550 BCE, Carthage made its first intervention in Sicily, intending to damage Greek trade and improve the position of Phoenician trade. The campaign in Sicily led general Malchus, who achieved some victories over the Greeks there, and then set out to support the Phoenician cities of Sardinia and Corsica, too. These events show that Carthage was now taking control of the Phoenician colonies in the Western Mediterranean.[25]

During the same period, a large-scale war broke out in North Africa between the Greeks of Cyrene and the Carthaginians. Cyrene had been founded by Laconian Dorians of Thera (now best known as Santorini) in 631 BCE, as had four other smaller cities that together made up the Greek 'Pentapolis' in Libya. Having grown in strength to a remarkable extent, Cyrene clashed with Carthage in the mid-sixth century BCE in a war that probably involved various land and naval battles. The Cyreneans wanted to expand as far westwards as possible. On the other hand, Carthage was in its nodal expansion phase and wished to eliminate the presence of a powerful Greek competitor in Africa. At the war's end, the Carthaginians had not achieved their aim, but neither had the Cyreneans, as the frontier drawn between the territories of the two cities was much closer to Cyrene.[26]

The field of conflict between the Greeks and the Carthaginians would then move to the Tyrrhenian Sea, where in 535 BCE, the increase in competition and tension led to a major naval battle between the Carthaginian–Etruscan alliance and the Greeks of Corsica. The naval battle took place off the city of Alalia and saw some 120 ships of the allies (60 each) pitted against around 60 Greek ships. The ratio of crews was, respectively, 20,000 to 12,000 men.[27] It is very significant and characteristic that no other Greek city sent help to Alalia, not even the Massalians. Massalia was itself in a confrontation with the Carthaginians in Iberia and was directly interested in the competition in the Tyrrhenian. Yet it preferred to remain neutral, perhaps trying to maintain a balance with all sides – something that its geographical position allowed, as it was at a considerable distance from the centre of the conflict – or there may have been other strategic reasons that prevented it from helping.

The naval battle ended with a narrow victory for the Greeks of Alalia, who drove the enemies into flight but lost forty of their sixty ships. As a result, they were forced to withdraw immediately from Corsica before the Carthaginians and Etruscans had time to regroup and return. The Phocian colonists temporarily settled in Rhegio, eventually occupying Elea in southern Italy. On the other hand, Massalia maintained its control on the Gaul coast after the Battle of Alalia, pushing back Carthaginian attempts to challenge the Greek dominance there too.[28]

Back in Africa, Cyrene was under pressure from the West from the Carthaginians, while at the same time, the Persians, with Cambyses II as Great King, had conquered Egypt and threatened it from the east.[29] The Cyreneans, therefore, accepted with relief and supported the mission of the Spartan Dorieus, who arrived in the region in 515 BCE with forces consisting of Lacedaemonian *perioeci*, that is, inhabitants of the Spartan state without the Spartan citizenship, and other Peloponnesians, and perhaps a few Spartan citizens. They aimed to establish a new colony in Libya. After arriving in Cyrenaica, Dorieus was joined by exiles from Croton, and the force marched westwards to settle on the river Cinyps in 514 BCE. Over the next three years, Dorieus' forces clashed with Libyans and Carthaginians and, in the end, had to abandon the region and their attempt to settle there permanently after Carthage mounted a strong attack.

The Carthaginians succeeded in preventing Greek expansion westwards and the establishment of a new colony, but obviously, they understood that it was also preferable for them to abandon the pressure on Cyrene and the attempt to eliminate it, as there was a risk of intervention by the Greek metropolises, especially Sparta, in defence of the Doric colony. The Carthaginians, therefore, reconciled themselves to the presence of the Greeks in north-eastern Africa in order to concentrate their forces in their crucial and growing competition with the Greek cities of Sicily and Massalia, especially since the Cyreneans, in turn, had accepted the Carthaginian primacy in the region and had no aspirations to expand westwards.

Dorieus and his companions moved to Italy, where they fought alongside Croton's forces and destroyed Sybaris. However, they did not manage to settle there either, as the Crotonians eventually considered them a threat. Consequently, the adventurous Peloponnesians, with whom some Athenians had probably joined in the meantime, landed in north-western Sicily in 510 BCE. They established a colony at the foot of Mount Eryx, essentially on the border of the Carthaginian territories and within the Elymian lands. The Greek cities of Selinunte and Himera allied themselves with them, but the local Carthaginians and the Elymians, like the Sicani, moved against them. The war ended some three years later, again after a decisive intervention by Carthage, which brought about the destruction of Dorieus' forces and his death.

Meanwhile, in 509 BCE, as the great historian Polybius mentions, the first treaty between Carthage and Rome had been signed immediately after the Etruscan dynasty's expulsion and the establishment of *Res publica* in the future imperial city.[30] With this treaty, the Romans recognised Carthage's sovereignty over the seas, particularly in Africa, Sardinia, and the western part of Sicily. Apparently, after the constitutional change in Rome, the Carthaginians wanted to ensure that the city would continue the Carthaginian-friendly policy of the Etruscans. That was extremely important to them because Sardinia and Corsica were at the heart of Carthaginian policies, as they were the main links between Africa and the East and Iberia. Sardinia was also used several times to supply Carthage, particularly with wheat.

Political and Cultural Data

The Greek colonies were already independent cities from their foundation, and while they usually continued to maintain friendly relations with their mother cities, they were not directly linked to them politically. As already mentioned, the Greek colonists generally consisted of populations that had found themselves in distress or disfavour in the metropolis for economic or political reasons. Therefore, although among them there were usually also aristocrats, the city founders, the class stratification at the beginning of a colony's life was sparse and limited. The archaeological evidence does indeed show relative equality, and land ownership was quite egalitarian.[31]

Then, the colonies that managed to establish themselves began to spread into the surrounding area and conquer land at the expense of the eventual natives. The expansion process proceeded in concentric cycles of occupation and exploitation of territory and had two basic typologies. In one of these, the expansion of the city's territory was achieved through the establishment of peripheral villages and settlements, while in the other, the population remained concentrated in the urban centre, and farms were established around it. Therefore, the expansion was not only carried out due to decisions of the political leadership but also as a result of private actions. In any case, the locals were either pushed back to the hinterland or they were mixed with the Greek colonists, sometimes by force, and essentially becoming servants of the Greeks. That is what we deduce from extracts such as that said by Alcibiades in Thucydides' history, who was trying to convince the Athenians to invade Sicily in 415 BCE. Alcibiades claimed that Syracuse and the Sicilian cities had absorbed populations of any kind and heritage, and their citizen bodies and societies were in constant change and rearrangement, so they wouldn't have the cohesion to resist an Athenian intervention.[32]

However, Alcibiades' prediction turned out to be entirely wrong, and on the other hand, archaeological data indicates that in other cases Greek communities coexisted peacefully with native inhabitants according to their evolving needs and requirements, like in the case of Metaponto. Over time, as Metaponto grew, the Greek and the native populations became almost identical.[33] Some scholars think that the Phoenicians were not a compact ethnic group but a mix of various peoples, and that Greeks of the colonies had mixed genetics, as the initial colonists came in contact since their arrival with local populations.[34] On the other hand, the Greekness of the Western Greeks or those in other colonies was never questioned by other Greeks and, inversely, several populations not considered Greek were Hellenised not only culturally but also genetically to a certain degree in those adventurous times. Certainly, many cities and regions that are not mentioned as Greek were culturally Hellenised to various degrees, sometimes to the point of being almost perfectly incorporated into Greek culture. Similar areas often had mixed local and Greek populations, such as parts of central Sicily, or large Greek communities, such as some Etruscan cities.

The social and class stratification of the Greek cities of the West gradually became more complex, and significant inequalities emerged between the upper and lower classes. Indeed, it seems that the contrasts in the colonies were more acute despite the great wealth and generally high standards of living, which could explain the permanent tendency of Sicilian cities towards tyranny. The solid middle classes, which Aristotle already mentions in his *Politics* as the foundation of political stability for a society,[35] probably failed to establish themselves in the colonies. Furthermore, perhaps this was due precisely because of the initial equality, which created a tendency for the newly rich to concentrate on aggressive armouring of their power and privileges, with the result that the popular masses often placed their hopes in a tyrant saviour, who consistently overthrew the oligarchy in the name of the people.

It is telling, for example, that after the first period of settlement, the established colonists tended, as early as the seventh and sixth centuries BCE, to limit the possibilities of naturalisation for those Greeks who arrived afterwards, and, of course, for foreigners, excluding them from political life and power.[36] One could undoubtedly observe similar phenomena in the metropolises. In Athens, after the prevalence of democracy and its peak, stringent policies were followed regarding naturalisation. In the metropolises, however, the traditional aristocracy, perhaps precisely because it was long established, was more moderate. Moreover, there was a larger middle class, which created better political balance and stability, with the result that tyranny was considered an obsolete form of government at the same time as it was taking off in Sicily.

A typical Greek colony's constitution, however, would have provided for the existence of an assembly or senate of a limited number of citizens, the majority of them aristocrats, often around 1,000, as well as one or more elected governors general, who, as executive power were controlled by the assembly. The influence of the people varied from almost insignificant to crucial in cases and periods when there was a democratic constitution. It is, however, characteristic that even tyrants did not abolish the people's assemblies, maintaining at least formally the public dialogue and the participation of citizens in public affairs.

The Greek cities of continental Italy and Sicily over the centuries had developed a sophisticated cultural life, which produced many of antiquity's leading philosophical, technological, and artistic works. The abundance and aesthetic excellence of temples, statues, vases, mosaics, and relief art, which, despite the destruction that has occurred over time, remains immense, is undeniable proof of the very high level of art and architecture in the Greek cities of the West, while their philosophical and scientific thought was equally exceptional and pioneering. In Elea, in southern Italy, the Eleatic school of philosophy was born, with Parmenides and Zeno as its foremost exponents, while the philosopher Xenophanes lived and wrote in the same city. The philosopher and mathematician Pythagoras fled to Croton, where he taught for many years and created the famous Pythagorean communities, while the great philosopher Empedocles came from Akragas, and the famous engineer and mathematician Archimedes was born and lived in Syracuse.

The latter followed and developed an excellent and long-standing tradition, as the Sicilian Greeks had been renowned from previous centuries for the exceptional and innovative degree to which they had developed their technological capabilities. As early as the fifth century BCE, their mechanical knowledge and constructions were famous and sought-after in the Mediterranean. Significantly, the famous jurist Lysias mentions in one of his speeches that Pericles himself had proposed to the Syracusan businessman Cephalus to open a weapons production workshop in Athens. In the following centuries, the most impressive siege engines were to be built in Sicily, and complex battle tactics using many different armed bodies would be implemented.

For the Greeks of the colonies, just as for those of the metropolises, military service was fundamental to the concept of citizenship, and a career in leading positions in the army was necessary to be counted among the aristocrats. The primary mode of combat was, as in metropolitan Greece, the hoplite phalanx, whose presence in the ranks was compulsory for all citizens since the age of 18. Each citizen purchased the armour at his own risk and expense, and its quality reflected its owner's social status and prestige. As mentioned, the Greeks, of course, gradually adopted the habit of hiring mercenary troops.

Over time, the citizens of the Sicilian cities remained relatively more resilient than those of the Italian cities as the constant presence of the Carthaginians and the long conflict with them demanded military readiness and fighting ability. Nevertheless, it must be stressed that the Greek cities of Italy also participated in the wars against Carthage, which often supported their Syracusan and Sicilian compatriots by sending massive military forces and paying a heavy toll of blood, even though they were fighting far from their homelands.

Finally, it is important to remember – as in the case of the Greek-Etruscan competition and conflicts – that the rivalry and wars between the Western Greeks and the Phoenicians/Carthaginians were fierce and marked the history of the pre-Roman Western Mediterranean. However, it would be a mistake to consider that the relationship between the two ethnicities and cultures took an exclusively hostile form and that they were completely separated. It is clear that alongside the wars between them, the Greeks and the Phoenicians/Carthaginians had close commercial and cultural contacts but also multidimensional, shifting political relations, which several times complicated the ethnic composition of the warring factions even during wars.

In the Phoenician and Carthaginian cities, Greek communities very often, as in Carthage itself, had significant activity, especially in the technical and artistic sectors. Conversely, there were Phoenician and Carthaginian communities in the Greek cities, which played an important role in the commercial and banking sectors. In some cases, there were probably even cities with a largely mixed population, and mixed marriages were certainly taking place.

That mixed dynamic is illustrated by the contrasting opinions of two elders of Greek civilisation, Homer and Herodotus. In *Odyssey*, Homer gives a very negative view of the Phoenicians, describing them as inclined to fraud and cheating.[37] However, Herodotus provides a contrary, positive view, describing the Phoenician merchants as righteous and trustworthy.[38]

Chapter 3

The Rise of Syracuse and the Battle of Himera

In 491 BCE, the tyrant of Gela, Hippocrates, defeated the army of Syracuse at the Battle of the River Helorus, having already extended his rule to Naxos and Zancle.[1] Thanks to this victory, he conquered the neighbouring city of Kamarina, but he soon died. Subsequently, the aristocratic general Gelon seized power in Gela, succeeding in imposing himself on the sons of Hippocrates.[2]

A few years later, social unrest and conflicts broke out in Syracuse, during which the demos allied with the Cyllyrians (Killirioi), a class of slaves similar to that of the Helots in Sparta, and expelled from the city the aristocrats, called *gamoroi*, establishing a democratic constitution.[3] The *gamoroi* then fled to Gela and sought Gelon's help. Gelon interceded and persuaded the citizens of Syracuse to accept the *gamoroi* back into the city, possibly reaching a compromise. His successful mediation and the trust shown to him by both sides allowed him to emerge as a guarantor of stability and social peace, effectively imposing his authority. Consequently, in 485 BCE, the Syracusans awarded him the newly created office of emperor general, that is to say, the supreme ruler of the city with full powers.

Gelon did not abolish the assembly. However, from then on, it had a more formal and advisory role, and its primary function was limited to ratifying the decrees of the emperor general, who had effectively established a tyranny. In this way, Gelon became the leader of what was now an enlarged hegemony in Sicily, as he also allied with the tyrant of Akragas (modern Agrigento), Theron. To ratify the alliance, they arranged marriages between the two families.

For Syracuse, this would be the beginning of a rapid rise that in a few years would make it the most powerful city in Sicily, and one of the most powerful in the entire Mediterranean region. Until then, the city of Syracuse, although ancient and located in a strategic geographical point, was of secondary importance and weight among the Greek cities of Sicily and mainland Italy, being smaller and less potent than Gela, Akragas, Rhegio, or Taras (modern Taranto). However, Gelon, realising the strategically crucial position of the city at the eastern end of Sicily, decided to move his headquarters to it, drastically upgrading its importance and leaving his brother Hieron governor of Gela.[4]

Gelon then greatly enlarged Syracuse by building markets and harbours and constructing strong walls that covered a larger area than the city had previously occupied. It is indicative of the massive works that took place and the extent of Syracuse over centuries in antiquity that it had a pervasive aqueduct system, which was so well made and preserved that some of its parts have in modern times contributed to the city's drinking water supply and agricultural irrigation needs.[5]

The tyrant aimed to create a great naval and commercial power by promoting the city's trade and maritime might. Understanding that to achieve these goals he needed a much more significant population than the one Syracuse had at the time, Gelon transferred half the people of his homeland, Gela, and almost the entire population of Kamarina to Syracuse.[6] In addition, he wiped some smaller cities in the north off the map, transferring their nobility to Syracuse and giving them citizenship with full rights while at the same time selling their poor inhabitants as slaves. The population increased even more thanks to the arrival of immigrants from metropolitan Greece at the invitation of Gelon, among them many Arcadian mercenaries.

In this way, within three years, Gelon transformed a city of no particular power and importance into a great international power, similar in size to Sparta and Athens, and capable of confronting the most significant power of the Western Mediterranean, Carthage. The two cities were to create a competitive bipolar international system in the West for over two centuries until both finally succumbed to Rome.

During the same years that Gelon was creating a new great power in Syracuse, the tyrant of Rhegio, Anaxilaus, had increased his influence. Rhegio was located at the southernmost tip of the Italian peninsula, and Anaxilaus wished to conquer Zancle, which lay on the opposite Sicilian coast, in order to grasp complete control of the strategic position of the strait between Sicily and mainland Italy, the modern Strait of Messina. Securing complete control of the strait would make him a ruler with broader ambitions.

In 493 BCE, Anaxilaus occupied Zancle using Samian and Milesian refugees who had recently fled to Sicily after the end of the Ionian revolt and the defeat that brought about the subjugation of the Greeks of Asia Minor to the Persians. However, the tyrant of Gela, Hippocrates, also wanted to maintain control of the geostrategic hub of the strait. For the opposite reasons, he could not allow the establishment of a hegemonic power based on the strait. He, therefore, persuaded the Samian and Milesian refugees to cross over to his side, ultimately keeping Zancle in the sphere of influence of Gela.

Anaxilaus reacted a few years later. In 486 BCE, he intervened forcefully and conquered Zancle, expelling the Samians and Milesians and installing Messenians originating from the Peloponnese in their place. The city of Zancle was then renamed Messene, as it is still called today (Messina). By extending his influence to the Sicilian side of the strait, Anaxilaus was emerging as the leader of a second rising powerful Greek pole in the region against the one that the Syracuse–Akragas alliance was forming at the same time. In this, he collaborated with his father-in-law and ally Terillus, the tyrant of Himera, in northern Sicily.

A new great power was thus beginning to rise, sited on the Sicilian north and the Italian south. However, the impressive strengthening of Syracuse achieved by Gelon in those same years would prove unrivalled and decisive for the interstate order of Sicily and the Greek West. The hegemonic alliance of southern Sicily effectively declared war on Anaxilaus' 'Kingdom of the Straits' when Theron attacked and captured Himera with the Akragantine troops, forcing Terillus to flee to his son-in-law and ally at the edge of the Italian peninsula.

The action foreshadowed that Gelon and Theron intended to subjugate Messene and Rhegio, extending their hegemony northwards. Anaxilaus, sure of this development and fearing that he did not have sufficient forces to meet an attack by Syracuse and Akragas, called for help from the region's greatest power, i.e. Carthage.

Having certainly watched with concern in previous years the sudden emergence of a peer competitor in the rising Syracusan power, the Carthaginians responded immediately to Anaxilaus' appeal, finding the opportunity to carry out in Sicily an intervention that they had most likely been planning either way.

The ancient sources and opinions probably do not allow us to be sure whether the Persian invasion of metropolitan Greece and the Carthaginian invasion of Sicily in 480 BCE were thoroughly combined and coordinated actions, coincidental, or something in the middle. What is certain is that in the early fifth century BCE, Persians and Carthaginians perceived the Greek world as their common main rival and had allied relations with each other. Most probably, the Great King did not recognise the Carthaginians nor anyone else as equals but as subordinate allies.

It is also certain that the Spartans and the Athenians asked Gelon for support in the face of Xerxes' terrifyingly robust campaign, but the tyrant of Syracuse refused. According to Herodotus, Gelon demanded to be the supreme commander of either the army or the fleet to assist, but the Spartan and Athenian envoys refused.[7]

More precisely, the ambassadors told Gelon that the Persians' claim that they invaded Greece only to punish Athens was just a pretext. In reality, they wanted to conquer the entire country. So, as Gelon had become very powerful as the ruler of Sicily, that is, a substantial part of Greece, he should support their aim, the ambassadors said. If Greece as a whole was united, the gathered force would be large, and it would manage to push back the invaders. Gelon became furious, responding to the ambassadors that a few years earlier, he implored the Greeks to send troops so they could co-operate in liberating the commercial ports that the Carthaginians had occupied, and seek revenge for the death of Dorieus. Yet, they did not send any troops either to help Syracuse with the ports – although they had excellent profits from them – or even to exact revenge for Dorieus' unfortunate expedition. He had to do everything by himself, but now that the war had come upon them, they remembered Gelon.

Herodotus' description of the dialogue is intriguing because of not only Gelon's complaints and accusations but also because the Syracusan ruler talks almost as if there is a unique interconnected war with various fronts.

That's more evidence favouring the notion of a Persian–Carthaginian alliance against the Greek world. Lorenzo Braccesi adds[8] that the picture can become even more expansive if we consider that the first treaty between Rome and Carthage dates to around 509 BCE, according to Polybius.[9] That is, precisely in the same years as Dorieus' second expedition and the possible first diplomatic connections between Persia and Carthage. Moreover, the treaty between Rome and Carthage coincides with a whole set of agreements between the Etruscan cities and the Carthaginians, documented by Aristotle[10] and confirmed by modern archaeology, with the finding of the three golden Pyrgi Tablets in 1964 during the excavation at the site of ancient Etruscan city Pyrgi, 30 miles north of Rome. The tablets are dated the end of the sixth century or the beginning of the fifth century BCE and contain a text commemorating the founding of a temple dedicated to the Phoenician goddess Astarte, identifying her with the Etruscan goddess Uni. The text is written in Etruscan on two tablets and in Phoenician on the third one.

Returning to the dialogue written by Herodotus, Gelon went on to say that he was however magnanimous and he would not repeat the metropolitan Greeks' indifference. On the contrary, he was ready to send a mighty fleet of 200 triremes and a robust army of 28,000 soldiers immediately to mainland Greece – 20,000 hoplites, plus 2,000 heavy cavalry, 2,000 light cavalry, 2,000 archers, and 2,000 slingers, and also to supply grain for the entire Greek army until the war's end. This would be under one condition: that he would be the supreme commander of the army, the commander of the Greeks against the barbarians.

The Spartan ambassador was indignant to hear this, and he said that Agamemnon would scream if he learned that Gelon and the Syracusans had the nerve to take away hegemony from the Spartans. 'If you want to help, you must know you'll be under Lacedaemonian leadership. Otherwise, do not help at all,'[11] declared the Spartan ambassador. Likewise, the Athenian ambassador excluded the possibility of Syracusan leadership in the sea.

Either way, we can suppose that if the description corresponds to what was actually said, Gelon's attitude was probably a pretext for refusing, without showing that he did not wish to render assistance. The real reason for his refusal could only be the enormous preparations that were taking place at the same time in all the Carthaginian possessions, with the gathering of immense troops such as Libyan, Iberian, Sardinian, Corsican, and other mercenaries.[12] Preparations showed that Carthage's aim was not a limited intervention in Himera to strengthen its presence in Sicily but the imposition of its complete domination of the large Mediterranean island.

The Carthaginian army that landed at Panormus in the summer of 480 BCE was indeed massive, supported by 200 warships and 1,000 transport ships. Even though modern estimates consider it reasonable to think of a fighting force of about 100,000 soldiers instead of the 300,000 who landed in Sicily according to tradition, the invading Carthaginian army was, in any case, immense by the ancient world's measures. Numbers mentioned by ancient historians about enemy armies may sometimes be excessive and unrealistic, but that should not raise questions about the credibility of ancient historians in general, in the sense of their good faith and honesty regarding their sources. We can imagine that the descriptions of those who fought in those battles were excessive – sometimes because they wanted to brag about the strength of the armies they fought against, other times in good faith – as it is normal for our perception of reality to exaggerate when intense emotions of excitement or fear are in play. It can happen even in a concert or a sporting event. Even today during wars, armies and governments tend to exaggerate or reduce numbers for propaganda purposes despite all the technological means we have at our disposal to verify their claims. Although in this case I agree with critics that 300,000 seems indeed way too much, I also think we often have an underestimation bias towards the ancient world in general when it comes to sizes and technology. We don't really understand the sizes and the complexity of those cities, armies, and societies. Modern digital technology and AI can offer us closer looks, but they are always recreations and representations, not reality. All we can see is ruins, which subconsciously can create a minimalistic bias. Conversely, archaeology often reveals more significant sites, transports, and armies than modern minimalist estimates believed existed, proving that ancient sources were usually accurate and reasonable, not excessive or biased. The most important and indicative example is Moses Finley's primitivistic view on the ancient economy and trade, proven utterly erroneous in the last decades by archaeologists and economic historians.[13]

At the head of the Carthaginian army was Hamilcar Mago, a member of a prominent aristocratic family, who, after the landing, marched along the northern Sicilian coast towards Himera. The fleet sailed alongside him, and troops from the allied Sicilian cities, including the Greek city of Selinus, joined his forces. The plan also foresaw that Anaxilaus' forces would arrive from the east.

When the Carthaginians arrived near Himera, they built two fenced camps, one on the beach north of the city, where the ships withdrew, and the other frontally on its western side. The city of Himera was on a hill ascending above the west bank of the river Himera, from which it had taken its name, and at that time, the troops of Akragas, led by Theron, were inside it. The defenders attempted some exits to harass the Carthaginian forces, awaiting reinforcements from Syracuse. For their part, the Carthaginians awaited the arrival of their allies from Rhegio and Messene to close Himera in a crushing vice from the west and east.

In the meantime, Gelon had assembled a powerful army with forces from Syracuse, Gela, and the other allied Greek cities and was marching rapidly towards Himera. His forces totalled 55,000 men, including 5,000 horsemen. When he reached Himera, the Greek army encamped on the east side of the city and the river, ensuring its supply and preventing a possible blockade.

Then Gelon, taking advantage of the fact that he had a larger cavalry, although his army was inferior in total number of soldiers to the Carthaginian army, took the initiative and ensured, thanks to his cavalry, the control of the surrounding area. Nevertheless, the situation for Hamilcar was not bad at all. The Carthaginian general had the unique opportunity to face most of the Sicilian Greeks' forces concentrated in one place and to win the war and the dominion over Sicily with a single blow in a major battle. Therefore, he calmly awaited the arrival of the rest of his Greek allies and perhaps further reinforcements from Carthage to attack in better conditions. Instead, Gelon wished to crush the Carthaginian army as soon as possible before it had time to grow stronger.

The superiority of the Greeks in cavalry and the control they were allowed to exert over the area around Himera paid off when a group of horsemen captured a messenger of the enemy army. The information carried by the messenger stated that a military unit of soldiers from Selinunte was expected to arrive at the coastal part of the Carthaginian camp. The Selinunteans had allied themselves with Carthage because Theron had previously occupied Heraclea Minoa, which they had controlled until then, and also because one of the Sicilian cities that Gelon had eliminated in order to enlarge Syracuse was their metropolis, Megara Hyblaea. However, the fact that Selinus was located near Motya, the main Carthaginian base in Sicily, prompted the Selinunteans, after the defeat of the previous century, to seek good relations with the Carthaginians.

Gelon and his officers thought that this information gave them a great opportunity. They prepared a body of elite soldiers, who appeared in front of the Carthaginian camp pretending to be the Selinuntean equestrians the Carthaginians were waiting for. The guards were deceived, and opened the gate, allowing the Syracusans to enter the camp. The result was that the latter immediately rushed towards the Carthaginian ships and set them on fire. The Carthaginians tried to fight back, and skirmishes broke out, with the Syracusans killing several of the unprepared and unconcerned soldiers who were in the camp by the sea.

The confusion caused by the surprise attack and the fires on the ships spread to the entire camp of the Carthaginians. Instead, Gelon and his troops were ready to attack and awaited the predetermined signal. When the forces on the hill saw that everything had gone according to plan, they sent the message to Gelon, and he immediately moved the army towards the main Carthaginian camp, passing through the south side of Himera.

When the Greeks approached the camp, a very fierce battle began, in which the two opposing armies fought with unyielding stubbornness, knowing that victory or defeat would be total. The tide tipped to the Greek side when Theron, with the troops of Akragas, left the city of Himera, moved to the western side of the Carthaginian camp, and attacked the enemies from the rear. The trapped Carthaginians, who had also lost much of the fleet, fought desperately until night, when those who survived surrendered. The battle had turned into a triumph for the Greeks and a disaster for the Carthaginians, who saw the expedition's entire land and naval forces wiped out or captured.

Among the dead was Hamilcar, who, according to the Carthaginian tradition, during the battle was throwing carcasses into the fire as a sacrifice to the god Baal to help his troops, and seeing with despair the crushing of his army, he fell into the flames, sacrificing himself.[14] According to another version, however, the Carthaginian general was killed by the Syracusan elite troops who carried out the commando operation in the naval Carthaginian camp where he had happened to be.

The Battle of Himera is undoubtedly one of the most important military events in ancient history. If, in addition, one examines it in combination with the naval Battle of Salamis, which took place in the same year and perhaps at some nearby date in the autumn of 480 BCE, then it acquires world-historical significance. These two great Greek victories repulsed the coordinated or parallel attack of the two other major powers of the time, ensuring the survival and independence of the Greek world and paving the way for the spectacular further strengthening that followed.

From an even longer-term historical and geopolitical perspective, the repulsion of the Persian and Carthaginian attack in 480 BCE was the first momentous defeat of the most potent eastern nations and the beginning of the rise of the Greco-Western area to the role of historical protagonist. This rise would continue in the following decades. The Macedonians of Alexander the Great would complete it by establishing the first great Western hegemony in history, followed by the Romans.

Carthage's attempt to take control of Sicily had failed. Instead, the Carthaginians were in danger of losing their presence on the island altogether. Nevertheless, in the end, Gelon proved lenient enough to accept the defeated enemies' peace proposal, which mainly provided the payment of a war indemnity of 2,000 talents. The triumphant tyrant sent rich tributes to Delphi and Olympia for victory as a champion and defender of Western Greece, and built temples to Demeter and Persephone in Sicily.

After the victory at Himera, the Syracuse–Akragas alliance effectively took control of Sicily, with the Carthaginian possessions becoming, at least to some extent, its vassals. Anaxilaus and Rhegio also allied themselves with Syracuse, as did the city of Selinunte. Anaxilaus' daughter married Gelon's brother and tyrant of Gela, Hieron, as a corroboration of the alliance. The victory also triggered a significant economic and cultural boom, alongside that recorded at the same period in metropolitan Greece, as, apart from securing booty and war reparations from the Carthaginians, it also favoured an increase in the general influence of Greek cities and their commercial activity.

For the Carthaginians, on the contrary, the defeat brought a retreat of their influence and a relative economic and political crisis. What is also certain is that for decades, the Carthaginian leadership ruled out the possibility of a new intervention in Sicily, as Carthage was no longer confronting scattered Greek cities, disconnected and competing with each other, but with a solid great Greek power.

Gelon died two years after the Battle of Himera and was succeeded by his brother Hieron. In turn, he would soon become the protagonist of a great victory, this time against the other traditional rivals of the Greeks of the West, namely, the Etruscans.

The Naval Battle of Cumae

Cumae was founded around 730 BCE by Euboean colonists. The fertile land of Campania and the abundant fauna of its seas ensured high potential for prosperity for the city and the other Greek colonies built between the eighth and seventh centuries in the region. With its rich agricultural production and intense commercial activity, Cumae developed and became stronger.

During the same period, the Etruscans, who dominated central and northern Italy, were at their peak. Between the latter part of the seventh century BCE and the first part of the sixth century BCE, the Etruscans extended their influence southwards, imposing their rule on Latium and occupying lands in Campania. At the same time, the Etruscans were undoubtedly keeping a close eye on the development of Cumae and other Greek cities in Campania, which emerged as a potential counterweight to further Etruscan expansion.

Nevertheless, trade and cultural exchanges were highly beneficial to both sides. For the time being, the primary concern of the Etruscans was the growing influence of Massalia and its ambitions in the Tyrrhenian Sea. The situation changed in the mid-sixth century BCE when the intensifying rivalry between Greeks, Carthaginian Phoenicians, and Etruscans in the area culminated in the Battle of Alalia mentioned in the previous chapter. The prevalence of the Carthaginian–Etruscan alliance in the Tyrrhenian Sea opened the way for the Etruscans to expand further into the Italian south. Cumae was now their main rival.

Therefore, in 524 BCE, a sizeable Etruscan army attacked Cumae, intending to conquer it, but the Greek forces prevailed in the battle that followed in front of the city walls.[15] The halting of the southward expansion was the beginning of a series of adverse developments for the Etruscans in the following years, the most important being the overthrow of the Etruscan dynasty in Rome in 509 BCE and the establishment of the Roman Republic. The Etruscans responded with a campaign against Rome the following year under the leadership of King Lars Porsenna, who laid siege to Rome in order to retake it. Yet, the Romans managed to defeat and repel the Etruscans, with Cumae making a small contribution to the Romans' success, having sent supplies in aid of the Romans.

Even more decisive was the contribution of Cumae to another defeat of the Etruscans at Latium, this time during the siege of Ariccia. The Cumaens sent an army to reinforce the Latin city, and the Greek troops swept the besieging Etruscans away, contributing decisively to their final retreat from the region of Latium.

The defeats of the Etruscans at Latium brought about an increasing isolation of the territories they held in Campania, which ended up unconnected by land to the centres of Etruria. Since attempts to recapture Latin territories failed, the Etruscans set their sights on striking at Cumae, seeing its key supporting role in favour of the Latins. Should the Greek cities of Campania be subdued, the Romans and other Latins would find themselves trapped among Etruscan bases and armies, with no help from their Greek allies.

The Etruscan strategic plan envisaged a major attack against Cumae, carried out by the powerful Etruscan fleet stationed in the Tyrrhenian

Sea. The Cumaens, seeing the threat approaching, appealed for help to the tyrant of Syracuse, Hieron, who was continuing the policy of his brother Gelon. His goal was to make Syracuse the leading city of both the Sicilian and Italian Greeks, creating a powerful Greek alliance or federation that would dominate the Western Mediterranean.[16]

Consequently, Hieron immediately sent a powerful fleet to the area of Cumae, which confronted the Etruscan fleet in a great naval battle fought in 474 BCE. The naval battle ended with a decisive victory for the Syracuse fleet in the third Greek triumph in a short period, after those that had preceded it against the Persians and Carthaginians.[17] The Greek world celebrated three historic victories, seen as proof of the Greeks' destiny to dominate East and West.

Hieron sent gifts to Olympia and Delphi and was honoured as a champion of Hellenism against the barbarians, as his brother had been before him.[18] The victory at Cumae made Syracuse the ruler of Sicily and southern Italy. At the same time, the Carthaginians omitted to do any foreign intervention for decades, and the Etruscans never returned to the southern Tyrrhenian Sea.

During the same period, the city of Taras had achieved two important victories against the Italian tribes of Messapians and Peucetians, even sending honours to Delphi.[19] However, in 473/472 BCE, the Tarantines finally suffered a significant defeat at the hands of the Italian tribes, which prevented them from spreading their power even further in the region.[20] The indigenous tribes were often involved in wars with the Greek cities of Italy, but they also adopted many Greek cultural elements and had economic transactions with them. Of course, the same happened also between the Greek cities. Intra-Greek conflicts in Italy were as frequent, fierce, and bloody as those in metropolitan Greece and Sicily.

Indeed, precisely in those years, the two biggest cities in Sicily, Syracuse and Akragas, ended up in war between them. After Theron's death, his son, Thrasydeus, became very unpopular among the Akragantines, as he was violent and tyrannical as a ruler, unlike his father, whom the citizens considered fair and non-oppressive. Thrasydeus also turned against Hieron, believing that Akragas no longer should accept the Syracusan leadership. He mobilised Akragas and Himera's troops and hired mercenaries, assembling an army of around 20,000 men to challenge the Syracusans. Hieron responded by mobilising a large army of his own, and the two stronger Sicilian Greek cities clashed in a huge battle with heavy casualties and thousands of dead for both sides, since 'here Greeks were matched against Greeks', as Diodorus mentions. According to the Sicilian Greek historian, the Akragantines lost more than 4,000 men, and the Syracusans lost around 2,000 men. Syracuse confirmed its primacy by winning the battle, and Thrasydeus was exiled to the city of Megara in mainland Greece, where he was later condemned and executed in 471 or 470 BCE. On the other hand, in Akragas, democracy was restored. The war between Syracuse and Akragas was officially over three years later when the Akragantines sent ambassadors to Syracuse to ask for a peace settlement and to come to terms with Hieron.[21]

Chapter 4

The Second Major Carthaginian Attack in Sicily

Hieron died in 467 BCE and was succeeded by his brother Thrasybulus, who was inferior as a leader to his two glorious brothers. At the same time, despite the tremendous historical successes of the two tyrants during the previous twenty years, a faction had grown strong in Syracuse that sought to overthrow the regime of the Deinomenids. Consequently, only a year later, a revolution overthrew Thrasybulus and established a democratic regime in Syracuse similar to that of Athens.[1]

This development perhaps had an essential cultural outcome, as according to an ancient notion, rhetoric was invented in Syracuse right after the fall of the Deinomenids' tyranny, when, in 466 BCE, Corax persuaded the disorderly Syracusan demos and gained control over them. That was the beginning of democracy in Syracuse, which would last for sixty straight years, as we'll see. Later, Corax's pupil Tisias wrote the first treatise on rhetoric.[2]

Another product of this development with the rise of democracy was that Syracuse's foreign policy changed. The democratic Syracusans abandoned the soft policy pursued by Gelon and Hieron after the initial strengthening of Syracuse and the Battle of Himera, which aimed at creating a Greek federation of the West under Syracuse through the establishment of alliances and family ties. Instead, they adopted a more aggressive attitude towards the other Greek cities and the Sicilian tribes, aiming to conquest the entire region of Sicily.[3] In this way, while maintaining or even increasing the power and influence of Syracuse in the first instance, they undermined the unity of the Greeks that the Deinomenids had begun to build and, thus, the foundations of Syracuse's power in the long term.

In the following decades, the Syracusans completely subjugated the native peoples of eastern and central Sicily. They imposed their hegemony on the Greek cities, even occupying their ally Akragas in 445 BCE and making it their vassal.[4] From the Battle of Himera onwards, Selinus had also allied itself with Syracuse and was, in a sense, their surveyor in western Sicily, as was Himera itself.

In 431 BCE, the Peloponnesian War between Sparta and Athens broke out in mainland Greece. Ten years later, the Athenians and the Spartans signed the so-called Peace of Nicias, which, according to its terms, was to last for thirty years. Then Segesta, the largest city of the indigenous Sicilian people of the Elymians, which was at odds with the Syracusan ally Selinus and was being raided and plundered in its territories, called on the mighty Athens for help – as Leontini and the other Chalcidian colonies of Sicily had already done a few years earlier, when under direct pressure from the Syracusans.[5]

In the previous years, the Athenians initiated a Western policy under the leadership of Pericles, showing that they intended to spread their influence beyond the Aegean to Sicily and southern Italy. In 427 BCE, Syracuse's aggressive policy initiated a new conflict, this time with Leontini. The Ionian city asked for help from Athens, which then made its first dynamic entrance into Sicilian affairs, sending a fleet of twenty ships full of soldiers.[6] Two camps were created on the grand Mediterranean island. A coalition led by the Athenians, including Naxos, Rhegio, Kamarina, and Sicels, alongside Leontini. Syracuse, with its allies, including Gela and Locri, on the other side. The war between the two alliances went on for the next three years with various episodes, especially the capture of Messene by the Athenian coalition in 426 BCE and the recapture of the important city by the Syracusan alliance the following year. Eventually, in the summer of 425 BCE, Gela and Kamarina firmed a peace treaty between them, as the two traditional allies had suddenly become enemies because they were part of the opposing coalitions fighting for control of Sicily.[7] The two cities decided to enlarge the treaty to include the other parts of the conflict, too, to find a peaceful solution and not let turmoil and war keep falling upon the Sicilian Greeks and the different peoples of Sicily. So they invited all the other cities to send ambassadors

The Second Major Carthaginian Attack in Sicily 39

to Gela to participate in a big congress aiming to find a diplomatic way out of the war impasse. Very acutely, the Syracusan delegation, led by Hermocrates, used the presence and involvement of Athenian troops in the war to rally all the Sicilians behind Syracuse. They portrayed the Athenian presence as a foreign intervention in the internal Sicilian affairs and a threat to the freedom of all the Sicilian cities, proposing a general peace and collaboration of the Sicilian cities under the leadership of Syracuse.[8] Being united under Syracuse's leadership would guarantee that external interference would not threaten Sicilian cities again. Syracuse also offered a deal to Kamarina, exchanging control over the Sicel city Morgantina with money. The representatives of the various Greek cities of Sicily accepted this ancient 'Monroe Doctrine' of Hermocrates and Syracuse, and the Athenian fleet departed. The first Athenian military intervention in Sicily had thus the opposite effect, paradoxically uniting the island behind Syracuse when it was a part of the island that had asked for Athenian help against Syracusan hegemony.

However, within a few years, in 421 BCE, Athens effectively emerged victorious from the ten-year conflict with Sparta since the Peloponnesian invasion of Attica failed to achieve its strategic objectives, and the Athenian alliance continued to dominate the Aegean and significant parts of mainland Greece fully.

It should be stressed that the fact that the Elymians had asked for the help of Athens and not of their traditional ally and much closer Carthage is indicative of the Athenian power at that time, as well as of the weakening and introversion that the crushing of Himera had caused in Carthage. Indeed, this period was the longest in which Carthage did not make extensive use of military power to advance its interests, having accepted the primacy of Syracuse in the region.

On this occasion, Athens found the opportunity to intervene in Sicily, aiming to implement a plan of conquer and consequently to further increase its power, to the extent that it would allow it to subjugate Sparta and the Peloponnese, but also Carthage, and to become the ruler of the entire Mediterranean. The Athenian Ecclesia of the demos decided enthusiastically in favour of the campaign in Sicily, following the urging of

Alcibiades, the new star of the democratic party and nephew of Pericles, and voting against the opposing position of the oligarchic Nicias.

However, the Sicilian campaign that took place between 415 and 413 BCE ended in a crushing defeat for Athens, which saw its expeditionary force almost annihilated after the impressive and stubborn resistance of the Syracusans. It also saw the decision of the Athenians to condemn Alcibiades to death in absentia for a religious scandal shortly after his departure with the expeditionary force. During the disastrous Sicilian campaign, the Athenians, or better, the Athenian alliance, lost from 40,000 to 50,000 men and 216 triremes.[9]

The failure of Athens led Segesta to ask Carthage for help subsequently, but the latter initially refused and proposed to Syracuse that they should take charge of the matter. Although more than sixty-seven years after the defeat of Himera, Carthage had undoubtedly fully recovered, and there was a solid political faction within Carthage that supported an interventionist policy in Sicily, the Carthaginian leadership remained hesitant. On the other hand, rehabilitated and traumatised by the war against Athens, the Syracusans refused, too, arguing that Selinus and Segesta should find a solution between themselves.

After this development, the Selinunteans continued to raid and pillage the lands of Segesta. That helped the Carthaginian interventionist faction to prevail and take control of Carthage's foreign policy after decades. The leading figure of the faction was Shophet Hannibal Mago, grandson of Hamilcar and son of Gisco, who had been defeated and died in Himera, and son of Gisco, who had spent most of his life in Selinus as a hostage after the defeat. Hannibal argued that the intervention in favour of Segesta was necessary to protect Carthaginian interests in Sicily; otherwise, the Syracusans would soon take complete control of the island and occupy the Carthaginian cities there.

The Carthaginian Senate felt that the time was right for a dynamic return to Sicily because of the weakening of Syracuse caused by the Athenian siege. Therefore, they decided initially to send 5,000 Libyan mercenaries to Sicily, in addition to 800 Campanian mercenaries, who had initially come to Sicily to work – that is, to fight for the Athenians – and had been left unemployed.

The mercenary Carthaginian troops and the army of Segesta defeated the army of Selinus,[10] and then the two cities turned to their patron powers. The Syracusans regarded Carthage's intervention as a hostile action against them and a declaration of war. On the other side, the Carthaginians, between 410 and 409 BCE, prepared for a massive invasion of Sicily.

Hannibal made meticulous preparations, paying attention to every detail and equipping his forces with the most sophisticated technical means. The army he assembled and finally left Carthage for Sicily in the spring of 409 BCE numbered over 100,000 men, according to the ancient sources,[11] or 54,000–64,000 according to modern estimates.[12] It consisted of Carthaginians, Libyans, Iberians, and Campanians, supported by a war fleet of 60 triremes, plus some 1,500 transport ships.[13] The Carthaginian army landed at the western end of Sicily, near the artificial Gulf of Lilybea, and settled a little further north, near Motya.

In making this move, it was not clear whether Hannibal intended to attack Selinus or Syracuse by sea after Syracusan troops had left their city to come to help Selinus. The result was that the Syracusans did not grant the request of the Selinunteans for military aid, as in addition, a part of their forces were busy fighting against the Chalcidian colonies, namely Catania, the Leontini and Naxos, which had joined the Athenians in the previous years.[14] Apart from this, the Syracusans somewhat underestimated the strength of the Carthaginians and overestimated Selinus's ability to resist for a long time. Syracuse's inertia also left the forces of Akragas and Gela unused; instead, they were ready to move to give assistance to Selinus.

Having succeeded in confusing the Greeks, Hannibal marched against Selinus and laid siege to it. The city's population, which according to an estimation was 30,000 inhabitants, excluding the slaves,[15] joined in the defence in every possible way, creating many problems for the besiegers. At some point, the latter managed to open a breach in the walls and tried to penetrate the city. However, the Selinus response was immediate and forceful and repelled the attackers outside the walls with hand-to-hand fighting and bows, slingshots, and stone throwing. Then, the Carthaginians, with the Campanians and Iberian mercenaries carrying out the attack, enlarged the wall's opening further by using siege rams and made massive attempts to invade the city. The Selinunteans fought desperately and repulsed the attacks. However, the number of available forces was steadily decreasing, while at the same time, the vast Carthaginian army was constantly replenishing their fighting forces.

On the ninth day of the siege, the defence of Selinus broke, and the Carthaginian troops entered the city like a flood. Battles ensued in the streets, the town's central square, and in front of the doors of the houses. Yet nothing could contain the momentum and massiveness of the invaders, who carried out a horrible massacre without distinction between men, women, and children.[16] At the end of it, 16,000 inhabitants were dead, 5,000 were prisoners, and only 2,600 had managed to escape and make their way to Akragas.[17]

In the previous days, the Syracusans had finally withdrawn their forces from Catania, the Leontini, and Naxos, and sent a military corps of 3,000 men to reinforce Selinus. However, it could not reach the city before the disaster. Consequently, they could only propose to liberate the prisoners and request that the temples be respected. Nevertheless, Hannibal rejected the proposal and their request, being determined to sell the survivors as slaves, as well as to plunder the city thoroughly. He only proposed that the pro-Carthaginian exiles return to Selinus and rebuild it, with an obligation to pay tribute to Carthage.[18]

The Carthaginian army then marched towards Himera and on the way was reinforced by about 20,000 soldiers of the Sicani and the Sicels who considered that they had found the opportunity to free themselves from Greek domination. The city had a population of perhaps as many as 60,000. It was the main objective of the campaign, as Hannibal was determined to avenge his grandfather's crushing in the same place seventy-one years before to restore his family's honour. The elderly Carthaginian aristocrat had waited all his life for the opportunity to dismantle Himera and wipe out its population.

The Carthaginian attack began this time not with siege towers but with digging tunnels under the walls and siege rams. The city at that time had 12,000 soldiers, half of whom came from other Greek cities. In addition, shortly afterwards, the corps that the Syracusans had already sent during the siege of Selinus arrived from Akragas, reinforced by about 1,000 soldiers from other cities. At the head of the corps, which consequently increased the total number of Greek forces to 16,000 men, was Syracuse's Diocles, who, after he arrived in Himera, assumed the chief command.

The Carthaginians continued to try to undermine the stability of the walls and eventually succeeded in causing part of them to collapse, thanks to underground tunnels. However, the Greek forces repelled the attempts of Carthaginian troops to enter the city until sunset, which interrupted the attack. The defenders made a makeshift repair to the wall, but the new situation made it more difficult to defend the walls. Consequently, Diocles and the other Greek commanders, given that they had a reasonably large army, decided to do something other than wait for the Carthaginian attack behind the walls and attack them in the open at dawn.[19]

The Greek exit surprised the Carthaginian troops, preparing to resume efforts to breach the walls. The solid column inflicted heavy losses on the enemies and drove them into flight. In their excitement, the Greeks thought they had won and pursued the retreating Carthaginians by breaking their lines, believing they had a chance to annihilate them. However, the provident Hannibal had kept several forces in the hills, and after the Greeks had withdrawn from the city and the phalanx had lost its formation, he unleashed them against them. This time, it was the Greeks who were taken by surprise before the onrushing attack of the enemy; they fled in disorderly fashion towards the city, having suffered heavy losses, equal to about 3,000 dead.[20]

The death toll on the Carthaginian side was more than twice as high, but the blow to the Greek camp was hefty, and there was a great deal of concern about what the next moves should be. At the same time, a fleet from Syracuse was arriving at the bay of Himera in those hours, and a rumour was spreading, it is not clear by whom, that the Carthaginian fleet was about to set out from Motya to strike Syracuse.

Diocles – wanting to rule out the possibility of another massacre like that of Selinus and to avoid risking the safety of Syracuse in case the rumour was true – decided to evacuate the city of Himera, amidst heated arguments and accusations of treason. During the night, the inhabitants were to be hurriedly embarked on board the ships with whatever possessions they could carry. Those who could not find room there were to depart at once on foot to march to Syracuse under cover of the army, who were also to retreat. A few forces would remain in Himera to ensure the Carthaginians did not take the city fast enough to make a case for pursuit. There also remained some older men and the sick, and those who decided not to leave the city but to stay to the end.[21]

With the break of dawn, the Carthaginians initiated their assault, persisting until the day's end, when the final pockets of resistance collapsed and the attackers entered the city en masse. There followed widespread looting and destruction, during which the Carthaginians burned all the temples and demolished the victory monument to the battle of 480 BCE.[22] Hannibal led the 3,000 remaining men to the spot where his grandfather Hamilcar had died, and killed them after torture. This is not surprise as, at least according to Greeks and Romans, the Carthaginians showed no mercy to prisoners; on the contrary, they displayed a complete lack of sympathy, crucifying some of them and subjecting others to unspeakable abuse.[23]

Hannibal also gave orders to his troops to capture any women and children who remained in the city. Having thus completed his revenge, the Carthaginian general left some forces in Sicily to aid his native allies and returned with countless spoils to Carthage, where he received the highest possible honours from his compatriots as a national benefactor.[24]

The Siege of Akragas

The levelling of the two Greek cities caused political turmoil in Syracuse. In the following period, the movement of Hermocrates – a member of one of the most prominent aristocratic families of the city and a hero of the resistance to the Athenian aggression in the previous years but who had been exiled as dangerous to democracy – manifested itself.[25]

Hermocrates returned after the Carthaginian invasion of Sicily, secured the support of about 1,000 Syracusan hoplites and several survivors of Selinus and Himera, and recruited mercenaries using his considerable fortune. Eventually, he assembled an army of about 6,000 loyal men determined to follow him. With this force, he began a personal war against the Carthaginians, wishing to prove his love for his country and worth to his compatriots, in contrast to the incompetence and meanness of its governors, who had engineered his exile. Hermocrates and his followers denounced them as responsible for the destruction and humiliation that the Greeks of Sicily had suffered and presented themselves as those who would restore the honour of the Greeks and take revenge on the barbarians.

Hermocrates' first action after the formation of the army was to recapture the deserted Selinus and fortify the city's citadel, making it his base.[26] He then invaded the Carthaginian territories and plundered the countryside of Motya and Panormus, even prevailing in battles over the city guards and forcing them to take refuge within their walls. These bold actions and victories boosted the morale of the Greeks to some extent and greatly enhanced the image of Hermocrates among his compatriots. Many of them began to think that they had made a great mistake in exiling him and that he was just the man the city and all of Greek Sicily needed in the critical and dramatic situation in which they found themselves.

The Syracusan noble tried to strengthen the sympathy towards him further and prepare the ground for his return by moving his forces to the region of Himera and collecting the unburied corpses of those who had fallen in the previous year's battle.[27] He loaded the dead into decorated carts and sent them to Syracuse to be buried as befitted fallen men for the homeland. At the same time, his followers contrasted his action with that of the leadership of the city, who had left the bodies of the soldiers unburied. The developed climate led to the exile of Diocles from Syracuse, but it was not enough to recall Hermocrates as well. The latter and his followers reacted by trying to seize power in the city in a *coup d'état*. Still, their attempt failed and was suppressed after the authorities' immediate reaction and the battle inside the city.[28]

At the same time, the Carthaginians, encouraged by the successes of the previous years and having large sums of money at their disposal thanks to the plundering of Greek cities, began in 407 BCE to form a vast army to conquer the entire Greek part of Sicily. The head of the invasion force would be the experienced but elderly Hannibal Mago again, this time accompanied by the younger Himilco.[29] The Carthaginian expeditionary force was to consist of Libyans, Iberians, Numidians, Campanians,

Maurusians, and Carthaginians, and the total extent of the troops would eventually reach perhaps 120,000 men or even more.[30]

The Syracusans sent a delegation to Carthage but its efforts to persuade the Carthaginian Senate to call off the invasion were ultimately fruitless. Consequently, the Syracusan fleets began patrolling the western coast of Sicily to confront the Carthaginians at sea and prevent the invasion. In the spring of 406 BCE, forty Syracusan triremes did indeed clash with an equally powerful Carthaginian fleet off Eryx at the island's western end and prevailed. However, the victory had no strategic significance since the particular Carthaginian fleet had, as it turned out, sailed westwards for diversionary purposes, precisely to facilitate the army's landing on the southern coast of Sicily. Hannibal and Himilco did indeed land undisturbed with their numerous army, causing great alarm among the Sicilian Greeks, who called for help from the Greek cities of Italy and the metropolitan Greek area, where the Peloponnesian War was still raging.[31]

The first target of the Carthaginian campaign would have been the city of Akragas, the second-largest Greek city in Sicily, with a population that according the ancient sources reached or exceeded 200,000 inhabitants.[32] Akragas stretched over an area of about 5,000 acres and had very high walls, a total length of 12 kilometres.[33] It was known for its inhabitants' luxurious lifestyle and famous for its temples' unique beauty. The city also had an excellent irrigation network, a famous extensive water park, magnificent gardens, and well-organised vineyards and olive groves, the produce of which was exported to many regions of the Mediterranean, including Carthage. For all these reasons, the ancients considered Empedocles' homeland one of the most beautiful cities in the world, and the moderns a prime illustration of how genius the Greeks were in choosing exceptional natural sites and designing their cities around them.[34]

In April 406 BCE, the Carthaginian forces reached Akragas, finding its entire population sheltered behind the city's walls. Hannibal and Himilco divided their forces into two corps. The bulk of the army camped near the city's southern walls, where they constructed a fortress surrounded by a deep moat. From this point, the Carthaginian generals intended to launch their attack, as the northern side of the city was unassailable because of the rocky hills that covered it. The other corps, consisting of

40,000 Libyans and Iberians, was positioned on the mountain south-east of Akragas. Hannibal thus repeated the deployment that had given him victory at Himera three years before.[35]

The Carthaginians proposed to the Akragantines to accept their suzerainty, allying themselves with Carthage or remaining neutral, as their big target was Syracuse. However, the Akragantines had confidence in their city walls, and in their reasonably strong army as well as in the help of Syracuse, and rejected the Carthaginian demands. Moreover, they further strengthened their military force by buying off the Campanian mercenaries from the Carthaginians and, most importantly, with the arrival of the Spartan Dexippus with 1,500 more mercenaries from Gela. Dexippus was one of the many Greek military leaders of that time who assembled mercenary troops and worked for anyone who could pay them. Diodorus informs us that according to Timaeus, Dexippus was famous in Sicily at the time.[36]

The Carthaginian attack began with two tall siege towers, from which archers exchanged arrows with the Akragantines on the battlements of the walls. The Carthaginians returned to their camp, leaving the two towers outside the moat, resulting in a group of Akragantine soldiers firing on them in a swift midnight exodus.[37]

This fact made the work of the besiegers even more difficult; it was difficult enough already as the walls of Akragas were not only high but also, in many places, built on hills. Hannibal, therefore, ordered the building of a large mound, enabling the siege engines of the Carthaginians to be placed at a greater height so that they would be more effective and would cease to be easy prey for the defenders' projectile machines and archers.[38]

The Carthaginians obtained the materials needed for the construction from a nearby cemetery. But the opening of graves and the scattering of bodies, combined with the concentration of many thousands of people in a limited geographical area and the fact that the valley was crossed by the products of the sewerage system of Akragas, caused an epidemic that led to the death of a large part of the Carthaginian army. Among those who became infected and died was Hannibal himself.[39]

The Greeks naturally believed and spread the word that the epidemic was divine punishment for the desecration of the tombs by the Carthaginians, and the latter were even more terrified when a thunderbolt fell near the tomb of the tyrant Theron, victorious with Gelon at Himera in 480 BCE. Being extremely superstitious, they did not doubt that the incident meant that the great enemy of their country was fighting against them from the other world and defending his city. At the same time, there were accounts and reports of apparitions of spirits at night, which the Greeks probably took care to feed.

Himilco, who had now assumed command, seeing that the heavy losses and fear threatened to lead his army to complete disintegration, reacted by carrying out sacrifices, including the human sacrifice of a teenager, a practice not uncommon in Carthaginian and Phoenician mores. The ceremonies reassured the soldiers, who then completed the construction of an embankment, probably along the Ipsas River, shifting the line of attack to the south-west, where the walls reached a lower height. There, they placed siege towers, which they laid against the walls.

Despite the efforts of the Carthaginians to improve their position, Akragas's resistance remained firm. In the meantime, a mighty army had finally been assembled in Syracuse, with the participation of Greek cities of Sicily and Italy, which numbered 35,000 soldiers, of whom 15,000 were Syracusans. The Greek army set out for Akragas under the command of Daphnaeus of Syracuse. Himilco responded by mobilising all his forces not directly involved in the siege, which amounted to a force with a similar number of soldiers at that time. The Carthaginian troops met the Greek army after crossing the South Himera River, about 55 kilometres west of Akragas. The 15,000 Syracusans were positioned in the northern part of the formation, and the 20,000 Sicilians and Italians were in the southern part, near the sea.[40]

The battle was fierce and long, and at one point, the Carthaginian forces in the coastal part of the conflict seemed to outnumber the Sicilians and Italians. Daphnaeus, seeing that the cohesion of his left flank was in danger, ran through the Syracusan lines, shouting instead that the Sicilians and Italians had prevailed over their opponents and that one last push would suffice to win the battle. This utterly false information gave the Syracusan hoplites enthusiasm and momentum, helping them to break through the enemy line and put it to flight. The right of the

Carthaginian army suddenly found itself in imminent danger of being surrounded by the Syracusans. Consequently, although the Sicilians and Italians with whom it was fighting were in a marginal situation and could scarcely maintain cohesion, it fled.

The Carthaginian forces had left 6,000 dead on the battlefield and were retreating towards Akragas while the Greeks pursued them.[41] The Greek forces in the city had an excellent opportunity to make an exit and finish off the disorganised and retreating enemy troops, who were also forced to pass in front of Akragas's walls to return to their camp. However, the Akragantine generals hesitated to take such an action, fearing that the city would be uncovered while the Greeks were already approaching and pursuing the Carthaginian forces. Many inhabitants and soldiers watched from the walls, shouting out suggestions that the army should make an exit and ultimately crush the enemies in a disorderly retreat, but the order was never given.[42]

The Greeks had probably lost an excellent opportunity to win the war that day, and the atmosphere in Akragas was agitated. The generals were accused of treason, and after a popular assembly in which the anger overflowed, they were summarily executed by stoning, carried out by the raging crowd.[43]

The allied Greek army then settled in the city, and the siege became even more difficult for the Carthaginians, given the heavy losses they had suffered from the epidemic and the fighting. On the other hand, conditions for the inhabitants of Akragas gradually became more complex, and they were even used to a very comfortable way of life. They were, therefore, anxious to be rid of the Carthaginian presence and the nuisances it brought, believing also that victory was inevitable, and underestimating the threat of the barbarians.[44]

The Greek military leadership finally gave in to this mood and decided to attack to break up the Carthaginian army in a pitched battle. Still, the attempted exodus failed utterly in its objective. Using the technique of deception, Himilco made the Greeks believe that a body of his army had secretly entered the city and was setting it on fire while they were advancing towards the Carthaginian territory. Thus, the Greek troops hurriedly returned to the city, suffering blows and casualties from the

Carthaginian forces in their hasty retreat, only to find that, in reality, the fires had been lit on the outside of the walls by a small group sent by the Carthaginian general on this mission.

However, from a strategic point of view, the situation was not bad for the Greeks. The fortifications of Akragas had proved far superior to the siege engines of the Carthaginians, while the Greek forces remained solid and ready for war. The only problem was that the Akragantines continued to consume at rates too high for the circumstances, without taking care to conserve and store resources, despite the recommendations and efforts of the Allied Greek military leadership. This was while the city could not meet its basic food needs due to the siege and was critically dependent on supplies from Syracuse.

Towards the end of 406 BCE, the unpreparedness of the inhabitants of Akragas, combined with the recklessness of the government of Syracuse, resulted in a complete reversal of the strategic situation. For the entire duration of the siege, the Carthaginians had kept their warships at Motya and Panormus in their naval bases, which had caused the Syracusans to lower the intensity of their attention on the transport fleets supplying Akragas.

In their certainty that there was no danger, the Syracusans sent a large cargo of wheat to Akragas without any military cover. What they did not know was that the Carthaginian fleet was on the high seas, as Himilco had learned earlier from his spies or informers of the arrival of the ships from Syracuse, and had mobilised his triremes from the western end of Sicily in good time.

The defenceless Greek transport fleet became easy prey for the Carthaginian triremes, and the entire cargo of wheat was stolen. The result was that suddenly Akragas found itself unable to meet the population's nutritional needs, as there were insufficient stored supplies, and an equally large cargo of wheat would take a long time to prepare.[45]

The Akragantines pressed for a new exit, which would have broken the siege by defeating the Carthaginian army in a battle of array. Still, Daphnaeus and the other Syracusan officers considered it too risky to fight a war of such magnitude under the walls of a city that had lost the ability to withstand a siege. In the event of defeat, a complete disbanding of the Greek army was possible, which would have been a massive blow to Syracuse and jeopardised the survival of the Greek presence in Sicily.

At the same time, the Greeks of Italy, who had already wanted to leave for their homelands to return to their crops after months of absence, announced their immediate withdrawal. The Campanian mercenaries also defected to the Carthaginian side, agreeing to be paid 15 talents.[46]

The deadlock was complete, and so, in a repetition of the Himera scene and despite the strong protests of the Akragantines, Daphnaeus decided to evacuate the city immediately and transfer the population to Gela and Syracuse under the cover of the army. The evacuation took place during the night amidst the weeping and wailing of people who were leaving the city and their properties, taking with them only what they could carry at the time. Some forces remained within the walls so the Carthaginians would not realise what was happening. Before dawn, they, too, left the city, leaving behind the old and sick who could not move, along with those who had voluntarily decided to stay to the end. The Akragantines also had to leave behind enormous wealth.[47]

In the morning, the Carthaginian troops entered the almost deserted city, killed everyone they encountered, and engaged in unprecedented looting and destruction. Akragas was one of the wealthiest cities of that time, and nobody had ever looted it. The Carthaginians had the opportunity to grab an enormous number of luxury objects and unique art treasures, such as high-quality paintings, drawings, and statues, which the Akragantines, known for their exquisite aesthetic taste, had collected or created. Himilco sent the most precious pieces of art to Carthage and sold the rest of the spoils.[48]

One of the tragic stories of the disaster was that of Tellias, a prominent citizen patriot and esteemed gentleman. He refused to leave his city; instead, he went to the temple of Athena with some other Akragantines. They thought they would be safe there, as they expected the Carthaginians to respect the temples. But they were terribly wrong. Himilco and his army slaughtered those who had sought refuge in the temples of the city while they were looting temples and houses without any distinction. Tellias, taking notice of all that destruction and disaster, set fire to the temple of Athena, thus killing himself with it, as he wanted to eliminate the Carthaginians' chance to sack that temple too and get possession of the dedicatory offerings and the propriety of the temple. As for himself, immediate death seemed preferable to torture, which was sure to happen if he fell into the hands of the Carthaginians.[49]

The spoils brought to Carthage from Akragas were so numerous and prosperous and made such a profound impression on its inhabitants that they sparked a natural cultural development in the great city of North Africa in the following years. Greek art, dress, and decoration, already held in high esteem in Carthaginian society, were even more widely adopted as synonymous with taste and luxury.

Things had turned out magnificently for Carthage, which only a few years ago was in the sights of Athenian expansionism, and now had occupied great part of Greek Sicily. Moreover, from 414 BCE onwards, given the difficulties they faced in the war against Syracuse, the Athenians chose to forgo any intentions of taking action against Carthage. Instead, they focused on cultivating positive relations with the North African city. In 406 BCE, heralds from Carthage made their way to Athens, where the Athenians graciously received them. The Athenians extended their hospitality by inviting the heralds to entertain at the *prytaneion*, the official banquet hall of Athens. Then, they likely dispatched an embassy to Sicily to meet with Himilco and Hannibal.[50] By then, things had become even more challenging for Athens, and in a period such as that, forming alliances was crucial for the city's survival. In addition, the Carthaginian invasion of Sicily benefited Athens as it prevented the Syracusans from providing additional support to their Spartan allies. In 406 BCE, there was a Syracusan squadron in the Aegean supporting the Spartan fleet,[51] and the Athenians, who were still superior in the sea but not in their best shape, preferred no more Syracusans to come eastwards.

The Rise of Dionysius to Power and the Battle of Gela

The fall of Akragas, on the other hand, was a massive shock for the Greeks, and the new situation was dramatic for them. Hundreds of thousands of refugees were moving towards the eastern side of Sicily, and some of them were settling roughly around Syracuse or in the northernmost Sicilian cities, while others were migrating to Italy.[52] Alongside the humanitarian drama came enormous economic damage, as the loss of Akragas, after the loss of Selinus and Himera, marked a hefty blow to Greek trade. All this while, the Carthaginian threat remained in Sicily, spreading like a black cloud over Gela, but now also in the distance, over Syracuse itself.

As a natural consequence, the political climate in Sicily's largest city was highly volatile. The people were furious with the leadership, which had not proved capable of defending the Greek cities, and many believed that there were traitors in its ranks.

In the first assembly of citizens in Syracuse after the destruction of Akragas, Dionysius, a young army officer, made his dynamic entry into the political arena. Dionysius was not of aristocratic descent but had distinguished himself during the war in progress. He emerged as a leading figure in the political space of the former Hermocrates' followers, expressing a political tendency that believed the root of the problem lay in the democratic constitution and institutional framework itself. The latter could not respond in a timely and adequate manner to emergencies such as the one that the Greeks of Sicily were facing because of its structural procrastination in decision-making, its pluralism and disunity in leadership, its promotion of personal strategies and interests, and the endless debates and controversies that characterised it.

Dionysius fiercely attacked the generals, calling them outright traitors, and with his passion, he won the enthusiastic support of the angry Syracusans, who decided to depose Daphnaeus and other generals and proclaim him general.[53] Soon afterwards, the new general advanced and still further deepened his theory of conspiracy, falsely declaring that Himilco had attempted to bribe him and his colleague generals, the latter accepting, while he did not. Consequently, he concluded that he could do nothing but resign lest he should become an accessory to treason. Dionysius' falsehood was vulgar and ruthless, but it fitted in perfectly with the psychology of the mob, who, in their anger and fear, were looking for scapegoats on one side and saviours on the other.

The most respectable citizens suspected that Dionysius was, in fact, trying to overthrow democracy and establish a dictatorship of his own, and they opposed him vigorously in public meetings. Yet, the populace did not have similar worries about democracy and tyranny and became enthusiastic about this new young leader, feeling that he was the one Syracuse needed to become great again.

Dionysius' rhetoric struck hard against the state of fear caused in Syracuse after the Carthaginian march and the enormous failures of the city's government to derail it. He noted that the Syracusans were terrorised by the situation and pushed for the return of oligarchic exiles who knew better about war and had repeatedly refused proposals of rich awards to join the enemy, preferring to stay at the sidelines as wanderer emigres instead of turning against their homeland. He added that it was foolish to ask for and expect help from Italy or the Peloponnese while at the same time insist on keeping their own citizens away from Syracuse and Sicily.

The people were excited about Dionysius' argument and voted in favour of his proposals. At the same time, the other generals or political opponents did not dare to oppose them, as they would only receive hatred from the citizenship and the returning exiles alike. Dionysius' move was clever, as he secured the support of influential and wealthy citizens who had been exiled from the city and politics, and now they were to return thanks to him.[54]

Then, Dionysius used a letter that came from Gela and asked for military help from Syracuse as a justification to begin his military preparations. He marched quickly to Gela, where the Syracusans had previously placed Dexippus, a Lacedaemonian, to lead the city's military forces and protect it. Dionysius arrived in Gela with 2,000 foot soldiers and 4,000 horsemen. As soon as he arrived, he took advantage of the internal strife in the city. Before the assembly, Dionysius denounced the affluent elite and arranged for their conviction and execution, taking their possessions to cover the salaries of Dexippus' garrison. Concurrently, he promised to increase the pay of his soldiers to gain their allegiance and gain favour with Gela's ordinary people, who welcomed him as their saviour from the despotism of the ruling class.

Satisfied that he had his back covered, having Gela's support, Dionysius left the city and arrived in Syracuse during an assembly. Taking advantage of the occasion, as thousands of people were gathered, he harshly indicted the city's officials, charging them with disloyalty to their responsibilities and public betrayal. His passionate speech struck a chord with the gathered assembly, causing unrest and inciting demands for his nomination as supreme commander.

Consequently, the citizens' assembly solemnly anointed Dionysius, the general emperor, i.e. the sole supreme commander with full and extraordinary powers, and later approved a personal bodyguard of 1,000 men to protect him from the alleged plots against him. Dionysius also doubled the pay of the mercenaries to ensure their loyalty to him, brought back to Syracuse exiles and various adventurous men, and, of course, placed persons of his very close circle in the most critical governmental positions.[55] His nearest associate was the active behind-the-scenes writer Philistus, whose historical works were to become a primary source for ancient Sicilian history and, among other things, were read very carefully by Alexander the Great.[56] Finally, Dionysius married Hermocrates' daughter, while some of the officials of the previous leadership were found murdered, such as Daphnaeus, and others were exiled. It was essentially the establishment of a tyranny that had the support of the vast majority of the people.

Meanwhile, the Carthaginians spent the winter at Akragas and continued the campaign in the spring of 405 BCE. After plundering and destroying the surrounding countryside, they appeared before the city of Gela and set up camp in June. The camp was enclosed, and surrounded by a moat except on the side where it was next to the sea, which is where the support fleet anchored.[57]

The Carthaginian forces destroyed the countryside without attacking the city. They carried out acts of intimidation or demonstration, most notably the removal of the towering bronze statue of Apollo on the beach, which they sent as a prize to the Phoenician metropolis of Tyre. At the same time, they were building siege engines and eventually began attacking the walls by striking them with battering rams. The walls were damaged and began to collapse in some places, but the Geloans resisted valiantly and repelled the attacks. In the evenings, with the participation of civilians, they repaired the weakened parts of the walls, too.

Gela was a city of 80,000–100,000 inhabitants, with an area of about 2,000 acres and a significant aristocratic tradition. From there descended the priestly family of the Deinomenids, whose members were Gelon and Hieron, the two tyrants of Syracuse who had led the Greeks in the historic victories of Himera and Cumae, respectively. The Geloans resisted proudly, trusting in the coming help of the Syracusans.

Dionysius arrived with a formidable army comprising Sicilian and Italian Greeks along with mercenaries, which might have numbered over 50,000 troops and included at least 30,000 infantry soldiers and 1,000 cavalrymen.[58] He camped along the coast on the eastern side of the city, near its citadel, and for the next twenty days, he used his light infantry to repel Carthaginian raids in the countryside. The army supported fifty triremes from the sea, preventing the Carthaginian camp from being supplied by ships.

The battle plan that the young Syracusan general drew up, having studied the area very well, provided for a triple surprise attack by the Greek army. The Italian Greeks would march along the beach with the Geloans on their right, to invade the Carthaginian camp directly from the sandy beach in the narrow unfortified passage between the fence and the sea. The fleet would support them and create a diversion, landing soldiers inside the camp. At the same time, the Syracusans and Sicilian Greeks would march on the north side of Gela, keeping it on their left, and attack the north-eastern side of the enemy camp under cover of the cavalry. With the mercenaries, Dionysius would cross the city and charge from the main gate frontally against the Carthaginians, while the Geloans would secure the defence of the walls. The Carthaginians could not perceive the three moves before the last phase.[59]

The attack started at dawn. The fleet approached the opening of the Carthaginian camp at sea and disembarked some soldiers, with the result that the Carthaginians concentrated the bulk of their forces at the point, believing that they were under general attack from there. At the same time, the Italian Greeks were marching rapidly along the beach, and thanks to the successful diversion of the fleet, they succeeded in penetrating the camp. A fierce battle commenced in which a large number of the Carthaginian troops were engaged while the Greek fleet fired a mass of arrows from the sea against them, and the Syracusan and Sicilian Greek corps on the northern side of the field advanced.

Dionysius' plan had been going perfectly so far. The first difficulties arose when the Libyan forces, which rushed to meet the Syracusan and Sicilian Greeks' attack on the northern side of the front, proved highly challenging for the Greeks. Although the Greeks had the advantage, they could not break through their resistance and approach the camp.

The execution of the plan was, however, to fail utterly under Dionysius' command. The young leader of the Greek army started to march with the mercenaries to cross the city of Gela towards its western gate. Still, contrary to his orders, the streets had yet to be kept clear, and indeed, there was a heavy movement of carts of supplies moving in the opposite direction from him and his forces. The result was that Dionysius and his troops were excessively late.

The Geloans, seeing the hard-fighting Italian Greeks forced to retreat towards the city since Dionysius' attack was not taking place and the Carthaginians were gathering more and more forces against them, decided to come out of the walls themselves to support their comrades-in-arms, but without moving far away. At the same time, the Sicilian Greeks also suffered a counterattack by a numerically superior force consisting of Iberians, Campanians, and Carthaginians, who forced them to retreat into the city.

When Dionysius and his forces finally emerged through Gela's central gate the battle was effectively over as the other two Greek armies sought refuge inside the walls, having left behind about 1,000 dead. Consequently, Dionysius and his soldiers immediately returned to the city's interior without engaging the enemy.[60]

The atmosphere in the war council that followed at Gela was weighty and cold towards Dionysius. The latter naturally asserted that somebody had committed treason, as the streets of the city, contrary to his orders, were crowded with people, which prevented his exit. However, the objective fact was that under his leadership, the Greeks had again finally been defeated, and indeed, he and his forces were the only corps of the army that had not even engaged in battle. The frustration intensified when it became clear that now the disposition of the forces, with all the Greek forces concentrated inside the city and with no possibility of manoeuvre, precluded an attempt at a new surprise attack and that the fortification of Gela could not keep the enemy out of the city much longer. Accordingly, the Italian Greek corps commanders, who had paid the most significant toll of blood on the battlefield during the day, decided to depart for their cities.

Once again, mirroring the situations at Himera and Akragas, the Greek leadership encountered a familiar deadlock, and for the third time, the decision was the same. Dionysius, who had risen to power by denouncing the previous leaders for having surrendered the Greek cities to the barbarian hordes and left the dead soldiers unburied, decided to evacuate the city of Gela immediately in the middle of the night. Again, a unit would remain on the walls, so that no suspicions would be raised among the Carthaginians, and leave the city at dawn, while the army's main body would cover the long lines of refugees on their way to Syracuse. At that time, Syracuse possessed a population of 500,000–600,000. Still, no one can know what the exact demographic situation was after the destruction of Selinus, Himera, Akragas, and Gela, and the hundreds of thousands of refugees who had moved precisely towards Syracuse and eastern Sicily.

The only Greek city standing between the Sicilian megalopolis and the Carthaginian army was now Kamarina, a town smaller than Gela, which could only resist if there was time to strengthen its walls significantly. However, this was impossible. Seeing that the enemies were retreating, Himilco did not stop at Gela at all but left a small part of his forces in the city to plunder it and continued to march eastward in pursuit of Dionysius.

With the only alternative now being to risk everything in a battle away from the walls of Syracuse, Dionysius gave the order to evacuate Kamarina immediately before he even reached the city. Its population was to be incorporated with that of Gela as they passed through the area, and the following army was to continue marching towards Syracuse without stopping its march at all. Some took as many things as possible – gold and silver, or just their children and old parents.[61]

The developments had naturally created intense doubt towards the young commander-in-chief, whom many in Syracuse and the army called a tyrant, but now also incompetent, or even a traitor who abandoned the Greek cities to the barbarians to strengthen his power in Syracuse.[62] In this climate of resentment and questioning, a considerable part of the cavalry, composed of nobles, broke away from the rest of the troops without seeking Dionysius' approval and moved swiftly towards Syracuse. On arriving there, the cavalrymen tried to incite a rebellion against the tyrant and killed his wife after first abusing her.[63]

Upon noticing the horsemen's departure, Dionysius hastened back to Syracuse with a contingent of a few hundred soldiers. Bloody fights ensued in the streets and houses of the city, during which Dionysius, enraged by the sight of his wife's corpse, killed several of the rebels with his own hands. Eventually, the government forces prevailed and suppressed the equestrians' movement, while those horsemen who survived had to flee Syracuse to save their lives. After that, they occupied the city of Etna.[64]

While the interior of Syracuse had again become a theatre of civil strife, the crowds of refugees were creating chaos in the eastern part of Sicily, and the Carthaginians were advancing and occupying Kamarina.

The Greeks of Sicily were experiencing a real tragedy. However, the strategic situation was not as desperate. With the evacuations of the three cities and the retreat of their armies to Syracuse, the forces concentrated there were even more significant, and combined with the strong fortification of the great city, its large fleet, and its general size, made it virtually impossible for the Carthaginian army, weakened by the plague and the fighting, to threaten it. Moreover, while the Carthaginians were approaching Syracuse, a new epidemic appeared in their ranks, which again caused thousands of casualties, and the Greeks attributed it to Apollo's punishment.

Thus, after having conquered almost all of southern Sicily, paradoxically, Himilco could only offer a peace treaty when he arrived in front of the walls of Syracuse.[65] The Carthaginian general made it a condition that Dionysius and Syracuse should recognise the Carthaginian sovereignty in the territories of the Elymians and Sicani, i.e. inner western and central Sicily, and that Dionysius' power should be limited to Syracuse and the surrounding areas. Also, the destroyed Greek cities could be rebuilt and inhabited, provided they completely demolished their walls, did not build new ones, and paid regular tribute to Carthage. Dionysius accepted, as he wanted to eliminate the Carthaginian presence as soon as possible and consolidate his power.

The departure of the Carthaginian army brought relief to most Greeks in Sicily, but they had a long way to go to regain their old standards of living, something that for many of them was never going to happen. For their part, the Carthaginians were returning home victorious and laden with rich spoils. However, they had lost at least half their soldiers and carried with them a deadly contagious disease.[66]

Chapter 5

Dionysius I of Syracuse against Carthage

At the end of 405 and the beginning of 404 BCE, while the great war between Sparta and Athens in mainland Greece was coming to an end, with the former prevailing, Dionysius proclaimed himself governor of Syracuse for life. This move confirmed the fears of the democrats, who claimed that since he had been given extraordinary powers, he would not relinquish them at the end of his term of office and they accused him of being a tyrant. Following in the footsteps of Gelon, Dionysius did not abolish the assembly of citizens, but he instituted the office of lifelong ruler, which concentrated the powers of the council of generals in a single person. He also fortified the island of Ortygia exceptionally well and settled there with his mercenaries and closest friends and supporters.[1]

He donated significant land to them in the Syracuse countryside, while other estates were divided equally between citizens, free former slaves, and foreign residents, to whom Dionysius granted citizenship.[2] In this way, the proclaimed lifelong governor of Syracuse further strengthened the support of his entourage but, above all, secured the sympathy of large masses of people, weakening the influence of the democrats who opposed his rule.

However, not a long time later, during a campaign against the pro-Carthaginian Sicilian town of Herbessos, a large part of Dionysius' troops mutinied against him to overthrow him. Then, they moved to Etna, where they joined the rebellious horsemen who had already settled there.[3] Dionysius fled to Ortygia while the mutineers headed for Syracuse, reinforced by additional forces from Rhegio and Messene. The latter saw the ongoing rebellion against Dionysius as an opportunity to prevent the establishment of a new robust regime in Syracuse, which could pose a threat to them.

An actual siege of Ortygia began, with the situation becoming increasingly tricky for Dionysius and many of his mercenaries deserting him and joining the enemy. The young tyrant was to be brought out of the impasse thanks to Philistus' idea to approach the Campanian mercenaries whom Himilco had left as a garrison in the Carthaginian territories of Sicily. The Campanians accepted the proposal as they were paid handsomely, and attacked the mutineers by surprise, forcing them to break the siege of Ortygia and retreat. Then Dionysius, wishing to smooth the situation, did not resume hostilities but practically promised amnesty to the mutineers, as reconciliation was necessary to deal with the enemies of the state. Eventually, he admitted them all back to Syracuse; the only ones expelled were the defecting mercenaries.[4]

After the peace in the interior, Dionysius went on the offensive with a large army against Etna and the Chalcidian cities.[5] The Syracusans were already hostile to the latter because they had supported the Athenians, but now they also held them responsible for the delay in sending aid to Selinus at the beginning of the drama of the last Carthaginian invasion. Consequently, the strengthened tyrant of Syracuse quickly conquered Etna and then Catania and Naxos, enslaving their populations. He also transferred the inhabitants of Leontini to Syracuse, offering them citizenship.

Dionysius then upgraded the defence of Syracuse by enlarging and significantly strengthening the city walls, which he extended both in the northern and southern parts to cover a much larger area, and by constructing new fortifications. Many new towers and a large fortress were built at Euryalus, at the junction of the additional sections of the southern and northern walls.[6] The works were carried out in an impressively short time, through the intensive endeavour of thousands of engineers and workers who enjoyed high wages, which increased in proportion to their productivity.

When they completed the works, Syracuse had become impregnable. Fully satisfied, Dionysius could now prepare his forces for the counterattack against the Carthaginians, which almost all the Greeks of Sicily desired and expected. Gunsmiths and artisans worked on creating the most sophisticated weapons, arrows, projectiles, and projectile machines until then, including catapults, which were appearing for the first time. They also repaired damaged ships and built new ones, including, according to Diodorus, the first-ever quadriremes and pentaremes, bringing the Syracuse fleet to 300 warships.[7]

Diodorus mentions that the workers had high wages, and the managers gave bonuses to those who were more productive. Moreover, Dionysius himself visited the workers daily, talked with them in a friendly way, and offered gifts to those who worked with more zeal, even inviting them to have lunch with him. That favourable treatment made the workers highly devoted and hard-working, creating faster war machines and missiles.[8]

In addition to the preparations for war, Dionysius strengthened his political position in view of the impending new war with Carthage by simultaneously contracting two marriages in 399 BCE. The first was to Aristomache of Syracuse, a member of a prominent aristocratic family, through whom the now 31-year-old tyrant wanted to improve his relations with the Syracusan aristocracy. The second bride was Doris, the daughter of a prominent family in the city of Locri in Greek Italy. By marrying her, Dionysius intended to promote allied relations with the Italian Greeks.[9]

In reality, Dionysius proposed marriage to Locri after the city of Rhegio rejected a previous wedding proposal.[10] As previously mentioned, Rhegio and Messene controlled the strategic point of the strait between Sicily and Italy, and the two cities allied themselves with the opponents of the new Syracusan regime. Dionysius tried to win them over, eventually succeeding in signing a peace treaty with them.

The Siege of Motya

With his position in Syracuse and eastern Sicily more firmly established, his relations with the cities of the strait improved, and with the discreet support of the Greeks of Italy, Dionysius could now turn against the great enemy.

Having prepared intensively in the previous period, Dionysius, the Syracusans, and the other Greeks of Sicily could reasonably hope that they would succeed in liberating the Greek cities under Carthaginian suzerainty, as well as in eliminating the Carthaginian threat for the future.

The timing was right because also the epidemic that the Carthaginian army had brought to Carthage and Libya had led to the death of a significant part of the population. Dionysius spoke of the impending campaign against the Carthaginians in the Syracusan assembly, winning the enthusiastic cheers of the citizens.[11]

The decision of Syracuse was received with enthusiasm by the rest of the Greeks of Sicily, who on hearing it expressed their anger against the Carthaginian merchants who lived or were located in Greek areas.[12] Outraged crowds slaughtered thousands of them and stripped them of their property as a prelude to a war, which, for the Greeks, had the explicit aim of revenge for the massacres and destruction of Selinus, Himera, and other cities by the Carthaginians. Dionysius sent an ultimatum to the Senate of Carthage, demanding its immediate renunciation of any claim to suzerainty over the Greek cities of Sicily. The Carthaginians rejected it and began war preparations, recruiting Iberians and other mercenaries.[13]

Thus, in the summer of 398 or 397 BCE, the Greek troops invaded the Carthaginian territories of Sicily. The army that Dionysius had assembled with forces of Syracuse and other Sicilian Greeks, plus mercenaries and allies from other Sicilian cities was mighty. His total force amounted to 80,000 infantry and 3,000 horsemen. Moreover, the army had many siege engines, a fleet of 200 warships, and 500 transports to support it.[14]

The campaign's main target was Motya, which was Carthage's most substantial base in Sicily and the central hub connecting the metropolis with the Carthaginian regions of the island. Panormus was an equally sized or even larger city, but its location on the northern Sicilian coast and its consequently greater distance from Carthage made it of secondary strategic importance for promoting Carthaginian policy in Sicily compared to Motya. Thus, it was less militarised throughout time than Motya.

Since the eighth century BCE, Motya was the main Carthaginian base in Sicily, chosen because of its geographical location and topography. It was located at the westernmost tip of Sicily, the shortest possible distance from Carthage, and was built on a small island in the interior of a bay, which was connected to the open sea by a very narrow channel. It therefore resembled an island situated inside a lake. The Carthaginians had formed it into a fortress city. The fortified island of Motya had some 15,000 permanent residents. It was about 2 kilometres in circumference and was connected to the Sicilian mainland by a 1,200-metre-long artificial road, which the Motyans destroyed when the Greek army approached their city.[15] The Motyans were hiding, expecting Carthaginian reinforcements.[16]

The other Carthaginian Sicilian cities, Panormus and Solus (modern Solunto, while the Carthaginians called it Kapara), naturally sided with their fellow Carthaginians of Motya, but so did Alykes, Entella and Segesta. On the other hand, the Elymian city of Eryx, north of Motya, sided with the Greeks, as did the nearby towns of the Sicani.[17]

Dionysius caused destruction in the countryside of the cities that sided against him, while on the Carthaginian side, Himilco sent a small fleet of ten triremes to attack the port of Syracuse by surprise and destroy ships that had remained there. He aimed to create a diversion so that part of Dionysius' fleet could return to Syracuse and somewhat reduce the strength of the troops besieging Motya.

There was indeed a night raid, during which the Carthaginians set on fire some of the ships in the port of Syracuse, but the forces remaining in the harbour fought back and even destroyed five Carthaginian triremes, forcing the others to flee. The diversion also failed, as Dionysius remained calm and did not move any of his forces towards Syracuse. Instead, he continued undeterred with the preparatory phase of the siege, which aimed to construct an artificial embankment that would reconnect Motya with the land, thus enabling the siege engines to attack the walls and the enemies who threw projectiles against them. The city's inhabitants were awaiting on their side the reinforcements that they knew Carthage would send.[18]

Indeed, shortly after the failed diversionary attempt, Himilco departed with 100 triremes for the western tip of Sicily. He hoped that on reaching the area, he would have the opportunity with a surprise attack to destroy Dionysius' anchored fleet before he could react, as the Spartan commander Lysander had done a few years earlier against the Athenian fleet in the decisive naval Battle of the Aigos Rivers (Aegospotami). Dionysius did not commit the same mistake as the Athenian admirals; consequently, when the Carthaginians arrived, they found only a few Greek ships lying on the beach. They destroyed them and closed off the bay, in the interior of which the bulk of the Greek fleet anchored. In this way, Himilco wanted to neutralise Dionysius' numerical advantage, forcing him to fight in the strait.[19]

However, Dionysius did not rush to attack with his ships but mobilised archers and projectile weapons and struck the Carthaginian fleet from the land. At the same time, he ordered his engineers and craftsmen to construct a wooden trackway, through which he transported in one day eighty ships from the bay's interior to the open sea by land, breaking the Carthaginian blockade. Himilco attempted to attack directly the ships passing from the land to the open sea but failed as he received massive arrows and projectiles from both land-based units and the ships themselves, on which Dionysius had taken the precaution of embarking many archers and projectile weapons during their transport from the trackway.[20]

In this way, the Carthaginians found themselves in a challenging position since they were in danger of being surrounded and annihilated by the two parts of the Greek fleet. Faced with this danger, Himilco gave orders for an immediate withdrawal to Carthage, leaving the inhabitants of Motya to their fate; due to the numerical disadvantage, he had hesitated to face the entire Greek fleet on the open sea, even though by moving away from the bay he could have avoided being surrounded.[21]

Thus, Dionysius was able to concentrate on the siege of Motya. When the embankment was constructed, the Greeks moved the siege towers and catapults to within striking distance and began attacking the walls. The city's inhabitants fought with all their might, knowing what fate awaited them in case of defeat.[22]

The walls of Motya were solid and well built; however, at some point, the siege engines managed to cause them to collapse in one section, and the Greeks began to enter the city. The defenders continued to fight behind a makeshift second wall they had constructed, and the battle continued for some days, with several casualties for the Greek army. Eventually, however, the resistance of Motya was finally broken, and the Greeks poured into the city, carrying out massacres and looting. Those with the most particular zeal were the Selinunteans and Himerians. Thirsty for revenge, they persecuted and killed the Carthaginian people, as they had now the opportunity to retaliate for the massacres of the Carthaginians involving their relatives, friends, and fellow citizens.[23]

For his part, Dionysius, having secured the strategic capture of the main Carthaginian base in Sicily and exacting historical revenge, thought that some inhabitants would be better off being rescued and sold as slaves, with the profits contributing to the costs of the campaign. However, he could not demand that his angry soldiers should stop the massacre and therefore sent heralds into the city, who called upon the inhabitants to take refuge as supplicants in such Greek temples as were in it.[24]

On the other hand, the triumphant Dionysius was simultaneously adamant and relentless towards the Greek community of Motya, which had resisted the Greek army by fighting alongside the Carthaginians. He ordered that those members of the community who had survived the occupation of the city be crucified as traitors.[25] In this way, Dionysius wanted to emphasise that the struggle was Panhellenic and aimed at the Sicilian Greeks' final liberation from the threat of the barbarians. Therefore, he would not tolerate any collaboration with the Carthaginians against the fighting Greeks by other Greeks.

The Carthaginian Counterattack and the Siege of Syracuse

Dionysius then established a garrison at Motya, possibly made of Sicels allies,[26] and left 120 ships patrolling the sea area under the command of his brother Leptines while he returned to Syracuse to prepare for the next campaign, which was to subdue those cities that had remained allied with Carthage. The campaign began the following spring when Dionysius moved his forces into western Sicily again. This time, Alykes accepted his rule, but Segesta continued to oppose it. Dionysius raided and destroyed the surrounding countryside, aiming to take Segesta and then attack Entella.[27]

For their part, the Carthaginians, after the destruction and loss of Motya, had begun to prepare a new campaign, realising that there was a clear danger of them being wholly eliminated from Sicily. They assembled forces even more extensive than Dionysius', both on land and at sea, and put Himilco at the head again.[28] The plan was for the army to land at

Panormus and, from there, recapture Motya, bring back into the sphere of influence of Carthage those Sicilian towns that had passed over to the Greeks, and march towards Syracuse.

Himilco managed to avoid Leptine's fleet at the western end of Sicily and cross to the northern side, reaching Panormus. His success was not total, as part of his transport fleet was spotted and sunk by Greek warships, carrying with it some 5,000 soldiers to their deaths. However, the bulk of the Carthaginian army managed to land at Panormus and immediately marched towards Motya, first capturing Eryx.[29]

While Dionysius' army was operating in Segesta, Himilco and his troops arrived at Motya and laid siege to it. They soon evacuated the deserted city, as the Greek garrison there was not strong enough to deal with an army of that size, and Leptines and at least most of his fleet had probably already left after the fall of Eryx.[30]

Seeing this development, Dionysius decided to leave western Sicily and not fight a battle far from the lands and cities of his territory. By doing so, he would have lost the alliance of the Alykans and the Sicani, who would necessarily cross over to the side of the Carthaginians, but he would have secured much better conditions in terms of supply, and he would have been able to retreat inside the upgraded fortifications of Syracuse.

Indeed, Dionysius' former allies or vassals allied themselves with the Carthaginians, unable to deal with them alone, and then Himilco, in turn, moved further east. The Carthaginian general did not immediately head for Syracuse but advanced to the northern side of Sicily, which he took control of, and then captured Messene.[31] However, the Messenians had managed to evacuate the civilian population from the city in time to move them to the neighbouring towns. Moreover, many of its warriors escaped and barricaded themselves in the surrounding fortresses after the powerful Carthaginian army overcame their brave resistance.

The capture of Messene ensured that the Carthaginians could use its port as a base for their fleet near Syracuse, making it very difficult for the Italian Greeks to transfer reinforcements to the Syracusans. The latter, however, managed to reinforce their fleet by building 60 new warships, and Dionysius freed some 10,000 slaves to handle them and asked for help from Sparta, which responded by sending him 1,000 mercenaries.

Dionysius also strengthened the garrisons of the forts in various parts of the territory. In this way, he weakened the bulk of his army, from which the Sicilian allies had already withdrawn, but he created problems for Himilco since the latter could no longer plunder the countryside and cause destruction undisturbed. In fact, after the capture of Messene, the Carthaginians had tried to conquer the nearby fortresses, but the Messenians defending them repelled the attacks.

At the same time, Dionysius prepared his army and left Syracuse to approach Himilco and the Carthaginians in the north. Alongside the military, the fleet, consisting of 180 ships and led by Leptines, was sailing at sea.

Himilco marched backwards in a southerly direction, wanting to meet Dionysius, with his fleet sailing in parallel under the command of Mago. But as he was near Naxos and approaching the Greek army, the volcano of Mount Etna erupted. The lava that poured out to sea made it impossible for the Carthaginian army to continue its march along the coast and forced it to detour through the interior.[32]

Himilco ordered Mago to anchor in the sea area off Catania and wait for him there, as he did not want to separate his land and sea forces for a long time. For the same reason, Dionysius, when informed that the Carthaginian army had moved away from the coast, thought it an opportunity to attack the enemy's fleet directly and hastened towards Catania. On arriving there, he ordered Leptines to attack the 250 warships of the Carthaginian fleet with all his ships while he deployed the army on the beach to create more pressure and intimidate the enemies. Dionysius knew that with a victory at sea, Himilco's task would become complicated, and the possibility of putting Syracuse under siege would fade away since the Carthaginians would not be able to block the city from the sea.

However, the ensuing naval battle turned out to be disastrous for the Greeks, who, with the great responsibility of Leptines, committed significant tactical errors and ended up losing about 100 ships and 20,000 men.[33] The Carthaginian losses were also heavy, but Dionysius had now lost the ability to confront them at sea. Thus, despite the allies' urgings to fight a land battle against Himilco, he decided to retreat to Syracuse. His decision was prompted by his close advisors and the fear that if he stood to fight in the vicinity of Catania that Mago with his Carthaginian fleet might sail towards Syracuse and attack it while it was almost defenceless. However, the bulk of the Sicilian Greeks abandoned Dionysius because they were displeased with his refusal to engage Himilco. Some returned to their lands, while others went to fortifications in the surrounding area.[34]

Himilco arrived in Catania two days later, and then the Carthaginian forces headed towards Syracuse by land and sea simultaneously. When they approached the city in the summer of 397 BCE, they camped near the Olympiaeum on the south bank of the Anapo River and built a perimeter wall around the camp. The Carthaginians again obtained the necessary materials from nearby tombs, including that of the tyrant Gelon, i.e. the victor of Himera and his wife. At the same time, the fleet occupied the large harbour, and the transport ships displayed the spoils of the naval battle to Syracuse's inhabitants, aiming to influence their psychology negatively. Dionysius instead retained control of the northern harbour and the maritime station of Ortygia.

Himilco's troops plundered the surrounding countryside and caused destruction, demolishing, among other things, the temples of Demeter and Persephone in the region of Achradina. They also built two forts around the perimeter of the harbour, at the positions of Dascon and Plemmyrium, and another at Polichni, a bit further west of their camp. In this way, Himilco believed he would secure complete control of the harbour.[35]

However, the Carthaginians had not managed to strike a blow to the Syracuse defences by winter. The fortifications of the Greek metropolis of Sicily remained too strong for the resources available to the Carthaginians, so Himilco arranged for large quantities of supplies to be transferred to his troops from the North African territories of Carthage and from Sardinia, assuming that the siege would last for a long time.

Dionysius intended to avoid exiting the city to expel the Carthaginians after a battle and had asked for help from Greek Italy and the metropolitan Greek area.[36] Indeed, some cities responded to his request and assembled a fleet of thirty ships, led by the Spartan Pharacidas, loaded with soldiers. The fleet arrived at Syracuse in the spring of 396 BCE and captured nine patrolling Carthaginian ships on arrival. However, this good news was offset by a growing shortage of supplies. Dionysius decided to carry out a supply raising operation himself at the head of part of the fleet with Leptines. In his absence, Pharacidas, with the rest of the fleet, engaged forty Carthaginian ships on the high seas and achieved a significant victory, sinking twenty-four of them.[37]

The victory boosted the morale of the Syracusans, some of whom, after Dionysius' return with the supplies, raised the issue of overthrowing his tyranny, hoping that Pharacidas and their soldiers would support such a movement. However, in the discussion made in the assembly, Pharacidas supported Dionysius and instructed his men to remain loyal to him. Consequently, the dissidents had to abandon their plans, as they did not have enough support to claim a regime change.

At the same time, on the Carthaginian side, poor sanitary conditions again led to the outbreak of an epidemic that, in the process, caused thousands of deaths. The Greeks, and maybe the Carthaginians themselves, saw the plague as divine punishment for the new sacrileges committed by the Carthaginians by destroying temples and tombs.[38]

In particular, the plague hit after the Carthaginians pillaged the temples of Demeter and Kore. Rationalist Diodorus points out, though, that in addition to the catastrophe that the demon had delivered, there were, most importantly, other factors at play that caused this new plague, such as the large number of people assembled and the sweltering summer. The location probably contributed to the disaster's disproportionate results as well, as the area had a swampy and hollow topography, and the Athenians had suffered a similar plague some years before there, too.[39]

First to be affected, the disease killed a great number of Libyans. The illness started as a catarrh and then spread to the throat, causing burning feelings, backache, and heavy limb pain. Eventually, it became dysentery, and the whole body collapsed in pustules. Diodorus mentions that some lost their minds due to the disease, and they began roaming the camp and hitting out at everyone they came across, similar to our zombie movies. Death came typically soon, on the fifth or sixth day of the illness. The disease was transmitted very quickly, and it only took someone to stand near a sick person to become infected themselves. The lack of adequate medical aid and the disease's great severity and fast transmission made the situation dramatic for the Carthaginian army, as even friends and brothers were compelled to give up one another to protect themselves. Because of the sheer number of corpses and the disease's hold over those who cared for the sick, the Carthaginians stopped burying the dead and disregarded them.[40]

Learning of the disaster that the Carthaginians were facing and the weakening of the enemy troops, Dionysius decided that the time had come to strike back. He planned a combination of attacks in several places at once, involving both the army and the fleet, designed to confuse and divide the Carthaginian army, allowing the conquest of the fortresses. Leptines and Pharacidas would mobilise a fleet of eighty ships to attack the enemy's ships before dawn. Meanwhile, already some hours before, Dionysius would start at the head of the army to march with the aim of the Carthaginian camp. He would approach it from the west, using the absence of moonlight to move his forces, drawing a circular course past nymph Cyane's temple so as not to be seen, and arriving at the enemy camp before daybreak.[41]

By sunrise, Dionysius had reached the western side of the Carthaginian camp undetected and ordered a unit of mercenaries to assault the extending part of the camp even sooner, before the attacks of the principal naval and land forces began. This was a diversionary attack intended to pin down the main body of the Carthaginian army near their camp and thus facilitate the capture of the forts. Initially, the cavalry supported the attack to reinforce to the Carthaginians the impression that they were facing the main Greek army, but after the first skirmishes, the horsemen abandoned the post and galloped towards the fortress of Dascon. Maybe for that reason, Diodorus gives a different version about that move of Dionysius, claiming that he had not mainly tactical military goals. When the mercenaries approached the camp, and the Carthaginian troops moved against them and they engaged in battle, instead of entering the fight to support the mercenary foot soldiers, the horsemen withdrew immediately without engaging the enemy even minimally. The mercenaries were left alone in a deliberate suicide mission and were exterminated. According to Diodorus, that was precisely what Dionysius wanted because they had previously become very hostile to him, taking place in factional disputes and riots in Syracuse.⁴² Perhaps the ruler of Syracuse hit two birds with one stone, in that case.

Meanwhile, the actual attacks of the fleet and the army began. The land troops besieged the Carthaginian camp and the forts that the Carthaginians occupied. The attack succeeded perfectly in taking the Carthaginians by surprise, and they had severe problems in moving enough reinforcements and forming an orderly defence. The combined attack was perfectly successful, as the cavalry, supported by a few triremes from the sea, raided the area around Dascon. Then, the whole fleet and land troops joined the attacking action, and the Syracusans started to conquer one fort after another. At the same time, Dionysius, with other forces, attacked the fortress of Polichni and conquered it just as quickly.⁴³ Shortly afterwards, he attacked the Carthaginian camp, reinforcing the troops already fighting there. The Carthaginians remained assembled to defend the camp, thinking again that almost all the Greek forces were fighting against them, and realised too late that a large Greek fleet was simultaneously attacking their ships and destroying them.

When the Carthaginians realised what was happening, they sent part of their forces to the naval station, but so did a part of the Greek troops led by Dionysius. The Carthaginians moved hurriedly in support of their ships. However, the quick pace of events surpassed them, and their rush proved in vain. Even where they managed to man their triremes and raise the decks to resist the attack, the Syracusan triremes assaulted fast and neutralised the Carthaginian ships before they were able to move.

Fear and panic completely overtook the Carthaginian camp under the pressure of the Syracusan all-out surprise attack. The sound of the crushing aggression shattering and ripping apart the battleships was incredible, Diodorus wrote. Corpses covered the shoreline.⁴⁴

Diodorus says that the Syracusans fought with high zeal, competing on who would assault on board the Carthaginian vessels. At the same time, they were eager to support each other and enhance the success of their fellow combatants. On the other side, the Carthaginians were even more horrified seeing how dreadful their situation was. However, it was only about to get worse. The Syracusan land forces entered the scene, assaulting the port from land with the same zeal as their compatriots of the fleet, and they put to fire many enemy triremes that were still at anchor, as well as the fifty pentaremes situated along the coast, in addition to commercial ships that were next to the warships. The fire always grew more robust, making it impossible for the Carthaginians to react, and it spread quickly due to the intense wind, causing massive destruction also of the commercial ships anchored away from the coast and having nothing to do with the conflict. Rough waves completed the destruction as they caused ships to clash, and they ended up wrecked. People were jumping from the vessels all over the place, trying to escape the fire and, before that, the smoke, which caused asphyxia. According to Diodorus, the destruction of the barbarians seemed like men struck down by lightening for their impiety, and the Syracusans were delighted to watch the destruction of the enemy fleet from the city's walls and the flames rising to the sky, which seemed like a spectacular scene out of a theatrical play. Women, children, and families came out of their homes as news of the triumph spread across Syracuse, and they hurried with enthusiasm to the highly crowded walls. Moreover, despite contrary orders, some children and older people approached the port to enjoy the spectacle more closely.[45] After the fire was extinguished, the Syracusans pillaged the remaining ships and took whatever they could from them, and seizing the ones that were undamaged or could be repaired.

The Carthaginians found themselves blockaded in their camp, while a few of their forces remained in the isolated fortress of Plemmyrium.[46] They had lost their fleet and the two forts closest to the camp, while the Greek army had assembled at Olympiaeum and the Greek fleet was occupying the harbour. There was no hope of victory or escape for the Carthaginian troops. Himilco sent a delegation to Dionysius, proposing to hand over the 300 talents he had in the camp in exchange for allowing the retreat of the Carthaginian army.[47] Dionysius looked favourably on an easy, immediate end to the war without further risk, and of course, he needed money to repair the damages. He therefore replied to Himilco accepting the proposal on condition that the Carthaginian civilians left secretly, so that the allies could not accuse him of allowing the enemies to escape.

The departure of the 8,000–10,000 Carthaginian citizens of Himilco's army occurred four days later, during the night, with 40 ships rescued, but in the end, it was not bloodless. Some Corinthians noticed that the Carthaginian vessels were departing, and while Dionysius, pretending to be clueless, stalled to allow their escape, the Corinthians pursued them with only their ships, managing to sink some of them. Himilco was among those who managed to return home. However, his countrymen would later condemn him as being responsible for the disastrous defeat and stripped him of all office, driving him to suicide.[48]

Dionysius then attacked the Carthaginian camp with the entire army, where only the mercenaries remained since the Sicilian allies of Carthage had hastily departed for their cities after the flight of the Carthaginian citizens. The Greeks occupied the enemy camp, and then Dionysius sold those mercenaries who had survived the battle as slaves, except for an Iberian corps, whose soldiers, by agreement with him were recruited and were accepted among his troops.[49]

The defeat brought dramatic developments in Carthage, which suffered a very heavy military and economic blow. As a result, even its position in North Africa would become dangerous and precarious. Various subjugated Libyan tribes rose against Carthaginian rule, threatening the city of Carthage itself, when they learned about the disastrous Carthaginian defeat in Sicily. They had long hated the Carthaginians' oppressive rule over them, and now they felt they had the chance to overthrow it. They also wanted revenge for the betrayal of their men in Sicily by the Carthaginian leaders. The Libyan tribes assembled a large army, and many slaves joined them, making their numbers and the threat to Carthage even more significant, as the Phoenician and Punic metropolis of North Africa had its rule challenged just a few years after, hoping Sicily would have become theirs. The rebels seized Tynes, a town not far from Carthage, while the Carthaginians, confused and afraid, gathered inside the city's high walls.

In that dramatic time, in 396 BCE, a critical and indicative shift took place in the cultural history of Carthage. The Carthaginians decided that they should include the Greek cult of Demeter and Kore in their religious practices. They consecrated statues of the two goddesses, conducting the rites following the Greek traditions. The importance of this decision is evident also by the fact that the Carthaginians appointed some of their most acclaimed citizens as priests and priestesses of the two goddesses, along with prominent members of the Greek community of Carthage. The Carthaginian response to the crisis was not only spiritual but also practical, as they hastened the construction of new ships and reinforced the existing fleet in order to secure all the needed supplies for the city through the sea for as long as the war with the rebels would go on.

Those moves brought back calm, unity, and confidence to the Carthaginians. At the same time, things were not going equally well on the rebels' side, as their lack of cohesion, supplies, and capable leaders for an enterprise of similar proportions began to undermine their unity. Soon, they started squabbling about who should be the supreme commander. The Carthaginians were ready to take advantage of this situation, using their wealth to buy off some tribes or their chiefs, further deepening the dissolving tendencies. Ultimately, after a few months, the rebels' rabble dissolved completely, and everybody returned to their lands.[50]

In Sicily during the same period, Dionysius launched campaigns against the Sicilian cities that had allied relations with the Carthaginians, while the victory enabled the Sicilian Greeks to start rebuilding their destroyed cities and towns and to restore, to a certain extent, their economic and cultural activities.

Dionysius had also further problems with his 10,000 mercenaries and their commander, named Aristotle. To deal with them, he first took advantage of the commander's issues with the law and sent him to his homeland, Sparta, where it appears they accused him of something and wanted to put him on trial. Then he satisfied the mercenaries by offering them lands and properties in Leontini. Following that settlement, Dionysius recruited other mercenaries, and he helped people return to their lands after the disaster brought to their cities by the Carthaginians. He also established in Messene 1,000 people from Locri and 4,000 from Medma, a Locrian colony in Bruttium, and 600 Peloponnesians in a newly established town on the coast named Tyndaris, which accepted people from elsewhere, too, numbering more than 5,000 citizens.

Military operations went on, too. Dionysius invaded the territories of the Sicels, occupying Morgantina and Menaenum, and took control of Greek cities such as Solus and Enna. On the other side, he concluded peace treaties with other cities and local tyrants.[51]

The Plans of Dionysius and the New Wars with the Carthaginians

The Carthaginians reacted by immediately sending Mago back to Sicily with a limited force to harass Dionysius. As it turned out, they were ready to assemble a new large army.[52] The Carthaginian leadership was determined to maintain a strong presence and influence in Sicily, not to let Dionysius develop into the absolute ruler of the island and spread his dominance into Italy. It is also likely that the Carthaginians planned those operations and carried them out in consultation with Rhegio. The Greek city at the southernmost tip of mainland Italy had a grand strategic alliance, and the influential Syracusan leaders always aimed to establish their complete dominion over it to control the strait between mainland Italy and Sicily. For this reason, Rhegio, on the other hand, was inclined to interact and collaborate with the Carthaginians, as had happened in the Battle of Himera in 480 BCE.

Mago plundered the countryside of Messene with his forces and then camped near the Sicel city of Abacaenum, which was also fighting the rule of Syracuse.[53] Dionysius moved his troops directly against the Carthaginian forces and their Sicel allies and defeated them in a battle in which the Carthaginian troops lost 800 soldiers. The Syracusan leader then plundered the countryside of Rhegio and put pressure on the city.

Following this development, a powerful Carthaginian army consisting of Libyans, Sardinians, and Italian mercenaries landed in Sicily and invaded the mainland, arriving near Morgantina. However, the city's tyrant, Agyris, did not ally himself with the Carthaginians but sided with Dionysius, who had departed from Syracuse with an army of 20,000 men.[54] The Carthaginian forces were equal to or even more significant than those of Dionysius and Agyris. However, the latter, knowing perfectly well the location as opposed to the enemy, succeeded in gaining a tactical advantage through their movements. Dionysius then avoided engaging in battle, considering that the positions he had occupied ensured victory in the event of an attack by the Carthaginian troops. However, this wait-and-see attitude caused discontent within the Greek army. Several soldiers lost patience and abandoned Dionysius, while he tried to compensate for the losses caused by this strange mutiny by freeing slaves and recruiting them.[55]

Despite Dionysius' difficulties, the tactical advantage he had secured was crucial, as the Carthaginians did not dare to attack but instead made a peace proposal to the Syracusan tyrant. Dionysius accepted, so the war ended in 392 BCE, with Carthage effectively accepting the primacy of Syracuse in Sicily. That was the first step towards creating the mighty Greek state of Sicily and Italy that Dionysius had envisioned.[56]

Dionysius' basic strategy was to unite all the Greeks of Sicily and mainland Italy into a single state under his leadership and, in this way, to gain the necessary power to eliminate the Carthaginian presence in Sicily and then subjugate Carthage.[57] As part of this strategy, he also established several colonies on both coasts of the Adriatic, which he effectively turned into a Syracuse Sea. Among these cities were Ancona (387 BCE), and Adria (385 BCE), which is located near modern Venice. In addition to controlling trade routes, securing resources and the general expansion of Syracuse's power, Dionysius' intensive colonisation of the Adriatic also enabled him to be in direct contact with northern tribes, such as the Gauls, and to recruit mercenaries from them. Around 385 BCE, Dionysius allied himself with the Illyrians, too, and helped them make a raid into the Greek kingdom of Epirus.[58]

Dionysius' plan was similar to the one that Philip II of Macedonia would carry out about half a century later in the mainland Greek area, and it would be continued by his son Alexander, with the Persian Empire as the primary opponent. The problem for Dionysius, as respectively later for Philip, was that the Greek cities of Italy had no intention of being incorporated voluntarily into the empire he was creating, but the only way for this to happen was to subjugate them by force. Furthermore, the Italian Greeks came together in a confederation to deter Dionysius' ambitions and better deal with the neighbouring Italian tribes simultaneously.[59] Dionysius then tried to take advantage of the war that had broken out between the Greek city of Thurii and the Lucanians tribe by allying himself with the latter. The tyrant of Syracuse sent a fleet led by Leptines to the region with orders to cooperate with the Lucanians to achieve the subjugation of Thurii and other Greek cities in Italy to Syracuse.

Opportunism and strategic assault characterised Dionysius' tactics. He decided to prioritise Rhegio to strengthen his position of power in southern Italy as he saw it as a crucial strategic location and the key to consolidating his hold in the area. The expedition corps consisted of 20,000 foot soldiers, 1,000 equestrians, and 120 ships, and they attacked Rhegio with such force as to put its fortifications under severe pressure and devastate its lands. The Italian Greeks rallied in defence of Rhegio against the Syracusan offensive, sending a fleet of sixty ships from Croton to support their struggling allies. The Syracusan fleet moved against the Crotoniate fleet, engaged it in battle, and destroyed it before it could reach Rhegio as a relief force. However, the Syracusans also suffered substantial casualties during that operation, mainly due to an unexpected storm. Dionysius' next strategic move was highly contested as he approached and partnered with the Lucanians to take advantage of the conflicts between the Greeks and the local tribes in the Italian peninsula. They joined forces to begin a combined campaign into Thurii's territory, which set off a chain of events that brought other Greek cities into the conflict. In compliance with a pact among the Greek cities of Italy for mutual defence, the Thurians assembled their army to thwart the Lucanian attack. But shortly after, their early victory was followed by disaster when they stumbled into a trap set by their enemies. The Lucanian host outnumbered their troops and cut them off from escape, resulting in a catastrophic loss for the Thurians, who lost thousands of men in combat.[60]

However, Leptines, seeing that the Thurians were in a challenging situation and had been decimated on the battlefield, intervened and achieved the cessation of hostilities by paying military compensation to the Lucanians so that they would withdraw.[61] Dionysius was furious at Leptines' initiative, which was utterly contrary to his orders, and banished his brother to a Syracuse estate on the Illyrian coast of the Adriatic. At the same time, Philistus, who disagreed with Dionysius' decision to collaborate with barbarians to subjugate Greek cities, had also been expelled and ended up in exile in Adria.

Dionysius continued his attempt to impose his dominance on the Italian Greeks, departing from Syracuse with a new powerful army under his personal command, which included more than 20,000 infantrymen, around 3,000 cavalry, 40 warships, and a sizable fleet for logistical support. After five days of travel, he finally arrived at Messene and rested his forces before moving further.

Dionysius quickly deployed his brother Thearides with thirty ships and the order to apprehend the Rhegian vessels and their crews near the Liparaean islands. The operation was successful, and Dionysius imprisoned the Rhegian sailors in Messene. After that, he sent his main land military force towards Caulonia, where he began laying siege using siege engines and attacking the city repeatedly.

The Italian Greeks raised troops in response to Dionysius' actions, with Croton playing a major part because of its large population and the fact there were many refugees from Syracuse, opposers of the Dionysian regime. Indeed, the commander assigned to lead the coalition army was Heloris, an exiled Syracusan distinguished for his vigorous nature and enmity against Dionysius. Heloris assembled an army of around 25,000 foot soldiers and 2,000 cavalrymen, leading them to meet Dionysius' army in Caulonia, 50 kilometres north of Locri.[62]

Knowing that the Italian Greek soldiers were stationed close to the Elleporus River, Dionysius, in a cunning move, launched an ambush before dawn that caught Heloris and his vanguard off guard. Heloris bravely fought, despite being outnumbered, and sent messengers to call reinforcements from the main camp. However, Dionysius' well-trained troops quickly routed Heloris' detachment and dealt significant losses. There was a brief relief for Heloris' men when reinforcements from the Italian Greek camp arrived. However, after Heloris was killed, morale collapsed and turmoil broke out. On the other side, Dionysius' soldiers remained cohesive, taking advantage of the situation to win decisively. The Italian Greeks made a heroic struggle but ultimately gave up and left the battlefield in disarray.

1. Relief depiction of what is thought to be an ancient Phoenician-Carthaginian ship from a sarcophagus of the second century CE. (*World History Encyclopedia; Wikimedia Commons*)

2. Ceramic representing the Phoenician deity Tanit, found in a necropolis of Ebusus, present-day Ibiza, fifth–third century BC. (*Archaeological Museum of Catalonia, Barcelona*)

3. Carthaginian amulets made of glass, fourth–third century BCE. (*National Archaeological Museum, Cagliari*)

4. Odysseus and the Sirens, on an Attic red-figure vase, made about 480–470 BCE.

5. Scene from an ancient Greek red-figure vase, 490–480 BCE. (*Museum of Fine Arts, Boston*)

6. The temple of Zeus in Cyrene (Libya) as it is today. (*Adobe Stock*)

7. Corinthian bronze helmet, sixth–fifth century BCE. (*Archaeological Museum of Olympia*)

8. The head of the Charioteer of Delphi, a statue donated to the Oracle by Polyzalos, tyrant of Gela and brother of Gelon and Hieron of Syracuse, around 470 BCE.

9. Modern reconstruction of the ancient port of Carthage.

10. Phoenician mask used to exorcise evil, found in Sardinia, fourth century BCE. (*National Archaeological Museum, Cagliari*)

11. Greek hoplites in battle, from the Nereid Monument in the city of Xanthos, Lycia, 390–380 BCE. (*British Museum, London*)

12. Effigy of Dionysius I of Syracuse, sculpted by the American sculptor and historian George Stewart, 1929.

13. Greek tragedy mask, fourth century BCE. (*Archaeological Museum of Piraeus*)

14. Two Phoenician glass vases, fifth–third century BCE. (*Museum Kunstpalast, Düsseldorf*)

15. Apollo of Belvedere. Roman copy of a bronze statue made by the famous Athenian sculptor Leochares, around 350 BCE. It is considered a model of aesthetic perfection. (*Vatican Museums*)

16. The Temple of Omonia in the Valley of Temples, at Akragas.

17. The Riace Bronzes. Two Greek statues of naked warriors, from 460–450 BCE. (*Museo Nazionale della Magna Grecia, Reggio Calabria*)

18. The ancient theatre of Syracuse as it is today. It had capacity for 16,000–20,000 spectators.

Dionysius I of Syracuse against Carthage 81

The Battle of the Elleporus in 388 BCE demonstrated Dionysius' skill at both military planning and tactical execution, as well as the difficulties and internal conflicts that the Italian Greeks' confederation encountered. Dionysius' campaign was relentless in its execution, as seen by the fall of Heloris and his army, which paved the way for further wars and power struggles in the area.

After losing the battle, the remaining Italian Greek soldiers withdrew to a strategically located hill where they took cover from Dionysius' oncoming army. Nevertheless, the trapped forces faced extreme heat and thirst due to water scarcity, despite the hill being defendable. They therefore had to negotiate. A herald from the embattled army delivered a message to Dionysius, recognising their dire position and requesting their freedom in return for a ransom.[63]

Dionysius, however, emboldened by his recent victory, replied that they had to submit unconditionally. At first hesitant, the withered and debilitated soldiers, numbering many more than 10,000, finally surrendered. In contrast to expectations, Dionysius showed surprisingly generous behaviour, negotiating peace with several Italian Greek cities and, furthermore, freeing the captives without demanding a ransom. He received tremendous praise and admiration for this deed of generosity, and many hailed it as the height of his leadership.[64]

Encouraged by his achievements, Dionysius switched his focus to Rhegio, intending to besiege the city as payback for alleged slights involving a marriage proposal. The siege went on for a long time, and the Rhegians eventually sent envoys to ask Dionysius for mercy and moderation since they were outmatched and lacked the military might or allies to stand their ground. Dionysius exacted a high price despite their pleas, occupying the city, seizing their ships, demanding 300 talents, and requiring 100 hostages as a guarantee.[65]

After the Rhegio campaign, Dionysius turned his attention to Caulonia, a city he planned to punish for its alleged wrongdoings. It seems that Caulonia's transgressions were very useful to Dionysius. He used them as a pretext to bring the city to the ground, offering its territory to the Locrians and moving its inhabitants to Syracuse, where he provided them with Syracusan citizenship and excluded them from taxes.[66] At the same time, Hipponio was also destroyed and its population deported to Syracuse. One could say that was a win-win situation: Locri became bigger, stronger, and wealthier, the Caulonians and Hipponians lost their cities, but they became citizens of the great Syracuse free from taxes, and of course, Dionysius eliminated a problem for himself in Italy, also satisfying and empowering his loyal ally in the peninsula, and gave a boost to Syracuse's demographics.

On the other hand, some scholars have considered that those transfers of people from conquered cities to Syracuse and the establishment of mercenaries from mainland Greece to their lands, made by Syracuse in various cases, such as during the Gelon or the Dionysius times, indicate a practice similar to those of Eastern empires and not Greek cities and the Mediterranean. However, there is a huge difference. As we've seen in various cases, the Syracusans offered citizenship, land, property rights, and even tax exemption to the people they relocated from other cities to Syracuse, while in the case of Eastern empires, nothing of the above was true, and instead, relocated people were enslaved or held to a semi-servile status.[67]

Dionysius' military campaigns in Italy prove that he had an aptitude for diplomacy and cunning planning, mixing brutal actions with indulgence. That attitude made him popular to some and terrifying to and hated by others.

After conquering Caulonia and Hipponio and transferring their populations to Sicily, Dionysius turned against the two largest cities in the region, namely Thurii and Croton. The two cities resisted stubbornly for quite a long time but eventually succumbed and submitted.[68]

An important role in those successes of Dionysius played his alliance with the Gauls, who had conquered and sacked Rome in the same period.[69] Dionysius recruited many Gaul mercenaries, while it is also possible that the Gaul raids towards the south were carried out in consultation with him and at his instigation. It is clear that Dionysius pursued alliances with non-Greek peoples of Italy and the northern regions to create as much trouble as possible in the Italian peninsula and to prevent the uninterrupted concentration of forces against him.

This situation caused contempt for Dionysius in the Greek metropolises, where they disparagingly began to call him 'philo-barbarian', while he had presented himself as the champion and leader of Western Greece against the barbarians. Of course, in reality, the mainland Greeks were not entitled to make similar characterisations, as at the very same time, Sparta had signed the Peace of Antalcidas (387 BCE), essentially abandoning the Greeks of Asia Minor to the Persian Empire, trying to consolidate its hegemony in mainland Greece. In any case, Sparta, Athens, Thebes, and other cities often competed to win Persian favour to use it against each other. A few decades later, Spartans and Athenians were to ally with the Persians against the Macedonia of Philip and Alexander.

Having largely imposed his rule on the Greeks of Italy, Dionysius turned against Rhegio. With the capture of Rhegio, the tyrant of Syracuse would now control the strait and thus the shortest sea routes from the Tyrrhenian to the Ionian Sea and the Adriatic Sea, and would touch his dream of building a Greek empire of the West. The siege of Rhegio lasted eleven months, and during that time, there were fierce clashes, some of which Dionysius himself was involved in, resulting in a severe injury to his groin. Eventually, Rhegio had to surrender, as they suffered from a dramatic shortage of supplies. With the surrender of Rhegio, Dionysius was now the ruler of a vast region, which included all the Greeks of Sicily and Italy and various other peoples and tribes of the peninsula.[70]

During this period of glory for Dionysius, the great Athenian philosopher Plato, who by then was about 40 years old and rising but had yet to become famous, visited Syracuse. Dionysius received Plato with honours and, at first, warmly hosted him personally. Soon, however, the two men strongly disagreed and quarreled vigorously. Plato was very strict and adamant against tyranny and did not hesitate to tell Dionysius that he considered him a tyrant and disapproved of his attitude towards the city's institutions.[71]

The enraged Dionysius expelled Plato, and during his journey, the philosopher was captured and sold as a slave. Plato eventually returned to Athens after his friends bought him from the slave traders. Nevertheless, it seems that the founder of the Platonic Academy and Platonism was particularly drawn to Italy, Sicily, and Syracuse, as he was to travel there several more times.[72]

Plato believed that the Greek cities of the West were more receptive and suitable for political reforms than the Athenian democracy, which he despised, believing that demagogues and the uneducated mob dominated it. Plato's second visit to Syracuse occurred while Dionysius was still alive and ruling. That time, he avoided meeting the philosopher, but he did not bother him either for the time Plato remained in the city. It seems that Dionysius had an ambiguous stance towards philosophers. He was probably interested in philosophy but also harboured a certain coolness towards those who studied and practised it. He perhaps believed that they were inclined to tiresome moralism, and to criticise and admonish without understanding the harsh realities of politics.[73]

On the other hand, the most powerful man in Sicily and Italy loved poetry intensely, which might seem paradoxical to some given his harsh, authoritarian, and often cynical political practice. Dionysius not only loved poetry but also wrote poems himself, which were received with contempt and scorn by the public during the first phase of his activity, while, of course, the flatterers in his entourage praised him as a great poet. Later, however, the tyrant of Syracuse's poetry improved, apparently also thanks to the benevolent presence and criticism of Philistus after he was recalled from exile. At the end of his life, Dionysius gained some appreciation for his poetry, even in Athens, where the public was more refined and snobbish than anywhere else.

Apart from his poetic attempts, Dionysius decided to wage a new great war against Carthage and began to prepare for it. At that time, Syracuse was likely the most populous city in the Mediterranean overall, and given its dominance over a large geographical area and its economic growth, probably the most powerful city in the West. The power of Syracuse now may have exceeded even that of Carthage and was undoubtedly far more significant than any other Western state, including the future great power of Rome, which was then undergoing the first phase of its historical rise.[74]

After his victory over the Greeks of Italy and establishing numerous Syracusan colonies along the Adriatic coast, Dionysius gained virtually complete control over this maritime area, allowing him to oversee the wheat trade in much of the Western Mediterranean. With the large profits flowing into Syracuse, Dionysius enlarged and further strengthened the walls and fortifications of the city, built new naval docks for his fleet, and gymnasium centres for military training.

In 384 BCE, preparations for the war, which aimed to eliminate the Carthaginian presence in Sicily, were in their final phase.[75] Dionysius decided to set sail himself with part of the fleet north of the Tyrrhenian, intending to put down the pirates who were interfering with Syracuse's trade with the northern Greek centres of the Mediterranean, particularly Massalia and Emporion.[76]

At the end of this mission, Dionysius found the opportunity to carry out a pirate raid of his own, at the expense of the Etruscans, by plundering the famous temple of Ilithyia in the town of Pyrgi, from which he seized valuable objects worth 1,500 talents to finance the forthcoming military operations.[77] Dionysius' simultaneous anti-piracy and piratical mission was thus completed with another raid, during which he extracted further booty, this time from Corsica.[78] There, Dionysius also established a base, probably in his plans to increase his influence in the Tyrrhenian more generally and possibly capture or develop bases in Elba and Sardinia.

Dionysius then hired several thousand mercenaries and recalled Philistus and Leptines from exile, understanding that in a war against Carthage, he needed them close to him and that despite the rupture that had occurred in their relations, they remained his most trusted men, and the only ones who always spoke to him honestly.[79]

In 383 BCE, the new war between Syracuse and Carthage was about to begin. The Carthaginians sent a delegation to Syracuse, but Dionysius refused to meet them, declaring war. Carthaginian diplomacy was instead successful in Italy, where several Greek cities and Italian tribes, wanting to escape the suzerainty of the Syracusans recently imposed on them, allied themselves with Carthage in anticipation of the conflict. On the other hand, the Sicilian cities outside Dionysius' territory crossed over to his side, turning against their Carthaginian neighbouring towns.

The Carthaginians assembled a powerful army and fleet and again put a general named Mago at its head. One can suspect that he was the same admiral Mago as before. In any case, forces were sent to Italy to secure Carthaginian control of the cities allied to Carthage and to extend its influence as far as possible, while the bulk of the troops landed in Sicily. Dionysius rushed with the Syracusan forces to confront the Carthaginian army and met it on the western side of Sicily, near the coastal town of Thermae Selinuntinae, a subcolony and port of Selinus. In the ensuing battle, the Syracusans repulsed some initial charges of the Carthaginian cavalry and managed to outflank the enemy forces and win a brilliant victory.

At the end of the battle, about 10,000 soldiers of the Carthaginian army were dead, and another 5,000 taken prisoner.[80] The remaining Carthaginian forces retreated and fortified themselves on a hill, at a location called Cronium, possibly near Panormus, while the Syracusans captured Thermae Selinuntinae. Dionysius and his forces then sealed off the Carthaginian camp. In the following negotiations, the Syracusan leader demanded the complete abandonment of Sicily by the Carthaginians and the payment of war reparations. The new leader of the Carthaginian army was Himilco Mago, son of Sophet Mago II and soon-to-be Sophet.[81] He replied that only the Senate of Carthage could respond to such a proposal and asked for a period of truce to transfer the demand to North Africa so the Carthaginian leadership could give its answer. Dionysius agreed, believing there was no danger and he was entirely in control of the situation.

However, in the following days, the Greek army relaxed too much, while the Carthaginians, knowing that there was no chance Carthage accepted Dionysius' demands, prepared for a hard battle with no way out.[82] At the end of the truce, the Carthaginian forces departed and engaged the Greek troops at the foot of the mountain. The Greeks divided themselves into two branches, one under the direct command of Dionysius and the other under the command of Leptines.

The corps commanded by Dionysius seemed to prevail over his opponents, but that of Leptines encountered difficulties, with him losing his life during the conflict. Leptines' death panicked his forces, many of whom fled, while Dionysius was shocked by the news of his brother's loss. Faced with the danger that his troops would be overwhelmed and his army would suffer significantly more damage, he ordered a retreat, effectively acknowledging that he had lost the battle.

In the end, the Greek army had 14,000 dead. Dionysius signed a balanced peace treaty with the Carthaginians, reflecting both sides' heavy losses during this war and their inability to prevail decisively over each other. The treaty recognised Syracuse's sovereignty over the territories east of the Alykos River but placed Selinus under Carthaginian control and imposed a war indemnity of 1,000 talents on Dionysius.[83]

For the umpteenth time, the two great powers of the Western Mediterranean had remained locked in the deadlock of an epic and tragic conflict that seemed destined to go on forever and bloodily without result. Thus, in the following years, Dionysius and Syracuse turned their attention to Italy and mainland Greece. The plan called for constructing a vast 35-kilometre wall south of Croton, from the coast of the Tyrrhenian Sea to that of the Ionian, which would thus geopolitically integrate the southernmost tip of mainland Italy with Sicily.[84] The point chosen was the shortest distance between the two coasts, approximately at the level of present-day Catanzaro. In this way, Dionysius intended to secure absolute control of the Italian territories nearest to Sicily and establish a secure base for expeditions to more northern territories, believing that he could achieve a considerable expansion into mainland Italy relatively quickly.

At the same time, the strongman of the Greek West proceeded to a greater involvement in the metropolitan Greek area, supporting the traditional ally Sparta with army and fleet, which saw its dominance threatened by the rising Thebes. Also, in cooperation with the Spartans, he supported the rise of Alcetas, a member of the Molossian dynasty, to the throne of Epirus.[85]

In the same years, Carthage suffered again from a severe epidemic, which had broken out in 379 BCE and, among other things, created huge strategic problems as the troubling situation in which the hegemonic city of North Africa found itself allowed the Libyans to rebel again. Moreover, this time, also the Sardinians did the same. Carthage met the rebellions with incredible difficulty. Indicative of the situation was that some 6,000 of its mercenaries in Sicily, being unpaid, mutinied against their commanders. Unable to pay them and fearing that they would turn against them, the Carthaginian leadership then put the mercenaries on board ships and, deceiving them, abandoned them on the desert island of Ustica in the Tyrrhenian Sea, where they all died of hunger and thirst.[86]

The weakness Carthage had fallen into prompted Dionysius to change his plans and bring back to the fore his great long-standing goal, namely eliminating the Carthaginian presence from Sicily, by again beginning preparations for a war against the Carthaginians.[87] In the summer of 368 BCE, Dionysius moved from Syracuse to the island's western side with an army that, according to Diodorus, consisted of 30,000 infantry and 3,000 cavalry, supported by a powerful fleet of 300 triremes. The Syracuse troops captured Selinus, Entella, and Eryx and then turned on the fortified city of Lilybaeum. The latter had been founded after the destruction of Motya and had developed into the new main naval and military base of Carthage in Sicily. The Carthaginians transported many people from Carthage and other places to Lilybaeum to raise its population.[88] Moreover, the city had probably a militarised structure and a military governor.[89]

The sea bordered the north-western and south-western sides of the city, while a wall forming a right angle covered the north-eastern and south-eastern sides. In previous years, the Carthaginians fortified the city with solid walls 6–7 metres thick and built towers 12 metres high every 38 metres along the length. In addition, they dug a large moat around the wall's perimeter, which was 30 metres wide and 9 metres deep but was also full of water, as both ends of the moat reached the sea.[90] In this way, Lilybaeum had become, in a way, an artificial island.

In addition to the mighty fortifications, the Carthaginians had stored vast supplies in the city, which made it capable of withstanding a long siege. At the same time, a relatively large military force defended it. When Dionysius arrived with his troops in front of the city, he found its capture difficult, almost impossible. An assault was out of the question, and siege engines could hardly have any effect against such fortified fortifications. Dionysius decided to carry out a naval and land blockade of the city, hoping to weaken its resistance and create more opportunities for the besiegers.

After a few months without any particular development, Dionysius learned of the destruction of the Carthaginian fleet after a fire had broken out in the great port of Carthage. This news led him to return to Syracuse with most of his forces, since the capture of Lilybaeum was still impossible, and to leave 130 triremes in the area. That fleet would continue to secure control of the trade routes and pressure the Carthaginian city.

Dionysius received intelligence from Eshmuniaton (Latinised as Suniatus by Justin), who was one of the dominant figures of Carthaginian politics at that time.[91] It is probable that Eshmuniaton controlled domestic Carthaginian politics and didn't want Carthage to be again involved in a war against Syracuse that would strengthen the interventionist party traditionally connected with the house of the Magonids and, by that time, led by Hanno.[92] Eshmuniaton wrote letters directly to Dionysius in Greek, informing him about the Carthaginian military preparations and moves. That would prove fatal for Eshmuniaton; eventually, the authorities intercepted him and he couldn't avoid being condemned to death for treason and conspiracy with the enemy.

However, the news of the destruction of the Carthaginian fleet did not correspond to reality.[93] The Carthaginian government had possibly staged a fire in the harbour of Carthage in which old and decommissioned ships had been set ablaze while they had secretly moved the real fleet to a safe distance. By this performance, the Carthaginian leadership had misled the spies and informers of Syracuse, who, thinking that they had seen with their own eyes the port and the Carthaginian fleet burning, had hastened to report the supposed event to their connections. By thus misleading Dionysius and his associates, the Carthaginians succeeded in launching a surprise attack with 200 triremes against the Syracusan fleet at the western end of Sicily, which was at that time docked carelessly at Eryx, and destroyed it.

A new mass invasion of Carthage occurred in Sicily in the same period. It is unclear whether this happened after or during the siege of Lilybaeum and whether Dionysius' withdrawal of the army from Lilybaeum related to it. What is certain is that having recovered from the plague and the challenging position in which it had found itself, the leadership of the North African metropolis was once again divided into two factions, one of which supported a vigorous intervention in Sicily while the other disagreed. The first managed to prevail, and subsequently, a mighty army was sent into Sicily led by Hanno, who, after the invasion, captured some Syracuse strongholds. Dionysius reacted by counterattacking and recapturing some of them, but the events and their exact timing are unclear. What is certain is that in 367 BCE, the situation was essentially unchanged from the beginning of the war.[94]

Dionysius was not to see his dream of a purely Greek dominion in Sicily realised, but he was to receive great satisfaction in his other field of activity, poetry. In December 367 BCE, one of his tragedies was declared the winner at the Lenaia, an annual festival held in Athens in honour of the god Dionysus, during which authors presented new tragedies and comedies, and competitions took place. The news brought joy to 62-year-old Dionysius, who organised a celebratory banquet. During it, the poet tyrant of Syracuse drank too much and suddenly sensed a strong feeling of indisposition, causing confusion and concern among friends and attendees. Dionysius then became seriously ill and died without his doctors even being able to understand what had happened. It has never been ascertained whether his death was caused through illness or some unintentional poisoning, or indeed was a murder perpetrated by the Carthaginians or Syracusan political opponents.

They say that Dionysius had earlier received an oracle, according to which his death would come immediately after the peak of his career. He had always assumed that the oracle meant that he would die after he had prevailed over Carthage in Sicily. As it turned out, the oracle referred to his peak moment as a poet, not a political and military leader.[95]

The unexpected end of Dionysius shook his political structure to its core. Since the latter had remained person-centred and had not developed a shielding of strong institutions that could survive their founder, everything depended on whether there would be a worthy successor. Unfortunately, Dionysius' son, Dionysius II, the so-called 'the Younger', as opposed to his father, 'the Great', did not possess the robust leadership characteristics of his father. Consequently, the great Greek empire of the West that Dionysius had envisioned and begun to build never became a reality. Instead, immediately after his death, a rapid process of disintegration of the state he had created began.

Chapter 6

Liberator Timoleon and the Battle of the Crimissus

In the years following the end of Dionysius, the political situation in Greek Sicily was agitated. At first, his son and successor, Dionysius II, made peace with Carthage and released the political prisoners, hoping that in this way he would be able to bring peace and consolidate his power. He also promoted friendly relations with Taras, wanting to present himself as a supporter of Italian Hellenism rather than a suzerain. However, the fact that he did not inspire as a leader and did not make sure his strength would increase and everybody would remember its extent meant that many perceived his attitude as a sign of weakness. Therefore, instead of greater consensus and understanding, what resulted was divisiveness and centrifugal tendencies.

At that time, Taras was a democracy, but for many years the city was effectively ruled by Archytas, a notable Pythagorean mathematician, philosopher, and scholarly friend of Plato. With Archytas' rule and Pythagorean principles permeating public life, Taras reached the height of its power. Taking advantage of Dionysius II's attitude and the fact that the Greek cities of Italy wished to escape the Syracusan hegemony imposed by Dionysius, Archytas made Taras the leading power of a Greek confederation in continental Italy and spread its influence into the Tyrrhenian Sea and the Adriatic.

The loss of the hegemony established by his father in the north was not the only negative development for Dionysius II. At the same time, a democratic faction also emerged in Sicily to challenge his authority. The democrats, led by Dion, gathered military forces, and in 357 BCE, launched a civil war to overthrow the tyrant and succeeded in winning. Consequently, Dionysius II left Syracuse and settled in Locri, the city that had been Dionysius' most loyal base in Italy for years.[1]

However, there was no political stabilisation in establishing functioning constitutions in Syracuse and the other Greek cities of Sicily. Instead, the situation remained chaotic, and the conflicts did not cease but multiplied, eventually leading, according to some sources, to a lack of people.[2] The essential result was the dissolution of the solid unitary Greek state that Dionysius I had created and the emergence of crowds of wannabe tyrants, rulers, and factionalists fighting for power in the various cities. Plutarch depicts in a negative light also the people of Syracuse during the years Dion was in power.[3] In the course of the controversies, Dion was himself accused of being a tyrant in Syracuse and was executed.

At the same time, Dionysius II, apparently realising that his previous mild attitude was inappropriate in an explosive political environment such as the one he was facing, committed the opposite mistake. Going to the other extreme, he ruled Locri cruelly and without respect for institutions and laws, causing an abysmal hatred against him among most inhabitants. This fact, along with the leadership vacuum created in Syracuse, made him decide to return to his native city and take power in it since the devotees and nostalgics of the Dionysian regime remained numerous and supported him.

Indeed, Dionysius II returned to Syracuse in 346 BCE and retook power, leaving his wife and daughters behind. The result was that the inhabitants of Locri unleashed their wrath upon them. The mob overpowered the small mercenary guard that Dionysius had left to protect them and then killed them after torture. Things did not go according to Dionysius II's wishes in Syracuse either, as the power of the resurgent tyrant soon became precarious. The reason was that another would-be ruler of the largest Greek city in the West had emerged, named Hicetas, the tyrant of the city Leontini.[4]

However, exiled Syracusans in Leontini sent a message to Corinth asking for help from the old metropolis to free Syracuse from tyranny. The Corinthians decided to respond to the request and sent a military corps of 700 mercenaries led by Timoleon.[5]

On the other side, after Dionysius' death, Carthage had also had similar problems of instability and internal conflict. Hanno plotted against the Carthaginian regime, leading around 20,000 slaves to revolt in alliance with Libyans and Numidians. The rebellion failed, and Hanno was crucified. Even worse, the Carthaginians executed all the male members of Hanno's faction, too.[6]

However, while the strife and conflicts in Syracuse and many other Sicilian cities were raging, the Carthaginians were talking and dealing with many parties and tyrants who had occupied positions of power, including Hicetas.[7] As the years passed and there was no solid leadership on the Greek side, the Carthaginians began to exploit the Greek disunity and anarchy to their advantage. In 345 BCE, the Carthaginian government sent a relatively large fleet of 150 ships loaded with troops to Sicily, under the command of yet another Mago. The Carthaginian troops landed and marched inland, where they captured the city of Entella.

Hicetas, for his part, moved against Dionysius II and managed to occupy a large part of Syracuse and settle in the quarter of Epipolae. At the same time, Dionysius II fled with his followers and mercenaries to the fortified citadel of the island Ortygia. Then, Hicetas asked for the help of the Carthaginian army to occupy Ortygia and fully take over Syracuse. Mago, of course, accepted the implausible invitation to enter freely with his army into the city, which for centuries had been the greatest enemy of his homeland, so a short time later, he captured the big harbour, and thousands of Carthaginian soldiers disembarked from the triremes and entered the interior of Syracuse. They then began to besiege Ortygia along with Hicetas' forces.

At the same time, Timoleon and his soldiers arrived at Rhegio, where people received them with enthusiasm, while a fleet of twenty Carthaginian ships was there to control the strait.[8] Hicetas intimated to the Corinthian general that Syracuse had been liberated from the tyrant, meaning Dionysius II, who was at the Ortygia fortress, and that Timoleon's mission had no longer any objective, so he should return to Corinth. However, Timoleon knew that Hicetas was as much a tyrant as Dionysius II, and furthermore, that Carthage was supporting him, so he ignored his claim to be allowed to rule Syracuse and departed from Rhegio. Timoleon and his men managed to escape the attention of the Carthaginian fleet and then landed at Taormina in Sicily, where people received him again with friendly feelings.

After consolidating his presence in Sicily, the Corinthian general accepted the invitation of one of the two factions fighting for power in the city Adranon, which was a city Dionysius the Elder founded around 400 BCE, and offered it to the Sicels to expand his leadership also among the non-Greek populations of the island.[9] Adranon had always had close relations with the Greeks, so the opposing faction had, for its part, called on Hicetas, who came to its aid with a military corps from Syracuse.[10] However, Timoleon prevailed by surprising his opponents, although he was vastly outnumbered. The Sicels of Adranon then honoured him and declared loyalty to him, as subsequently also did the Greek cities of Catania and Tyndaris.

Hicetas tried to eliminate Timoleon's presence and growing influence among the Sicilian Greeks and the other Sicilian peoples by organising an assassination attempt against him. The attempt, however, failed and instead reinforced the heroic and supernatural aura that had begun to build up around the name of the Corinthian general.

In 344 BCE, Timoleon strengthened his position decisively, convincing Dionysius II to hand over Ortygia to him while he settled in Catania.[11] The tyrant, exhausted and disappointed, agreed to leave the impregnable citadel of Syracuse and his 2,000 mercenaries under Timoleon's control in exchange for his safe removal and settlement with a small garrison and all his property in Corinth. The son of the most powerful ruler of the Greek West was to end his life in political obscurity and on the margins of the Peloponnesian city.

By moving another 400 men to Ortygia, Timoleon consolidated his position in the interior of Syracuse. At the same time, he managed to supply the island acropolis with the help of the tyrant of Catania, Mamercus, who sent small boats and fishing boats to penetrate the blockade attempted by the Carthaginian fleet. Seeing that the blockade was failing and Ortygia remained inaccessible, Hicetas moved his forces towards Catania to attack Timoleon and Mamercus. They cut off supplies to Timoleon's forces at the fortress of Ortygia. In this way, however, he reduced the strength of the troops besieging Ortygia. Thus, its defenders found an opportunity to make a counterattack and wrest the district of

Achradina from the control of the Carthaginians and the forces of Hicetas that had remained in Syracuse.

That forced Hicetas to return to Syracuse in haste. The Carthaginians also sent a fleet to prevent reinforcements for Timoleon from the Peloponnese and the city of Thurii in Italy, arriving at Catania. However, the Carthaginian fleet failed utterly, and the corps that had departed to reinforce Timoleon arrived without any problems, landing undisturbed in Sicily. The Peloponnese and the Italian Greeks who arrived to fight aside Timoleon combined in a force of at least 4,000 men.

The reinforcements' arrival helped Timoleon take Messina, and the Corinthian leader marched on Syracuse. Meanwhile, inside the city, the two Greek factions began approaching each other as the mercenaries met while fishing and began to discuss that they should unite against the barbarians.

Mago, realising that his Greek allies were likely to turn against him and join the enemies while Timoleon was also approaching the city with his forces, feared that he would end up trapped among enemy troops. He therefore took the not-unreasonable decision to abandon the effort and set sail for home so as not to risk the integrity of his forces. However, on reaching Carthage, he was severely blamed, and was driven to suicide, according to Carthaginian morals. Moreover, his fellow citizens were so enraged with him for the fact that, as they believed, he had missed an excellent opportunity to subdue Syracuse that after executing him, they also beheaded his corpse.

Back in Sicily, Hicetas, left with only his mercenaries and without any allies, suffered a well-organised attack and fled, resulting in Timoleon gaining complete control of Syracuse. After assuming the rule of Syracuse, the Corinthian general sought to reinvigorate the great city of the Greek West, which had been so severely tested in previous years and had seen its population greatly diminish. For this reason, he induced and favoured influxes of Greeks from anywhere on the map to Syracuse, increasing the city's population by tens of thousands of inhabitants so that it returned to its former size. Wanting then to pay his mercenaries without imposing taxes on the Greek populations, he sent a contingent of the army to plunder the Carthaginian territories on the east of the island,[12] led by

Deinarchus and Demaretus. Timoleon also sent troops to Entella, where they executed the fifteen most pro-Carthaginian renowned citizens, putting pro-Syracusan citizens in charge. After the soldiers returned with the loot from the Carthaginian territories, Timoleon sold everything and with the money, he paid his mercenaries.

At the same time, ambassadors from Greek and other Sicilian cities were arriving in Syracuse, as seeing its renewed strength, they sought to ally themselves with it. Practically all the Greek cities of Sicily entered voluntarily into Timoleon's Syracusan alliance, as also did the Sicels and the Sicani, who sent him ambassadors asking to be accepted.[13]

The Battle of the River Crimissus

The situation was developing in a particularly negative way for Carthage. Only a short time before, it had been on the verge of a final victory over the Greeks in Sicily but now was in a weak position and was watching its most potent enemy city increasing its power again and improving its general condition and situation. Consequently, the Carthaginian leadership decided to intervene vigorously and directly before the Greeks had time to heal the wounds that had opened up during the previous years. In the following period, Carthage assembled a large army, which, according to Plutarch, numbered 60,000 foreign mercenaries and 10,000 Carthaginians, including the elite soldiers of the Sacred Band, who numbered around 3,000 men.[14] The Carthaginian army then landed at Cape Lilybaeum in June 341 BCE to conquer the whole of Sicily.

Timoleon managed to gather a relatively small army and, thinking calmly and boldly, decided to strike the enemy first rather than wait for them at Syracuse, allowing them to advance into Sicily and secure resources and forces. Hence, the Corinthian leader of Syracuse and all of Greek Sicily rushed westwards through the frontier territories. According to Diodorus, Timoleon's army had only around 12,000 men. Moreover, during his march, some 1,000 mercenaries deserted him, worsening his numerical disadvantage against the sizeable Carthaginian army. The responsibility lay with a Phocian mercenary named Thrasius, who had participated in the plunder of the Oracle of Delphi a few years earlier. His sacrilegious ethics, which so disgusted Diodorus, prompted the mercenaries to desert Timoleon, saying that his plan was madness and would lead them to certain death. The mercenaries initially were enthusiastic about Thrasius' proposal, but Timoleon managed to keep most of them in the army with urgent pleading and by offering gifts.[15]

At the end of the route, the Greeks parked on a hill between Entella and Segesta, in front of which the river Crimissus flowed, from where they could watch the arrival of the Carthaginian troops on the other side of the river. Anxiety prevailed among the Greek troops because of the enemy's numerical superiority, and this intensified with the appearance of some worrying signs. For instance, some carts loaded with celery, customarily used in funeral rites, passed by. Trying to reverse the negative psychology in his men, Timoleon recalled that celery was also used for the wreaths worn by the winners of the Isthmian games. He therefore argued that the sign indicated that a great victory was imminent, and he even made a wreath of celery and wore it on his head, urging the soldiers to do the same.[16] He also raised their morale with fiery speeches and urged them to believe in victory.

The Carthaginians arrived and initially, their movements remained unseen by the Greeks as the morning fog covered them. The weather and visibility improved as noon approached, when Timoleon and his men could observe the crossing of the river by the enemies. The Sacred Company and other units composed of Carthaginian soldiers crossed first, with the sizeable body of the mercenary army following. Timoleon thought it best to attack right away in order to deal with those that had already crossed the river before the remaining troops could make the follow. The intention was to prevent the Carthaginian army being able to exploit its numerical advantage, and a victory over the Carthaginian elite unit would surely discourage or even drive the rest of the enemy forces into retreat.

The Greeks did indeed attack, and a fierce battle ensued between the Syracusan hoplite phalanx and the Carthaginian Sacred Band. Diodorus is certain that in the first phase of the battle, the Greeks were superior in bravery and skill, so there was a great slaughter of the barbarians. The tide began to tip towards the Greeks, but gradually, more and more

Carthaginian forces crossed to the other side of the river, and the outcome remained uncertain.

The Carthaginians – whom Diodorus calls at this point 'Phoenicians',[17] as in many other points of the text – began to take the upper hand against the Greeks due to their numerical advantage, when all of a sudden, sheets of rain and a storm of large hailstones erupted from the skies, along with lightening, thunder, and strong gusts of wind. The storm hit the Carthaginians head-on, hampering their efforts severely while leaving the Greeks unaffected, because they had their backs to it. This fortuitous circumstance helped the Greek side to repel the Carthaginians, whose first lines broke and retreated, causing panic among the rest of the troops.

Everyone was making for the river; horsemen and foot soldiers fought in chaos, while the chariots created even more havoc. Some Carthaginians met their deaths by being crushed beneath the feet of men or horses, or were accidentally pierced by their colleagues' swords or lances. Others were caught by the Greek cavalry and were eliminated in the riverbed. Yet more drowned trying to swim in their armour as the river raced downstream in the roaring torrent caused by the heavy downpour. The Sacred Band fought gallantly, but the Greek troops destroyed them.

The confusion that followed brought about the complete disorganisation of the Carthaginian army and its retreat towards Lilybaeum, having left behind some 10,000 dead and 15,000 prisoners.[18] According to Diodorus, the Greeks captured 200 chariots and most of the wagons of the Carthaginian army baggage train, while many other chariots were destroyed during the battle. The Greek soldiers carried around 1,000 breastplates and over 10,000 shields to Timoleon's tent, although most of the Carthaginian armour was lost in the river. Timoleon distributed some of the spoils among the soldiers, allies, and mercenaries and dedicated other parts to the temples of Syracuse. He also sent some of them to Corinth, with the directive to dedicate them to the great temple of Poseidon.

The victory of Timoleon and his soldiers was tremendous, and the acquisition of many rich spoils, which the Carthaginian troops abandoned in their hasty retreat, made it even more significant. However, the Carthaginian presence in Sicily remained strong, and Timoleon soon discovered that he now had to contend with the newly formed alliance between Hicetas and Mamercus. The tyrant of Leontini had not laid down his arms. Furthermore, Timoleon's former ally, the tyrant of Catania, was alarmed at the turn of events and the significant influence the Corinthian general now had in Sicily.

As a result, the two tyrants gathered troops, including Carthaginian forces. Then Hippo, the tyrant of Messene, also joined the alliance. Timoleon reacted by sending a mercenary corps against them, but it was crushed. This victory gave confidence and enthusiasm to Hicetas, who invaded and plundered Syracusan territory with his forces. In the end, however, Timoleon prevailed in a decisive battle against him, then pursued and captured him at Leontini. The tyrant's fate was to be executed along with his son.[19]

Timoleon then launched a campaign against Catania, and in 338 BCE, he crushed the troops of Mamercus and his Carthaginian allies at a battle near the stream of Abolus. As a result, Catania surrendered, while Mamercus fled to Messene and his ally Hippo. Timoleon and his forces laid siege to the city, and eventually, its inhabitants revolted against the authority of Hippo, whom they executed, and handed Mamercus over to Timoleon. The former tyrant of Catania was, in turn, executed shortly afterwards at Syracuse.

Timoleon went on to overthrow the other tyrants of the Greek cities of Sicily and establish democratic regimes, but also rebuilt Akragas and Gela. He also agreed to make peace with the Carthaginians if the latter accepted his terms, according to which the Alykos River on the western side of Sicily was redefined as the border between Greek and Carthaginian territories, and the Carthaginians pledged not to ally themselves henceforth with would-be Greek tyrants.

After overthrowing the tyrannies and attempting to bring a measure of law and order to the Greek cities of Sicily, Timoleon spent the last years of his life on a farm outside Syracuse, away from active politics, enjoying the recognition and honours of the citizens, and giving advice whenever he was asked, until he died in 336 BCE. His great work in Sicily and rare moral integrity secured him among the most outstanding personalities of the ancient Greek world and antiquity.

The Syracusans honoured Timoleon with gymnastic and musical games because he 'dethroned the tyrants, brought down the barbarians, and reconstructed the mightiest Greek cities, becoming the maker of the Sicilian Greeks' freedom'.[20]

However, eliminating the tyrannies did not lead to the formation and stabilisation of functional governments nor increased understanding and coordination between the Greek cities of Sicily. On the contrary, the political situation remained unstable, while no institutions capable of eventually containing the disruptive momentum of internal conflicts and creating essential political cohesion were formed. As a result, the political life of the Sicilian Greeks continued on its usual course, and very soon, a host of tyrants and would-be tyrants reappeared.

The Plans of Alexander the Great and Aristotle for the Western Mediterranean

Timoleon died in the same year (336 BCE) in which an event of great importance for world history took place, namely the coronation of Alexander III, King of Macedonia.

In previous years, Greek cities in mainland Italy had been facing problems from the attacks and pressure of the local tribes. The democracy of Taras, after the death of Archytas, had abandoned the prudent and disciplined government that had led it to the height of its power and, as the geographer and historian Strabo reports, had adopted a highly secretive way of life, simply enjoying the prosperity it had achieved in the previous period.[21] Not having at least taken care to maintain an adequate military capacity, the Tarantines asked the metropolis of Sparta for help in 342 BCE to deal with the problematic situation. The Spartans responded by sending a military corps led by Archidamus, one of the two kings, on a mission parallel to Timoleon's. Archidamus won some victories over the Messapians and the Lucanians but was eventually defeated and killed in 338 BCE.[22]

Finding themselves in danger again, the Tarantines turned to another state of metropolitan Greece, the kingdom of Epirus, asking for help from Alexander Molossus, uncle of Alexander the Great and brother of his mother, Olympias. Alexander Molossus landed with his troops in Italy in 334 BCE, the same year his nephew began his world-historical campaign in Asia. The Epirote ruler prevailed over the Peucetians, Messapians, Lucanians, and Bruttians, even liberating the city of Heraclea. Having, to some extent, emerged as the leader of the Greek confederation of Italy, Alexander Molossus allied with Rome to jointly dominate the Samnites, who were the most vigorous foes of both the Greeks and the Romans in Italy at the time.[23] Moreover, direct diplomatic relations between Alexander the Great and Rome were established at the same time.

From the Roman historians Trogus and Justin, we know that probably after the victory over the Italian tribes and the alliance with Rome, Alexander Molossus turned his gaze towards Africa.[24] However, the Tarantines and other Italian Greeks, who were under Tarantine influence, strongly resisted the prospect of an alliance with the Romans, as they regarded Rome as an enemy. For this reason, they subsequently turned their backs on Alexander Molossus, whom they had themselves called upon to help, fearing that he was tending to acquire too much power and authority, and even allied themselves with the Samnites against him. The Epirote ruler then tried to find some footholds in the land of the Lucanians but finally clashed with them and was killed on the river Acheron in Pandosia in 331 BCE,[25] the same year that his nephew subdued the Persian Empire with the magnificent victory at Gaugamela.

Alexander Molossus' campaign in Italy was certainly carried out with the consent of Alexander the Great, as Epirus was part of the immediate territories of his reign. It is also known that Alexander intended to continue his campaigns to the West when he had completed his conquest of the East and that there was a definite plan for the Western Mediterranean. Alexander Molossus' attempt to create a Greco-Roman union that would dominate Italy is combined with the fact that at that time, the influence of Aristotle, Alexander the Great's teacher, supported and propagated the idea that Rome was a Greek city. This position was, of course, political and propagandistic, and not entirely historically accurate. Nonetheless, it was based on racial, ethnological, and religious affinity between the Romans and the Greeks, as well as on the Greek-type Roman political institutions and legal systems.

I think it is therefore likely that Alexander the Great and Aristotle's plan at that time was to cultivate the idea of Rome's incorporation into the Greek world rather than confronting it, as it was the rising power of central Italy and could play a crucial dual role: on the one hand to act as a bulwark against the tribes of the north and south-central Italy, and on the other to add a critical mass to the power of the Greek cities of the Western Mediterranean, resulting in a decisive reduction of Carthaginian influence. The alliance of the Western Greeks with Rome under the aegis of the Macedonian throne would facilitate the submission of Carthage to the Alexandrian Empire and constitute its placeholder in the West.

Alexander the Great also used this kind of tactical approach extensively during the campaign in Asia, where he always approached the minor powers of a region in a friendly manner in order to join with the Greeks against the primary opponent,[26] which in the case of the Western Mediterranean would undoubtedly have been the Carthaginian Empire.

The history scholar can only travel with his or her imagination to what would have happened if the Tarantines had supported Alexander Molossus or if Alexander the Great had not died so prematurely in 323 BCE. What is certain is that the breadth and horizons of Aristotle and Alexander the Great's understanding, as well as their global vision of Hellenism, far exceeded the limits of understanding of Taras and any other Greek city-state.

Chapter 7

Agathocles and the Greek Attack on Carthage

In the years following the death of Timoleon, Syracuse and the other Greek cities of Sicily achieved no political equilibrium. Instability and internal conflicts again characterised social development – the constitutions and the governments that took over failed to stabilise the tense situation. In Syracuse, two decades after the victory on the Crimissus River, the generals were elected exclusively by an assembly of only 600 members in what was essentially an aristocratic new constitution, which caused the discontent of a large part of the population.[1]

Also, after the defeat at Crimissus, Hamilcar remained in Sicily as an ambassador of Carthage, and being probably much more capable as a diplomat than as a general, he succeeded in his efforts to increase Carthaginian influence on the island despite the military defeat that had preceded it. Taking advantage of the conflicts and disputes raging in Syracuse and the other Greek cities, Hamilcar ingeniously became the mediator or arbitrator to whom the various factions and parties appealed. By offering Carthaginian support now and then to one Greek faction and now and then to another, he sharpened the intra-Hellenic conflicts and strengthened the position of Carthage, serving its interests.

In this way, the militarily defeated Carthaginians managed to increase their influence considerably in Sicily to the extent that they could have gained a kind of suzerainty. At the same time, the failure of the political institutions of the Greek cities to define the constant power struggle brought about a complete lack of a long-term strategic vision. This fact constantly undermined their position, despite the enormous potential offered by their cultural and economic development, with the great wealth they possessed thanks to their fertile land, technical development, and trade.

For the third time in the history of Syracuse and the Greek West, after those of Gelon and Dionysius, political stabilisation and strategic strengthening would come only through the emergence and prevalence of a charismatic tyrant. Agathocles was the son of an exiled citizen of Rhegio, who had arrived and settled in Syracuse at the call of Timoleon in 356 BCE when his son was 5 years old. Agathocles' dynamic personality and impressive physique helped him make a successful career in the army, and he gradually gained political influence.[2] However, Agathocles' leadership and demagogic characteristics, appearance, and charm exerted on the citizens created concern among the oligarchic leadership of the city, who considered him a threat and exiled him. In doing so, though, they helped him become even more popular. So, when the people later banished those generals and their oligarchic supporters, Agathocles returned to Syracuse with an enhanced political role.

The oligarchic exiles fled to various other Sicilian cities and began collaborating with the Carthaginians to regain power, while the new Syracusan leadership declared war on their host cities. During this war, Agathocles, now a general,[3] distinguished himself further. However, fearing that his influence might enable him to establish a tyranny, the assembly did not re-elect him.[4] In his place, Acestorides, a Corinthian who tried to achieve a compromise between democrats and oligarchs to stop the civil conflict, was elected.

Acestorides also attempted to exterminate Agathocles as a politician with incendiary rhetoric, a would-be tyrant par excellence, and a protagonist of the civil war. Nevertheless, Agathocles escaped Syracuse and was rescued, while the previously exiled oligarchs eventually returned to the city.[5] Agathocles then contacted Hamilcar,[6] and the latter put pressure on the leadership of Syracuse to stop persecuting Agathocles and accept him back into the city, something that the Carthaginian general's compatriots considered suspicious because they feared the possibility of a new powerful ruler emerging in Syracuse. As it would turn out, the governments of both Carthage and Syracuse were right to be concerned about Agathocles' intentions and capabilities.

After returning to Syracuse and resuming his duties as general, Agathocles began to gather forces from parts of the population of Syracuse and cities of the hinterland that were hostile to the oligarchs. When the preparations were completed, Agathocles claimed that the oligarchs were preparing an ambush against him and unleashed his loyal forces against them.[7] The Syracusan general's surprise coup attack, carried out in 316 BCE, fully achieved its objective, as his cutthroats killed some 4,000 oligarchs, and 6,000 more of them fled Syracuse to safety.[8]

Agathocles then put the decisions in the hands of the people, knowing that they would elect him emperor general, which they did. Following the example of Dionysius I, after becoming the sole ruler of the city, he confiscated the property of his oligarchic foes and distributed it to the poor and needy, gaining even more enthusiastic support and loyalty from the lower social classes. It was the establishment of a new tyranny. After consolidating his power in Syracuse, Agathocles moved in 315 BCE against Messene, where many exiles and dissidents of his regime had taken refuge. He first captured Mylae (present-day Milazzo) and, in the autumn, laid siege to Messene with a strong force.

The Carthaginians were not happy with Agathocles' actions, which they considered a violation of the treaty they had signed with Timoleon. They therefore sent a delegation to formally protest to the new leader of Syracuse, asking him to lift the siege of Messene since the latter and other cities were autonomous under the treaty. Wanting to avoid a conflict with Carthage at this stage, Agathocles did indeed withdraw from Messene, but he captured the town of Abacaenum.

Then, Akragas, Gela, and Messene declared war on Syracuse with the support of other cities where Syracuse oligarchs had taken refuge and asked for help from Sparta to overthrow the new tyrant. The Spartans responded by sending Prince Acrotatus to take the role of the new Timoleon liberator. Acrotatus arrived at Akragas in 314 BCE with twenty ships of Taras, but things did not go well for him. Soon, the Spartan prince had to leave Sicily in haste, as the Akragantines accused him of being a tyrant, apparently because he tried to impose a Spartan-style discipline on the carefree Sicilian city and deposed its leaders. After his departure, the Tarantines also left Akragas for their homeland.[9]

Frustrated, the Syracusan oligarchs and their allies in Akragas and the other cities then turned to Hamilcar and Carthage. The Carthaginian aristocrat interceded and began negotiations with Agathocles, which resulted in the mutual recognition of transparent spheres of influence between Carthage and Syracuse in Sicily.

Agathocles recognised the sovereignty of the Carthaginians over Selinus, Thermae Himerenses (near former Himera), and in addition, Heraclea, i.e. essentially over the western part of Sicily, while Hamilcar recognised the hegemony of Syracuse over the rest of the island.[10]

The treaty caused the intense resentment of the Syracuse oligarchs and their allies in Akragas, Messene, Gela, and other cities as it recognised the rule of Agathocles in Syracuse and much of Sicily. Moreover, it was also considered treasonable by the Carthaginian Senate.[11] Indeed, Hamilcar was sentenced to death in absentia by his fellow citizens, as a faction had probably emerged that supported new military intervention in Sicily, and the Carthaginian general also bore the brunt of the defeat at Crimissus.

At first sight, the agreement may seem paradoxically favourable to Agathocles. However, in reality, Hamilcar had probably acted in the best possible way to serve the interests of his country, as he secured the formal extension of Carthaginian sovereignty over more territory than before without any cost or loss.

The fact that some Greeks opposed the Syracusan regime did not constitute a valid opportunity for a more significant increase in Carthaginian influence, as apparently considered those who criticised and judged the Carthaginian aristocrat from afar. The truth is that, despite the noise they had caused, in substance, neither the minority Syracuse dissidents nor the powerless other Greek cities could actually confront Syracuse. That is why, after all, they had ended up asking for help from the power that had flattened some of them a century earlier. Hamilcar eventually died mysteriously, however, before returning to Carthage.

After signing the treaty, Agathocles took advantage of the favourable situation that had developed for him and captured several cities and forts. At the same time, he recruited many thousands of mercenaries. He also created networks of supporters in the various regions and recruited strong forces from Syracuse and other cities.

However, the terms of the agreement regarding the Syracuse exiles were not entirely clear. Agathocles believed that since Carthage had recognised his hegemony over the Greek cities, he had, under the treaty, unlimited limits of action in the territories of the hegemony and could therefore pursue the Syracusan oligarchs who had fled to other cities. In contrast, the Carthaginians interpreted the treaty differently. They argued that the hegemony referred to foreign policy and did not abolish the autonomy of the cities; accordingly, Agathocles had no right to interfere in their internal affairs, such as whether or not to admit Syracusan dissidents.

Agathocles demanded that Messene and Tauromenio (now Taormina) surrender to him those Syracusan oligarchs who had taken refuge in them, and the two cities did so, fearing an attack against them. After the surrender, Agathocles executed all the oligarchs,[12] but he also captured the two cities, even tearing down the walls of Tauromenio. Having secured control of the Sicilian–continental Italy strait, the tyrant of Syracuse turned his attention to Akragas. In the spring of 312 BCE, he arrived in the city with a strong military force, demanding the surrender of those Syracusan oligarchs who had taken refuge there.

In the meantime, however, Akragas and other Greek cities, as well as the Syracusan dissidents had begun to act in concert with their Carthaginian allies. Consequently, upon reaching Akragas, Agathocles found many Carthaginian warships in the sea area. Considering the presence of the Carthaginian fleet as a declaration of war, Agathocles moved inland to the island, where he occupied various townships and forts, capturing and executing any Syracusan dissidents he spotted.

The Carthaginians raided the great port of Syracuse with a fleet of fifty ships, aiming to create a distraction and trouble Agathocles. Still, all they succeeded in was destroying two Athenian merchant ships, while the Syracuse fleet, which reacted quickly, crushed them.[13]

At the same time, the exiled Syracusans formed an army of about 5,000 men led by Dinocrates, with the support of Carthage.[14] Opposing them was a similarly sized Syracusan force under the command of Pasiphilus, who engaged the dissident troops in battle outside the town of Galeria and broke them up. The Syracusans then captured the town, which had sided with the rebels, and executed those who belonged to the faction opposing the authority of Agathocles.

The Carthaginians had sent a force of about 12,000 men consisting of mercenaries from Libya, Etruria, and the Balearic Islands, and 2,000 Carthaginians, among whom were several nobles. Sicilian allies reinforced the troops, and the Carthaginian army encamped on the fortified hill of Ecnomus on the east coast of Akragas. Agathocles camped on another fortified hill called Falarion, north-east of Ecnomus, with a large army of 45,000 men. He had previously entered Gela, where he had seized a considerable amount of property, executing some 4,000 of its wealthy citizens.

Agathocles then attacked the Carthaginian camp by surprise and began to besiege it. The Carthaginians were defending themselves, hoping for the soon arrival of reinforcements, which had already left Carthage for Sicily, something that Agathocles was unaware of. Indeed, the Carthaginian reinforcements had time to land at the rear of the Greeks while the camp's defences were still holding out, resulting in Agathocles' army being caught between two enemy armies. The result of the battle that took place in early August 310 BCE on the plain that stretched between the two hills was disastrous for the Syracusans, with their troops completely losing cohesion and fleeing in disorderly flight, scattered in every possible direction while being pursued by the enemy cavalry. At the end of the battle, the Greeks had 7,000 dead and the Carthaginians 500.

Agathocles retreated to Syracuse, trying to regroup his forces. On reaching Gela, he made the Carthaginians believe he intended to fortify the city and resist there. He even succeeded in an ambush to annihilate a body of 300 Libyan horsemen who were pursuing him. The Carthaginians prepared to lay siege to Gela. Yet, Agathocles had left only a small unit to delay them so he could have more time to better prepare Syracuse for the impending attack.

Indeed, the Syracusans provided their city with plenty of food and supplies, allowing it to withstand a long siege. On the other hand, the Carthaginian commander, whose name was also Hamilcar, recommended alliances with the Greek cities, approaching them carefully. The cities that could not resist nevertheless crossed over to the side of the Carthaginians, hoping at least that they would be liberated by the tyrant of Syracuse.

Their inhabitants who, on the contrary, supported Agathocles and were determined to fight against the Carthaginians fled to Syracuse.

With the enemies in control of Sicily and facing the walls of Syracuse, Agathocles conceived an extraordinarily bold and unprecedented plan, trusting in the mighty and impenetrable fortifications of the Greek metropolis of Sicily. Instead of remaining with the whole of his forces at Syracuse and resisting the siege, he decided to move with an expeditionary force to Africa and lay a parallel siege of Carthage.[15] In this way, he hoped either to have a chance to conquer the city, win the war with the Carthaginians once and for all, or at least force them to break the siege of Syracuse and accept a peace treaty.

Agathocles came to this choice because he had great military power and knew that apart from Carthage and Utica, the other cities of the Carthaginian territory in Africa did not have such solid fortifications. Also, many of Carthage's vassal populations harboured hatred for the city and would support an invader, as had conversely happened against Syracuse in Sicily.

Agathocles put his brother Antander at the head of the defence of Syracuse while he prepared the campaign in Africa.[16] To thicken the ranks of the army, he freed a large number of slaves and recruited them. At the same time, there was great discontent in the city with the tyrant's unorthodox choice, which was not even entirely clear since most of the army preparing for the campaign actually did not know where they were going. Wanting, therefore, to enforce absolute discipline to his orders and to boost the morale of his loyal followers, Agathocles announced, when all the soldiers had boarded the ships to depart, that anyone who did not wish to follow the expedition was free to leave. However, those who did so were put to death as soon as they got off the ships, while the rest were hailed as brave and worthy.[17]

In Front of Carthage

Agathocles' departure from Syracuse to Africa occurred on 14 August 310 BCE. Diodorus mentions that the following day after the departure of Agathocles with the fleet for North Africa, there was a solar eclipse.[18] In contrast, Frontinus[19] mentions a lunar eclipse. However, we know there was a solar eclipse on 15 August 310 BCE, so we can be confident that Diodorus' version is the most accurate.

The forces Agathocles took with him numbered about 36,000 men. For the ships carrying the troops to Africa to escape from the encirclement of the Carthaginian fleet without engaging in a naval battle, Agathocles had ordered sixty merchant ships, which, of course, moved much more slowly than the warships, to pretend that they intended to go out to sea.[20] Thus, the Carthaginians believed that the triremes that followed the merchant ships were to protect their exit from the harbour, which meant that they intended to engage in a naval battle with the Carthaginian fleet. So, they lined up their ships for a naval battle but were surprised to see the Greek war fleet swiftly fleeing. The Carthaginian triremes gave chase, but the distance was already considerable. Meanwhile, in this way, the merchant ships also returned intact to Syracuse.

The Greek fleet approached Africa after six days, probably having followed the longer route, i.e. sailing parallel to the northern Sicilian coast in a westward direction, before turning south. They thought that this way, there was more chance of deception and escape from the pursuit of the Carthaginians. Nevertheless, the Carthaginian ships were in pursuit when the Greek fleet approached the African coast.

Agathocles' army landed at the cape east of Carthage, the closest point in Africa to Sicily, today's Cape Bon, at 70 kilometres from the North African metropolis.[21] The Syracusan archers turned their arrows against the Carthaginian fleet as soon as they landed on land to force them to stay away and facilitate the landing of the rest of the Greek troops.

Agathocles' first action after the completion of the invasion was to order the burning of the ships.[22] In this way, the tyrant of Syracuse wanted to erase any thought of retreating and returning home from his men's minds and force them to devote all their efforts and strength to the pursuit of victory. In order to avoid the resentment against him and the possible wrath that his risky choice might provoke, he spread the word that he had promised Demeter and Persephone on board to offer them the ships by burning them if they managed to escape from the pursuit of the Carthaginian fleet, so he was obliged to keep his promise to the goddesses so that there might be favourable developments.[23]

However, we should stress that Agathocles' move, apart from the psychological interpretation attributed to it, although strange, was entirely rational from a strategic point of view. Maintaining a camp where the army should keep ships tens of kilometres away from the campaign's objective was unsustainable, as it would commit forces necessary for the decisive theatre of war without offering any substantial guarantee in case of defeat.

On the other hand, it is clear that the Syracusans wanted at all costs to avoid a naval battle, which, if lost, would have meant the destruction of the army and the fleet; otherwise, they would have already fought against the Carthaginian fleet in the open sea. Agathocles had probably decided from the start to land far from Carthage at the price of sacrificing the fleet, believing that staying away from Carthage would mean fewer problems when approaching and landing on the African coast. Equally or even more important was the fact that, in this way, he would also have the opportunity to plunder the regions on the route, strengthening his troops with valuable supplies. It is significant that before leaving Syracuse, he had instructed the horsemen to take saddles but not horses with them to facilitate the journey, apparently intending to procure horses in Africa before approaching Carthage.[24]

However, the sight of the fleet burning in its entirety filled the soldiers with fear. The psychology of the Syracusan troops improved when they plundered the rich countryside of Megalopolis (today's Soliman or Hammam-Lif) and Tunis during the march to Carthage.[25] The soldiers even wanted to take the two cities. Nonetheless, Agathocles flatly refused, ordering the march to continue, as he wanted the campaign to remain strictly focused on the main objective, namely Carthage itself. The plan did not provide for an immediate attempt to conquer the city since it was well fortified, and the Greek army did not have anywhere near adequate siege engines. Instead, Agathocles aimed to block Carthage's land supply by occupying the roads leading to its three western gates.

In Carthage, panic initially broke out as the city faced the presence of a Greek army on its territory for the first time. Two generals were then appointed to head the army instead of the usual one. This time, the

Carthaginian army was not to consist mainly of mercenaries accompanied by a small number of Carthaginian citizens but all Carthaginian citizens capable of fighting. The latter amounted to about 40,000 infantry and 1,000 cavalry, plus 2,000 chariots.[26]

The Carthaginian generals Bomilcar and Hanno took the army out of the city and deployed their forces on a hill near the Greek camp. Hanno commanded the right side of the formation, and there was the Carthaginian Holy Company. On the right side of the formation were also the cavalry and chariots lined up in front of the infantry. Bomilcar commanded the left side of the Carthaginian army, and there were the most significant infantry forces. However, the ground at that point was uneven, so the arrangement of the Carthaginian lines was not ideal, but there was some crowding and a greater depth of formation than usual.

Agathocles commanded the left side of the Greek army, having at his disposal 10,500 men, including 3,500 Syracusans, 3,000 Greek mercenaries, and a corps of about 4,000 Samnite, Etruscan, and Celt mercenaries. He was lined up with a corps of 1,000 selected warriors just opposite the Sacred Band of Carthage.

The right part of the Syracusan army consisted of about 25,000 foot soldiers under the command of Agathocles' son Archagathus. So, on one side of the front, where Agathocles and Hanno were, the elite units of the two armies were to be opposed. In contrast, on the other side, under the command of Archagathus and Bomilcar, the large masses of the two armies were to clash.[27]

The situation was critical for the Greeks, as they had no way of escaping in case of defeat, while their equipment was not entirely complete. Several soldiers did not have adequate equipment in their ranks, and of course, cavalry and chariots were absent. Moreover, in the opposite faction, the Carthaginians would fight to defend their city, knowing it might be in mortal danger if they failed.

Agathocles, in order to encourage his worried and troubled soldiers, used again a deceptive trick. He released some owls he had been secretly keeping, considerably boosting the soldiers' morale, as the owl is goddess Athena's sacred and lucky bird.

With the two armies lined up facing each other, the battle opened with an attack by the Carthaginian chariots. The chariots poured towards the phalanx; however, the Greeks had no particular problems and repelled them relatively easily. Knowing the example of Xenophon and the Ten Thousand near Babylon, after which almost a century had passed, and of course that of Alexander the Great at Gaugamela two decades earlier, the phalanx opened up at various points, letting the chariots enter and then enclosing them, while the archers and slingers hit them with arrows and stones when they charged, as well as when they then retreated.[28] The phalanx equally quickly met the attack of the Carthaginian horse riders that followed.

Then, the main battle took place, with the massive engagement of the infantry forces. The Sacred Band of the Carthaginians attacked in front of the remaining troops of the Carthaginian right flank, with Agathocles' 1,000 elite hoplites and the other forces of the Greek left wing trying to repel the attack. Their task was difficult, and the Carthaginians initially advanced. However, they received many arrows and projectiles from the rear of the Greek column, which also killed Hanno himself.

Nevertheless, the battle was to be decided at the other end of the front, where Bomilcar ordered his forces to make a tactical retreat after a fierce skirmish. However, the rear of the corps, seeing the front lines retreating, panicked, and thinking that the line had been badly broken, fled. The confusion and fear caused by the partial retreat of the forward sections became generalised, and under pressure from the Greeks, the left flank of the Carthaginian army fled altogether.

The Sacred Band and the other troops of the right wing of the Carthaginian deployment were at that time still holding their positions, but the general retreat of the left wing caused them to be overwhelmed and created an immediate danger of complete encirclement by the entire Greek army. In the face of this danger, and having lost their commander, the forces of the Carthaginian right wing also fled in haste.[29]

The battle had ended victoriously for the Greeks, who sacked the Carthaginian camp, while the Carthaginian troops found safe refuge behind the triple walls of their city. The death toll was, in one version,

200 for the Greeks versus 1,000 for the Carthaginians, or in another version, 2,000 and 3,000, respectively.[30]

During the same period in Sicily, Hamilcar and his troops intensified the siege of Syracuse, but without securing any positive result. Consequently, the Carthaginian general tried to deceive the Syracusans by showing the stern of a ship from Agathocles' fleet, claiming that the latter and his army had been crushed in Africa, so resistance was now futile. The Syracusans were very anxious, but their fear turned to great joy and relief when a ship managed to break through the Carthaginian cordon and arrived in the city carrying the news of Agathocles' victory outside Carthage.

At the same time, Hamilcar received an order from the Carthaginian Senate to send some of his forces back to Carthage immediately, as the battle had been lost and the Greeks were in front of the city and threatening it. The Carthaginian general then sent 5,000 soldiers, while his compatriots also appealed to the god Melqart for help, sending rich gifts to his great temple in the metropolis Tyre.[31] Besides, the Carthaginians, fearing that the gods had punished them with defeat because they had not been pious enough, also undertook, according to Diodorus, a massive human sacrifice, offering teenagers from the noble families as a sacrifice to the god Baal so that he would forgive and help them, plus 3,000 people who volunteered to be sacrificed.[32]

Modern historians treat information about human sacrifices in Carthage with scepticism, especially regarding children sacrifices. There may have been an exaggeration for propaganda purposes on the Greek side in the relevant historiographical references or just urban legends of the time erroneously taken seriously by some ancient historians. Furthermore, it is noteworthy that paramount ancient historians, such as Polybius, do not mention similar events regarding Carthage at all. On the other hand, however, human sacrifice was probably part of Phoenician religious practice, but only in very exceptional cases. I think we should accept the possibility of there having been a few human sacrifices, but it would be a huge surprise if those mentions of Diodorus about massive sacrifices of teenagers and 3,000 volunteers had anything to do with reality. They seem more like horror tales of the time, which Diodorus decided to include in his otherwise serious historical work to add drama for his readers.

In Syracuse, four-drachma coins commemorating the victory outside Carthage began to be minted, while the retreat of Bomilcar raised suspicions in Carthage, with many accusing him of planning a coup.[33] After the battle, Agathocles captured the strongholds around Carthage and imposed his control over the region, and subsequently, several cities accepted his rule, in some cases willingly, because they hated the Carthaginians and their hegemony over them.

The Carthaginians reacted by taking their troops out of the city again, reinforced by the forces that Hamilcar had sent from Sicily. The Carthaginian troops recaptured some towns, but Agathocles managed to mislead the enemies and attack them by surprise when they were not prepared for battle by moving his army at night. As a result, Greek weapons killed some 2,000 Carthaginians, while the Greeks captured several more thousands of them as prisoners. Even heavier than the first, this second defeat plunged the Carthaginians into frustration and consolidated the Greek occupation of Carthaginian territory. The situation had become complicated and deadlocked for the Carthaginians, especially since Agathocles had no intention of attempting to take the city by a direct attack on it.

In Sicily, Hamilcar and his forces had also managed to block Syracuse's supply to a large extent, creating considerable problems for them. Believing the time had come to conquer the city, the Carthaginian general planned a massive night attack. The aim was to capture the fortress of Euryalus and then advance with the troops to the sea, thus capturing the city.

According to sources, the forces that Hamilcar used for this operation exceeded 40,000 men, with a large part of them consisting of Sicilian Greeks. The Carthaginians thought that the Syracusans were not expecting the attack, but in the end, they themselves were the ones who were taken by surprise. The Syracusans realised the enemy's intent and stationed 3,400 soldiers at Euryalus and the surrounding area, who silently waited for the Carthaginians and their Greek allies in the dark.[34]

The operation was poorly organised, and a mob of would-be looters followed the besieging forces, aggravating their lack of organisation.[35] Consequently, when they reached the Euryalus fortress and met the sudden compact attack of the Syracusans, they lost their cohesion completely.

In the darkness and confusion, they considered the number of enemies much more remarkable than was actually the case.

The Syracusans struck them from the fortress, but they also carried out ambushes at various points on the roads outside the walls, trapping parts of the enemy forces, as well as from the roofs of houses. The Carthaginians and their Greek allies eventually retreated, after leaving behind at least 2,000 dead, some of whom were killed by the Carthaginian horsemen themselves, who, in their confusion and attempt to escape, trampled their fellow soldiers. Hamilcar did not manage to escape; instead, the Syracusans arrested him and carried him to the city. The Carthaginian general was subjected to torture and humiliation in front of the Syracusan citizens and was eventually beheaded.

The situation in Sicily after the defeat of the Carthaginians at Euryalus changed significantly, although the Carthaginian troops did not abandon the siege but continued to tighten and reinforce the blockade, creating major supply problems for Syracuse. The failure of the assault and the death of Hamilcar, however, prompted the Greeks who opposed Agathocles' authority to abandon the alliance with the Carthaginians, and a coalition of Greeks and Sicilians emerged. The Akragantines, watching the Carthaginian defeat and the relative vacuum of power in Syracuse with the absence of Agathocles in Africa, thought it was high time to bring down the tyranny and the Carthaginian threat alike.[36] Hence, they formed an alliance between Greek cities and the Sicel tribe under their leadership. Gela, Kamarina, Leontini, Erbessus, Enna, and Echetla joined the Sicels, who had become increasingly Hellenised, like other Sicilian and Italian tribes.[37] The goal now for the dissidents to the Syracusan regime was the simultaneous liberation of Sicily from both tyranny and the Carthaginian overlordship.

A few days after the failed Carthaginian attack on the fortress of Euryalus, Agathocles received news from the Syracusan messengers and, with them, the head of Hamilcar. The Carthaginians also learned what had happened, and their frustration and concern were further intensified when they saw Agathocles brandishing Hamilcar's head in front of the walls, showing it off to the soldiers and civilians watching.[38]

The Carthaginian leadership had begun to consider capitulation after all this, but an unexpected event intervened to divert the course of events again. During a symposium, Agathocles' son and deputy army chief Archagathus argued with the leader of a mercenary corps and murdered him. The dead warlord's men revolted, and the Greek troops were divided and plunged into disorder and confusion. During the next few days, intense quarrels and skirmishes occurred within the Greek camp, with cohesion and control almost wholly lost.[39]

The Carthaginians, masters in the art of negotiation and bribery, realised what was happening and approached the mercenaries and the disaffected of the Greek army. They offered to leave Agathocles, promising them better rewards, while the tension and conflicts in the Greek camp grew. Consequently, several were ready to defect by accepting the Carthaginians' proposal.

Faced with the visible danger of the disintegration of his army, Agathocles reactivated his inexhaustible resourcefulness and ability to manipulate the masses and the people psychologically. He appeared broken among the squabbling soldiers, and dramatically removed his royal robes, threw them to the ground, and declared that to restore peace and harmony among them, he was ready to sacrifice his life by committing suicide. He raised his sword, supposedly determined to end his life, and then some soldiers caught up and stopped him. Of course, one could assume that the soldiers' life-saving intervention was deliberate, as were the cries that began to rise to the sky from various parts of the camp, cheering Agathocles and celebrating the unity of the troops.

Like the previous ones, the performance of Agathocles achieved its purpose to perfection as emotion and new brotherhood spread throughout the Greek camp. Then, the demonic mind of Syracuse's tyrant conceived the best way to defuse and make ideal use of all that accumulated tension and psychological charge of the last few days: a sudden attack on the Carthaginian camp.

The Greek troops attacked with unprecedented enthusiasm and momentum. The Carthaginians, unsuspecting of what had transpired, were unprepared for the Greek army's general attack. Moreover, seeing troops approaching their camp, they thought they were mercenaries who had accepted the proposal and were coming to join them. So they allowed the Greeks to approach the camp undisturbed, and when they realised what was happening, it was too late. The Greeks attacked en masse, broke through the fortifications, and poured out in a roar into the camp's interior. Then, the Greeks looted the camp and killed many Carthaginians, while the rest of the Carthaginians fled back to their city, leaving behind many dead and much of their equipment.[40]

The End of the Campaign in Africa

A war of attrition characterised the next period. The Carthaginians did not attempt new offensive moves against Agathocles' army after the latest defeat. In his turn, he could not threaten the mighty walls of Carthage. The walls had three parallel rows, each taller than the previous one. The height of the innermost third wall was 13 metres, and turrets were built at close distances alternately into the first, second, or third wall. In this way, the attacker would receive a vast number of arrows and projectiles from all three wall lines simultaneously, and even if he managed to breach the first or second wall, he would still have a challenging task ahead of him to invade and occupy the city.

The Greeks obstructed Carthage's land communications and transport without, however, being able to cause substantial supply problems since the Carthaginian fleets sailed undisturbed throughout the Mediterranean. Agathocles' strategy was to create a sizeable anti-Carthaginian alliance in Africa, which would suffocate the city and force it to submit. The Carthaginians reacted in 308 BCE by launching a campaign against their former vassals, the Numidians, who, in the meantime, had allied themselves with the Greeks.

Agathocles left most of the army in Tunis under the command of Archagathus and set off with the rest of the forces in pursuit of the Carthaginian army.[41] However, one of the Numidian tribes agreed to pass with the Carthaginians, while already in their ranks were several oligarchic Sicilian Greeks who opposed the tyranny of Agathocles and had arrived in Africa to reinforce their Carthaginian allies. Consequently, when the two armies met on the battlefield, on one side, there were Greeks and

Numidians, a total of 8,000 infantry, 800 horsemen, and 50 chariots, and on the other, a similar-sized force of Carthaginians, Greeks, and Numidians, creating a confused and somewhat erratic picture.

The Carthaginian army camped on a hill, at the base of which a river flowed. The Greek forces moved towards the Carthaginian position, with Numidian archers and light foot soldiers harassing them. Agathocles sent his own archers and light infantry to meet them and marched with the rest of the army against the Carthaginian camp. The Carthaginian forces waited at the river crossing, where the first engagement occurred. Agathocles' forces prevailed, following the example and leadership of their leader, who fought in the front line, forcing the enemies to retreat and fortify behind the enclosure of their camp.

The Greeks attacked the Carthaginian camp and eventually managed to capture it, defeating the resistance of the Carthaginians and their Greek allies. However, simultaneously, the two armies' Numidian light infantry and archers stopped fighting each other and merged.[42] They then moved towards the almost unguarded Greek camp and began to loot it after overpowering the guards. Agathocles returned with some of his forces to the camp as quickly as possible, managing to salvage some of the equipment, as the Numidians withdrew as soon as they realised that the Greeks were approaching. However, most of the supplies were already gone, so Agathocles distributed the booty from the camp to the soldiers accordingly.

About 1,000 Greek allies of the Carthaginians were captured, among whom, 500 were Syracusans.[43] Nonetheless, they escaped from the camp during the night and fled to a nearby hill while Agathocles and his forces pursued them. The tyrant of Syracuse promised them that if they surrendered, he would spare their lives, but when they surrendered their weapons, he exterminated every last one of them. Agathocles' choice was cynical and cruel, but it is also evident from the ease with which the Greek captives had escaped from the camp that his initial attitude was particularly lenient towards them and that he had treated them as potential soldiers rather than prisoners. Forbearance and magnanimity towards the defeated enemy are as important a characteristic of great leaders as unrelenting cruelty when the benefactor turns out to be ungrateful.

After the Battle of Numidia, the war returned to its previous stalemate, with the Carthaginians unable to eliminate the Greek presence from their territories or regain control of some of them and the Greeks unable to threaten Carthage itself.

Agathocles tried to tip this balance to his advantage by approaching Ophellas, then ruler of part of Cyrenaica (but not the city of Cyrene, which was in the territory of Ptolemaic Egypt).[44] Ophellas had been an officer of Alexander the Great and subsequently served under Ptolemy, eventually being recognised as an independent ruler in the western region of Cyrenaica.[45] This development had been made possible by the fact that Carthage had bowed to the pressure of the mighty Ptolemaic Empire and had accepted the shifting of its borders to the west in relation to those previously established after the wars with Cyrene. The Carthaginians took care throughout time not to provoke tension in their relations with the Ptolemies so that the latter would not become involved in the Western Mediterranean but would remain focused on the East, on their conflicts with the other Hellenistic kingdoms, especially that of the Seleucids.

Agathocles proposed an alliance with Ophellas and the latter set as a condition that he should become the ruler of the Carthaginian territories after the victorious outcome of the war and the fall of Carthage. Agathocles would return to Sicily as its absolute ruler without the presence of the Carthaginians. The Syracusan tyrant accepted Ophellas' rather unabashed demands, as what immediately interested him was to mobilise the powerful forces that the Macedonian warlord possessed and meet his own near Carthage. Ophellas' forces comprised 10,000 infantry, 600 cavalry, and 100 chariots.[46] Several Athenian mercenaries and thousands of women and children joined them so that the Greeks would immediately colonise the lands they were to conquer.

In March 307 BCE, Ophellas and his troops arrived at the camp of Agathocles.[47] The two rulers had friendly talks for a few days, but suddenly, Agathocles accused Ophellas of plotting and preparing to betray him. Immediately afterwards, Agathocles' men murdered Ophellas, as Agathocles had taken care to surround himself with several of his men when he made the accusation. In this way, Agathocles secured control of the troops that Ophellas had brought into the area, which was probably the purpose of the proposed alliance from the beginning. At the same time, he sent the civilian population to Sicily. It is perhaps evident that Agathocles did so because his aim was not simply to get rid of Carthage by allowing another North African great power to emerge in its place, albeit a Greek one, but to strengthen his own influence and that of Syracuse as a whole, both in Sicily and in Africa. For his part, Ophellas should have realised that his ambitions far exceeded his capabilities and what he could secure from his involvement in the conflict between the two major powers of the Western Mediterranean.

Dramatic developments took place in Carthage during the very same period. Bomilcar, of whom many were suspicious, gathered army forces loyal to him and attempted to seize power by force.[48] After his movement began, there were bloody clashes inside Carthage, with the citizens turning massively against Bomilcar's *coup d'état* – the most significant attempt to establish a tyranny in the North African metropolis to date. The conflict turned out badly for the Carthaginian general, who lacked support from more comprehensive sections of society, and his forces ended up surrounded after suffering many casualties. The Carthaginians promised Bomilcar that they would spare his life if he surrendered at that moment and the civil bloodshed ceased. However, when the Carthaginian general agreed, and his men surrendered their weapons, the crowd of citizens brutally tortured and executed him in the main square of the city.[49]

Agathocles did not try to take advantage of the upheaval created in Carthage by Bomilcar's coup and civil strife, either because he was busy neutralising Ophellas and mobilising his troops or simply because he did not learn the news quickly enough. However, he turned against the second-strongest Carthaginian city in Africa, Utica.

He placed the city under siege, during which he even used a large siege tower, following the example of the Helepolis of Demetrius the Poliorcetes (Besieger), who at that time played a leading role in the political and military developments of the Hellenistic area.[50] The tower carried several archers and slingers, as well as catapults. Agathocles, having captured some 300 citizens of Utica, initially demanded the surrender of the city to free them. When the Uticans refused, he ordered his soldiers to tie up the captives against the walls of the siege tower. The purpose of this cynical and ruthless action by Agathocles was to use the prisoners as a human shield and to terrorise the population.[51]

However, the defenders of the city continued to fire en masse against the tower since they had no other choice, resulting in pinning the prisoners to its walls with arrows and spears. The repulsive sight may have affected the psyche of the besieged, but as the attack progressed, it became clear that the tower was not enough to penetrate the walls' defences. Consequently, Agathocles adopted another siege tactic, carrying out several attacks simultaneously on different parts of the wall. This option was successful as the wall collapsed at one point, and the Greeks finally rushed into the city. As in all such cases, massacre and looting ensued.

After the conquest of Utica, Agathocles and his troops moved again towards Carthage along the North African coast. Halfway between the two cities was a city that the Greeks called Hippo Diarrhytus (today's Bizerte). The Greek forces captured it, and consequently, all the territory previously held by Carthage had now passed under the control of Agathocles, and some of the nomadic tribes of the desert had allied themselves with him.

Everything seemed to evolve in the best way for Agathocles, who adopted the title of King of Sicily, following the example of the successors of Alexander the Great, who at that time divided the once unified empire into several kingdoms. However, while the situation in Africa was almost ideal, with Carthage alone and isolated and probably on the verge of capitulation, problems were to arise for Agathocles and a challenge to his dominant position in Sicily.

Akragas had rebelled against the suzerainty of the Syracusan king, forming an alliance that included Gela, Kamarina, Leontini, and other cities. Faced with this challenge, Agathocles returned to Sicily with a corps of 2,000 soldiers and put down the movement against him immediately before it grew stronger. He left Archagathus at the head of the army in Africa and set out for Sicily with a newly built fleet of seventeen ships consisting of quinqueremes and smaller transports.[52]

Meanwhile, a significant battle took place in Sicily between the Syracusan and Akragantine troops, with the Syracusan generals Leptines and Demophilus prevailing and the Akragantines leaving 1,500 dead on the battlefield.[53] The army of Akragas found itself in dire straits and entrenched in the city. However, the oligarchs' leader, Dinocrates, gathered many dissident Sicilian Greek oligarchs and assembled a strong army of about 20,000 infantry and 2,500 horsemen, among whom 8,200 infantry and 1,200 horsemen were Syracusans.[54]

At the same time, Agathocles landed in the western part of Sicily and took control of Selinus, Heraclea Minoa, Thermae, and Kephaloídion (today's Cefalù) in order. He then marched towards Syracuse and approached the Hellenised Sicel city of Centoripa in eastern Sicily to conquer it. Yet, the army that Dinocrates had assembled was approaching the area, and Agathocles, hesitating to confront him at that moment, as he was vastly outnumbered, retreated to Syracuse. However, the disparate army of the oligarchs, lacking the strong cohesion of a professional or national army, disintegrated very quickly. Those who remained war-ready were only the 10,000 or so infantry and 1,000 cavalry of Akragas, who returned to their city.

During the same period in Africa, some Greek troops under the command of Eumachus conducted a campaign in Numidia and other inland territories, where he captured several cities but also suffered a defeat. Meanwhile, the Carthaginians were preparing their counterattack. They planned to send 30,000 soldiers out of the city, divided into three brigades, to attempt to recapture different territories.[55] Perhaps this tactical choice was precisely to split the Greek forces to make them more vulnerable, given that they were fighting in territory foreign to them and the alliances they had formed were highly precarious. Many allies and vassals of Carthage, who had accepted Greek sovereignty, were quick to switch to the Carthaginian side again and reinforce the Carthaginian troops when they saw their mobilisation.

Archagathus chose to divide his army, too, seeing the triple attack of the Carthaginians, just as they had hoped. The results of this choice were disastrous. Eumachus and his troops were utterly annihilated in a battle where the Carthaginians misled them by pretending to retreat. The Greeks made the mistake of disorderly pursuing the enemies by falling into the trap, only to find that they remained solid and were waiting for the disintegration of the Greek lines. At the end of the battle, nearly 9,000 Greeks were dead.[56]

In a parallel second battle, fought closer to the coast, the Greek troops suffered another heavy defeat, losing over 4,000 men. Archagathus, with the rest of the army and the survivors of the two crushing defeats, sent a desperate appeal for help to his father in Syracuse from Tunis.[57] Most of the territory previously occupied by the Greeks in the region around Carthage was again in the hands of the Carthaginians.

Reflecting on this development, one can see that the achievement of a remarkable feat of international historical importance – such as the conquest of Carthage and the establishment of a western Greek empire similar to the Hellenistic empires of the East – requires not only the existence of a brilliant leader and a mighty army but also a group of competent officials. No matter how great a leader may be politically and strategically, he can ensure predominance in every theatre of an enlarged geopolitical region only with competent collaborators at his disposal. Two decades before Agathocles' campaign in Africa, Alexander the Great was fortunate to have generals like Parmenion and Ptolemy, as well as Antipater back in mainland Greece, who successfully carried out the missions assigned to them. They won battles and captured cities on occasions where Alexander himself could not be present, as he was at the war's most central and critical point. Things were different in Agathocles' case, though he would have no right to blame just luck for this, as the circumstances and nature of his power had nothing to do with those of a leader like Alexander. A few decades later, the Roman playwright Titus Maccius Plautus mocked Agathocles for his desperation to be like Alexander;[58] but in reality, Agathocles, like other tyrants, paid the price not for his ambition but for the fact that in order to consolidate his power, he had to persecute and exterminate people and social groups who possessed high qualities of education, experience, and political and strategic knowledge.

Upon hearing the dramatic news, Agathocles decided to return to Africa as soon as possible to rescue what he could. Before leaving, he made sure to free Syracuse from the thirty remaining Carthaginian ships that were still blocking the city's supply, thus facilitating his departure. To this end, he had aid from his new allies, the Etruscans, with whom he had previously agreed on cooperation.[59] In the same year (306 BCE), on the opposite side, the Carthaginians had diplomatically approached Rome.

After an arrangement, an Etruscan fleet secretly arrived near Syracuse's port one night. In the morning, Agathocles ordered the fleet he had brought from Africa to go out to the sea. When the Carthaginians moved against him, the Etruscan ships appeared, resulting in the Carthaginian triremes between two hostile fleets. Four of their vessels were captured, and the rest sailed for Carthage to avoid encirclement and escape.

Immediately afterwards, Agathocles turned his attention to Akragas, wishing to close this front before returning to Africa. Apparently, he entrusted the campaign against Akragas to general Leptines to prevent any longer delay. Leptines plundered the surrounding countryside with his troops, and when, at last, the forces of Akragas left the city to confront him, he won a decisive victory against them.[60]

The Akragantine leader Xenodocus, who opposed Agathocles, was accused by his fellow citizens of having led them into a dead-end war with Syracuse and that he was responsible for their suffering, as is often the fact in such cases. Consequently, Xenodocus was forced to take refuge in Gela,[61] while Akragas accepted again the rule of the Syracuse regime, as did virtually all the other cities that had previously rebelled against it.

The king of Sicily also thoroughly purged Syracuse of his opponents, carrying out yet another of his scheming and ruthless actions. Following the victory, under the pretext of reconciliation he held a festive dinner, which turned into a bloodbath as his mercenaries massacred some 500 of the guests, whom his collaborators had previously listed as oligarchic dissidents.

After consolidating his rule in Sicily, relieving Syracuse of the presence of the Carthaginian fleet, and further consolidating his power in the city, Agathocles departed again for Africa in November 306 BCE. This time, the forces at his disposal in Africa were equal to about 22,000 infantry and 1,500 horsemen. Of the infantry, only 6,000 were now Greeks, while another 6,000 were composed of Etruscans, Samnites, and Celts, and another 10,000 of Libyans.[62]

The Carthaginian army that moved to confront Agathocles' forces to expel him permanently from Africa outnumbered them. Moreover, the

Carthaginians occupied a bumpy terrain, which was difficult to attack. Nevertheless, Agathocles had to attack, as his supplies were running out, and his troops suffered from a lack of supplies. However, the battle's outcome was negative for the king of Sicily. The Greek forces suffered heavy losses, with thousands of dead and prisoners. Moreover, about half of the Libyans subsequently defected to the Carthaginian camp, creating a dramatic situation for Agathocles and his remaining men. At the same time, the mood on the Carthaginian side was jubilant.

According to Diodorus, the Carthaginians celebrated their victory by thanking their gods with a massive human sacrifice, in which Greek prisoners were burned alive in a great bonfire after dark.[63] Yet, things did not turn out favourably for the Carthaginian troops. Apparently, they had not taken enough safety measures before the human sacrifice. As a result, the flames got out of control due to the strong wind, ending up causing a fire to break out that destroyed a significant part of the camp and led to the deaths of several Carthaginians.[64]

And while the Carthaginian camp was becoming increasingly agitated because of the fire, the Libyans, who had initially sided with Agathocles, decided to defect to the Carthaginians. When they saw approaching troops, the Carthaginians considered that they were under a surprise night attack, and the already great confusion among them became even more intense. Soon, the Carthaginian army surrendered completely to panic and lost all organisation, and many sections of the army fled in disorder from the burning camp. As if that were not enough, the disorderly and hasty movements in darkness and fear resulted in bloody skirmishes between Carthaginian corps, who on both sides thought Greeks opposed them.

Therefore, while the Greek camp plunged into despair and Agathocles and his men were in an absolute stalemate and trying to sleep, the Carthaginians had burned and destroyed their camp by themselves and were retreating in a disorderly panic towards Carthage, having left behind them more than 5,000 dead, killed by themselves.[65] But, according to Diodorus, the grotesque events of that night were to continue. Seeing the situation, the Libyans, who had unwittingly caused great confusion in the Carthaginian camp, quickly moved back towards the Greek camp. Now that a troop was approaching their camp, the Greeks perceived that they were under sudden attack by night, as the Carthaginians had previously thought. The roar of the Carthaginian retreat added to the impression that a mass mobilisation was taking place, which the now diminished Greek army could not cope with. Panic prevailed, and a hasty and disorganised retreat began in darkness and confusion, during which fellow combatants clashed with each other, thinking they were being attacked and pursued by enemies.[66]

When Agathocles' men realised what had happened and returned to the camp, the army's strength was reduced to such an extent that they could not make any claim to confront Carthage or even survive for long. Consequently, Agathocles decided to return to Sicily immediately. He even tried to leave secretly, accompanied by a few close associates and his son Heraclides, so that the Carthaginians would not notice the movement of several ships and pursue them. But Archagathus was outraged by his father's intention and revealed it to the soldiers, and they arrested Agathocles as a traitor.[67] The king of Sicily managed to escape, persuading the jailers to release him, and fled to Sicily, eventually leaving both his sons behind.

The troops who remained in Africa unleashed their anger on Archagathus and Heraclides, whom they killed.[68] They then negotiated with the Carthaginians the surrender of what cities and territories remained in their possession for a sum of money and, at the same time, were hired as mercenaries of Carthage. The Carthaginian troops easily defeated those corps that refused to abandon the positions they held, and their leaders were crucified and their soldiers enslaved.[69]

Back to Sicily

Agathocles, returning to Syracuse, prepared himself to face immediately with terrible cruelty a rebellion of Segesta, wanting to send the message that he remained strong and sovereign in Sicily despite his final defeat in Africa, but also to raise money for his empty coffers. The Elymian city at the western end of Sicily had been pro-Carthaginian for centuries, but after Agathocles' victory outside Carthage and the repulsion of the Carthaginian siege by the Syracusans in 310/309 BCE, it had gone over to the Syracusan side. However, after the dissolution of the Greek army in Africa, the pro-Carthaginian party of the city regained political control, and the Segestians also failed to meet Agathocles' demands for funding.

Agathocles arrived in Segesta with a somewhat powerful army from Syracuse, declaring that he ought to punish its inhabitants for their dishonesty. He then captured the city and caused a general massacre of its population, also using horrific tortures as well as seizing all of its wealth. The only survivors were the young men of the city, who were sold as slaves. After this horrendous carnage, Agathocles renamed the desolate Segesta Dikaiopolis, i.e. City of Justice or City of the Just, indicating that he had now purified it for their dishonour and betrayal. Later, he settled in the city exiles, convicts, and various other deserters.[70]

By destroying and plundering Segesta and slaughtering its inhabitants, Agathocles confirmed his dominance in Sicily by spreading terror to would-be opponents and, above all, improved his economic state. Very soon, however, he received news of the killing of his two sons in Africa.[71] Mad with pain and rage, Agathocles made yet another terrible decision. He sent a message to his brother Antander, who had governed Syracuse all these years, to exterminate immediately all family members who were related to soldiers who had participated in the African campaign.[72] There was no distinction between men, women, children, and the elderly, with the result that many thousands of Syracuse residents were massacred. Soldiers piled up the corpses in the large harbour, and the sea was stained red with blood.

After all this unspeakable horror, Agathocles settled in Ortygia in a melancholy partial isolation. Perhaps disgusted and repentant himself of the hatred and blood that for so many years had defined the political life of the Greeks of Sicily, he, after a time, extended a hand of reconciliation to the leader of the oligarchs, Dinocrates. However, the latter refused, as he was assembling a powerful army again, making it a condition of peace that Agathocles should leave Syracuse. Agathocles reacted by concluding a peace treaty with the Carthaginians. As on other occasions in the past, the long and bloody conflicts between Syracuse and Carthage effectively resulted in a return to the status quo ante. Under the treaty, the Carthaginians were regaining control of the Sicilian territories they had held before the war. For their part, they paid 300 talents and vast quantities of wheat to Syracuse.[73]

After the agreement with the Carthaginians, Agathocles moved against Dinocrates, whom he met at Gorgio on the western side of Sicily, probably relatively close to Panormus. Agathocles' forces totalled only 5,800 men, while Dinocrates' totalled 28,000. Nevertheless, the battle, which took place in 305 BCE, turned out to be a triumph for the king of Sicily as his enemies fled.

Later, however, Agathocles not only did not eliminate Dinocrates but also appointed him general, which makes it reasonable to think that there had been an agreement between the two men and that the oligarchic leader deliberately led his far superior army to defeat. Perhaps Dinocrates' refusal of Agathocles' earlier proposal was a pretext to drive the dissidents into a battle with a predetermined outcome and thus crush their party, but also to get Dinocrates to side with the tyrant without any opposition. What is certain is that after the battle, Dinocrates carried out with great zeal his new duties as general of Syracuse, taking the cities where those who continued to oppose the authority of Agathocles had taken refuge and exterminated them. Among them was a former general of Agathocles and then associate of Dinocrates himself, Pasiphilus. It is also certain that the king and the general remained good friends and associates for all the following years and that the oligarchs never again challenged Agathocles' authority until his death.[74]

In the following years, Agathocles followed a strategy similar to that of Dionysius I after his own great war with Carthage. He tried to spread his influence to the north and east, that is, Italy, the Adriatic, and the Ionian, hoping this would strengthen his position and give him the power to prevail over Carthage.

He campaigned against the Bruttian tribe and the city of Croton in Italy, imposing his suzerainty on the region. Agathocles also intervened when the king of Macedonia, Cassander, tried to conquer Corfu, destroying his fleet and establishing the Syracusan control over this strategically important island in the Ionian Sea. Finally, he had contacts with Demetrius Poliorcetes and negotiated to establish some alliance with him.[75]

The king of Sicily also planned to build a powerful fleet that would allow Syracuse to dominate the sea against Carthage, believing that the root cause of his failure to subdue it was that the Carthaginians had always maintained naval supremacy. Yet Agathocles was never again to face the age-old enemy of the Greeks of the West and see his vision realised. In 289 BCE, he breathed his last at the age of 72. Agathocles died, probably poisoned by his grandson Archagathus, son of Archagathus killed in Africa, because Agathocles had appointed his youngest son, also named Agathocles, as heir to the throne. Before he died, he managed to secure the escape of his children, wife, and personal treasury to Egypt.[76]

After the death of Agathocles, the new rulers confiscated his property and demolished the statues representing him. Clearly, the successive political situation in Syracuse did not honour him as a popular king but condemned him as an evil tyrant. Nevertheless, as would be shown in a short historical time, the Greeks of Sicily and Italy could have maintained or improved their position on the international stage only if they had continued on the path Agathocles had blazed, consolidating and strengthening the imperfect unitary state he had tried to create.

Chapter 8

The Campaign of Pyrrhus

Agathocles' attempt had the same fate as that of Dionysius, as, after his death, Syracuse returned to a state of internal turmoil and conflicts, substantially abandoning their role as the leading power of the Western Greeks. At the same time, their general influence in the international arena was weakened. During the same period, in addition to the ever-powerful Carthage, Rome had now emerged as a significant power in the Western Mediterranean, having prevailed in the previous years over the other Latins and the Samnites and put the Gallic threat from the north under control. The Italian Greeks remained, to some extent, united in a confederation with Taras as the leading city. Nevertheless, they continued to face problems from rival Italian tribes, especially the Bruttians and Lucanians, who were raiding and pillaging Greek territories.

The Italian Greeks were extremely wealthy but were weak militarily, as they had adopted a more hedonistic lifestyle and tended to use mercenaries for their defence. Also, the death of Agathocles and the internal power struggles in Syracuse that followed had again eliminated any prospect of unity between the Greeks of Sicily and Italy under the leadership of Syracuse. Without the cover of the Syracusans and the Sicilians, Taras and the Greek Confederation of Italy saw their problems and dangers increase.

In this situation, the city of Thurii, feeling threatened and with Taras not ensuring its protection, turned to the rising power of Rome and, in 282 BCE, asked for its help. The Romans, having established their dominion in central and, to some extent, northern Italy, now saw an opportunity to spread their influence further into the south, where they had already established two colonies. They, therefore, sent to the Thurians a military unit, as well as ten warships, to reinforce them. The Tarantines considered these actions hostile, violating the agreement Taras and Rome had signed twenty years earlier, according to which Roman warships could not sail in the area, and responded with a direct attack on Thurii. The Tarantine fleet sank four Roman ships and captured another, and Tarantine troops struck the Roman garrison, forcing it to withdraw from Thurii and retreat.

As if this rather excessive reaction was not enough, the Tarantines, among whom, apart from wealth, also arrogance and conceit seemed to be in excess, rejected the Roman demand for compensation for the damage they had caused, even treating the Roman envoy with disdain and insult. The Roman Senate confined itself to responding by sending a corps to Samnium on the border of Taras's territory. Then, the terrified Tarantines, lacking a solid leadership in Syracuse, rushed to seek help from Pyrrhus and the kingdom of Epirus on the opposite coast of the Adriatic, following their fond habit of relying on mercenary armies and foreign leaders for their defence.[1]

Pyrrhus had considerable military and economic power at his disposal. He was destined to go down in history as one of the greatest military commanders on a tactical level. However, at that time, he was a relatively minor and peripheral actor in the Hellenistic world, which was still the central scene of international politics. Although the kingdom of Epirus was respectably powerful, it lagged behind the great powers that dominated the area that Alexander the Great had marked forever. Somewhat unable to make any severe claims in the Hellenistic strategic theatre and bordering Italy via the Adriatic Sea, Pyrrhus turned his attention westwards, believing that the Western Mediterranean could develop into a suitable area for the unfolding and realising of his ambitions.

Consequently, Pyrrhus accepted Taranto's invitation and landed in Italy in the spring of 280 BCE with 25,500 men and 20 war elephants.[2] His goal was not simply to defend Taras and reach a compromise with Rome but to establish his rule over Italy. His intention becomes more evident by his attitude towards the city, which had called upon him for assistance, for after he had settled in it, he imposed a strict government designed to strengthen its discipline and martial power and to restrain the excessive tenderness that had prevailed in its manners and customs.[3] For the time being, the Tarantine military force succeeded in increasing the strength of Pyrrhus' army by about 5,000 men. Still, the numerous reinforcements from Taras and other Italian peoples promised by the Tarantines were missing. Lucanians, Messapians, Bruttians, and other Italics, who had also begun to worry about the Roman tendency to spread southward, watched developments without wishing to side with either side yet. Consequently, Pyrrhus moved towards the Lucanians' territories to make the proposal of an alliance with him against the Romans more convincing.

The Romans reacted to the invasion of the Epirote army in Italy by forming an army of equal size led by the consul Publius Valerius Laevinus.[4] The Roman consul mobilised his legions to confront Pyrrhus quickly to prevent his troops from joining forces with those of the Lucanians. Eventually, the two armies clashed near Heraclea in the summer of 280 BCE.

The battle was fierce and deadly and ended with a victory for the Greek army, which, however, cost around 4,000 dead Greeks. On the other side, the Romans had around 7,000 dead.[5] Seeing the heavy losses suffered by his forces and the surprisingly excellent organisation and operation of the Roman legions, which proved far superior to the non-Greek armies the Greeks had been accustomed to facing up to that time, Pyrrhus proposed a peace treaty and alliance with Rome. He conditioned the coalition to include his Italian allies autonomously and not as subjects to Roman suzerainty, and indeed to include Taras. He promised to return the Roman captives without ransom.

The Romans understood that the proposal involved their entry into a confederation that would essentially place them under the hegemony that the king of Epirus was trying to build in Italy, and therefore refused.[6] Unlike the case of Alexander Molossus half a century earlier, when they had accepted something similar, they had now become strong enough to feel that they could be an independent great power. Moreover, on the Greek side, there was no unitary Alexandrian imperial leadership like then, but a multitude of empires, cities, and rulers in competition and wars with each other. On the contrary, several Italian tribes that had hitherto hesitated to side with Pyrrhus, seeing his predominance in Heraclea, eventually allied themselves with him. At the same time, the Romans also mobilised the potential of their Italic allies and subjects.

The following year, Pyrrhus briefly invaded Latium and then attempted to enter Samnium to wrest it from Roman rule. Then, the new consul, Publius Decius Mus, blocked his way with Roman troops near Asculum in northern Apulia, where the second major battle of the war took place.[7] This time, their Italic allies reinforced the two armies on either side. This way, the battle became huge as each army numbered over 70,000 men. The Epirote king again narrowly prevailed, inflicting on the Romans heavy casualties, some 6,000 dead, but again suffering heavy losses of his own, too, equal to at least 3,500 dead. Thus, according to Plutarch, Pyrrhus said the famous mocking phrase after the battle: 'If we win another battle with the Romans, we shall be utterly destroyed.'

The two marginal tactical victories did not give Pyrrhus and the Greeks a strategic advantage over the solid Roman force. Besides this, the king of Epirus soon found that the weakening of his troops was not the only problem he faced. The Tarantines, even though they had called on him to get them out of their predicament, were not prepared to support him beyond a certain limit and instead began to resent his requests for more significant funding of troops and campaign operations on their part. On the other hand, the Romans were also troubled after the two bloody battles with this powerful new enemy, and the Senate began considering the possibility of compromise.

At the same time, Pyrrhus received more and more appeals from the Greeks of Sicily for help against the Carthaginians, as the political instability and the division in Syracuse had upset the balance, allowing the Carthaginians to increase their presence and influence in Sicily again. Noting the growing and omnipresent demand of the Sicilian Greeks for Pyrrhus and realising the danger he posed to them, plus the fact that the Romans were discussing a compromise and alliance with him, the Carthaginians hastily sent a fleet to Rome, led by an admiral named Mago again. His mission was precisely to rule out the possibility of a Pyrrhus–Rome agreement and the coming of the Epirus king to Sicily.

Mago presented to the Senate a proposal for a Carthage–Rome alliance against the Greeks and Pyrrhus. The Senate initially rejected the Carthaginian proposal, and then Mago turned to Pyrrhus himself, possibly conveying some proposal of understanding or exploring whether he could negotiate a deal with Carthage. The core of such an agreement would be a commitment by Pyrrhus not to intervene in Sicily and, at the same time, some support from Carthage in his war against Rome.

Following this development and the ingenious diplomatic manoeuvre of Mago and the Carthaginians, the Romans, faced with the risk of a Pyrrhus–Carthage alliance against them even if the possibility of such an alliance was negligible, approached Mago and, as might be expected, finally accepted the Carthaginian proposal of a coalition against the common Greek enemy in the spring of 278 BCE. At the same time, contacts were made, resulting in the formation of an alliance between the Carthaginians and the Mamertines. The latter were mercenaries from Campania, assumed by Agathocles in previous years. After Agathocles' death and the resulting instability in Syracuse, the Mamertines had found an opportunity to seize power in Messene.[8]

With Messene on his side, the Carthaginian fleet and a Roman military corps attacked Rhegio on the opposite side of the strait. They also destroyed materials that Pyrrhus' forces had gathered to build ships in Locri. For his part, Pyrrhus, realising that threatening Rome was problematic and he probably didn't have enough forces for that at the time, decided to accept the Sicilian demands to escape the quagmire of the war in Italy and increase his power by seizing control of Sicily.

The Sicilian Campaign against the Carthaginians

The extent to which Pyrrhus had identified his ambitions with Italy and Sicily becomes manifest in the fact that he chose to intervene in Sicily, even though he had the opportunity to return to mainland Greece and seize the Macedonian throne, since at that time, 278 BCE, King Ptolemy Keraunos died and the Macedonian throne was left empty.[9] The Epirote king did so because by defeating the Carthaginians and conquering Sicily, he would have the opportunity to achieve the crucial strengthening of his forces to threaten Rome and Carthage, which may even have been his main target at that time.

Pyrrhus had campaigned as the defender of the Greeks of the West against the two major powers of the region. He claimed the creation of a robust Greek state in the West under his leadership, following the examples of Dionysius I and Agathocles. To strengthen his claims, he further declared that he was Agathocles' heir, as his ex-wife was indeed the daughter of the deceased tyrant of Syracuse.[10]

The Carthaginians had previously conquered the control of the entire island and the port of Syracuse after another reckless attack against the divided and warring Greeks, taking advantage of the fact that after the death of Agathocles in 289 BCE, political anarchy and instability prevailed in Syracuse. At that time, the largest Greek city in the West was in a civil war between two would-be tyrants. On one side was Theonon, who had been confined to Ortygia, and on the other was the Akragantine Sosistratus, who had occupied the main part of the city of Syracuse. In the face of the Carthaginian onslaught, the two tyrants, unable to meet it, were among those who constantly sent desperate petitions for help to Pyrrhus while he was in Italy.[11]

All that remained for the Carthaginians to complete their conquest of Greek Sicily was, therefore, as on other occasions, the capture of Syracuse, which they had placed under siege.[12] Pyrrhus landed at Taormina and marched rapidly towards Syracuse while other Greek troops joined him. That was enough to free the city from the Carthaginian pressure. Faced with the prospect of a clash with the approaching Greek army, the Carthaginians withdrew without fighting, although they had a considerable infantry force and 100 ships.

Pyrrhus entered the city as a liberator, and soon afterwards, the Syracusans and the rest of the Sicilian Greeks proclaimed him ruler. In the winter of 278/277 BCE that followed, celebrations were held, and the king of Epirus reorganised his army, reinforced it with more local Greek forces, and assumed supreme command of the Greek areas of Sicily. He also defeated the Mamertines and captured several of their fortresses but did not attempt to attack Messene.[13]

In the spring of 277 BCE, Pyrrhus began his campaign against the Carthaginians, departing from Syracuse and marching towards the western side of the island with 30,000 infantry, 2,500 equestrians, several siege engines and war elephants at his disposal, as well as a support fleet of 200 ships. Akragas willingly hosted him and offered him additional troops.

Then, the Epirus king invaded the territories of the Carthaginians and their allies and captured Heraclea Minoa, overpowering the Carthaginian garrison and Azona.[14]

After this development, Selinus, Alykes, Segesta, and other cities accepted Pyrrhus' suzerainty and joined his side. The first strong resistance against the advance of the Greek army on the part of the Carthaginians and their Sicilian allies occurred at Eryx. The city was well fortified, and it took hard fighting to break down its defences, but in the end, the Greek troops annihilated the Carthaginian garrison defending it.[15] Pyrrhus and his forces then approached Panormus. There, they did not meet any significant resistance, for the Carthaginians had decided to concentrate all their forces and efforts on the highly fortified Lilybaeum. Faced with the approaching danger, the Carthaginians both reinforced the city's defences as much as they could and, in violation of their agreement with Rome, offered Pyrrhus a large sum of money and several ships as a tribute, so that he would not attack Lilybaeum but return to Italy.

The Epirote king wavered as he thought the proposal allowed him to continue the war with Rome on a much more favourable basis and with Sicily effectively under his control. However, the Sicilian Greeks, who for their part were naturally averse to such a development, pointed out to him that it would be a mistake for him to leave behind him unscathed a powerful barbarian focus, which could always form the basis of another prominent Carthaginian intervention and foray into the rest of Sicily. The Sicilian exhortations paid off as Pyrrhus finally refused Carthage's proposal and decided to besiege and occupy Lilybaeum to achieve, after centuries of competition and wars, the elimination of the Carthaginian presence from Sicily and the final Greek dominance. The latter would pave the way for an attack on Carthage itself, which, if successful, would make the subjugation of Rome and Italy much more feasible.

However, these ambitious plans and dreams would soon prove to be unrealistic. During the siege of Lilybaeum, which began in late 277 BCE, the Greek forces encountered extreme difficulties.[16] The walls of the city were particularly strong and well designed, and the Carthaginians had taken care to enlarge the moat around the perimeter of the wall even further, as well as construct catapults that struck the besiegers from above, along with archers and other marksmen. Lilybaeum fortifications had underground galleries and trenches, and the defenders could launch surprise attacks on the enemies from behind.[17]

Furthermore, the position of the city and the strength of the Carthaginian navy ensured a continuous and uninterrupted flow of supplies to the besieged, which the Greek fleet could not interrupt. Pyrrhus used his siege engines to hit the walls and their defenders and undermine them so that they collapsed. However, the efforts of the Greeks were repulsed and failed to achieve their objectives because of the defenders' firepower and the design of the walls. The walls had several well-fortified turrets with battlements along them, and some more protruding from the line of the walls so that those who approached them were made even more vulnerable. Simultaneously, that structure made it more accessible for the defenders to fire at the siege engines.

After two months of siege, Pyrrhus and his army had not only failed to conquer Lilybaeum but also had made no progress whatsoever towards this goal, suffering losses of men and siege equipment instead. The Epirote king, who since the beginning was not, as has been mentioned, enthusiastic at the prospect of attacking Lilybaeum and, in any case, was probably not distinguished for his patience, became disillusioned and broke the siege of the great Sicilian Carthaginian city. Realising that to subdue Lilybaeum, he needed a much more powerful and battle-hardened fleet, he thought that if he had it at his disposal, it would be preferable anyway to attack Carthage itself directly, following the example of his former father-in-law Agathocles, and win the war against it outright. Moreover, being angry with the Sicilian Greeks, who he felt had led him to a wrong choice, he demanded that they surrender their fleets to him, build more ships, and generally cover the expenses of the African campaign.

The Sicilians refused to meet Pyrrhus' demands, as they wished to eliminate the Carthaginian presence from Sicily, but were not prepared to pay the price required for an all-out war against Carthage. The king of Epirus, therefore, hardened his attitude towards them, imposing the presence of his men in the most important administrative positions and confiscating money by force. Then, the Syracusans and the other Sicilian Greeks began to oppose him, considering that a dictatorship had been imposed on them by the leader they had summoned. They even approached the Carthaginians to ally with them against him and perhaps the Mamertines.

This impressive development is an excellent example of the fact that in international politics, each actor promotes what they recognise as their strategic interests, giving only relative and secondary importance to the observance of even what they had promoted and agreed upon and even less to ethnic, cultural, or economic ties. Between political entities and groups of people in general, yesterday's enemy can easily be tomorrow's friend, and vice versa, since relations' dynamics, criteria, and motives differ from those at the interpersonal level.

Of course, the fact that there is no point in blaming the Sicilians from a moral point of view for this attitude does not mean that it was strategically correct. On the contrary, as would soon be proved, with this move, they definitively downgraded the political importance of the Greek presence in Sicily, making it secondary. In the following decades, the large Mediterranean island would be the apple of discord between the Romans and the Carthaginians, with the Greeks as extras, and would eventually become a Roman province.

Pyrrhus reacted by executing Theonon and expelling Sosistratus from Syracuse, who had led the opposition against him and the rapprochement with the Carthaginians. Still, the opposition to him intensified instead of subsiding. At the same time, in Italy, the Romans intensified their pressure southwards, taking advantage of his two-year absence, and his allies there sought his help.[18]

Faced with the possibility of losing his few remaining Italian bases at Locri and Taras, while he would be forced to spend his time trying to control the Greeks of Sicily without even the possibility of attacking Carthage, Pyrrhus decided to return to mainland Italy in early 276 BCE.

Before he left Sicily, he probably won a battle of deployment against the Carthaginian troops there. Then he was certainly attacked by the Carthaginian fleet and suffered considerable damage as he crossed the strait between Messene and Rhegio.[19] Also, after landing in Italy, he attacked Rhegio, and his forces were engaged by a Mamertine force in the area, with the sole result that his army suffered further losses without gaining any advantage. The king of Epirus then regrouped his forces and gathered additional allied Italic troops to attempt a new campaign against Rome in the summer of 275 BCE.[20] The defeat by the Roman legions at Beneventum, as narrow and doubtful as his earlier victories, ended his ambitions for conquest in Italy and the West in general and forced him to return to mainland Greece, where three years later, he would meet his death during a war against Sparta.

As a military commander, Pyrrhus won the esteem and admiration of the most outstanding leaders who followed him in ancient history, including Hannibal and Scipio, who considered him inferior only to Alexander the Great. Yet his acumen and dynamism on the battlefield were not matched by a corresponding strategic and political wisdom. Ultimately, the trace left on history by the king of Epirus was more of a fascinating, adventurous warlord with opportunistic and mercenary characteristics than a statesman with the ability to conceive and implement long-term plans.

Chapter 9

The Rise of Rome

After Pyrrhus' final failure, the inevitable subjugation of Taras and all the Greek cities of Italy to Rome followed. By 272 BCE, Taras and the rest of the Italian Greeks were part of the Roman federation, which now occupied all of mainland Italy. That caused a rift between Rome and Carthage, as in the face of Taras's imminent submission to the Romans, the Carthaginians violated the 278 BCE treaty by sending a fleet to the port of the Greek city.

Rome was an ally for the Carthaginians, provided that its role was limited to opposing and containing the power of the Greek cities in Italy, which, after those of Sicily and the Western Greeks in general, were the great opponents of Carthaginian ambitions for dominance in the Western Mediterranean. On the contrary, the critical strengthening of Rome by annexing all the Italian Greek cities was a very negative development, which would have made Carthage's position more difficult, reducing its relative power in the international system. No longer would the Carthaginians be confronted with a galaxy of independent and autonomous Greek cities, often in competition and conflict with each other and sometimes in partial alliance with the Carthaginians themselves, but with a solid and robust power, which accumulated all the strength of the peoples and cities of the Italian peninsula.

The conditions were now set for the colossal conflict that was to follow. On the one hand, Rome was the ruler of mainland Italy but was also in alliance with the northern Greeks of Massalia, who had established good relations with Rome early on as they understood well the importance of getting along with as many Tyrrhenian actors as possible to prosper and flourish.[1] They had also long seen Rome as the centre of the anti-Carthaginian pole in the Western Mediterranean. On the other side was Carthage with its possessions in Africa and Europe.

Syracuse and the other Greek cities of Sicily were no longer comparable to the two great Western powers after the developments in Italy and their definitive failure to form a stable political entity. Rich but definitively disconnected, fragmented, and politically weakened, Greek Sicily was now geopolitically the bone of contention between Rome and Carthage and not even a potential international actor with claims of its own.

Pyrrhus' campaign's failure to decisively defeat either the Romans in Italy or the Carthaginians in Sicily would be crucial for the following evolution of the Greek presence in those regions, whose centrality for ancient Greek civilisation has often been underestimated, while in fact, it was equally important with that of mainland Greece. It is not a coincidence that the fall of mainland Greece to the Romans followed very quickly, from a historical point of view, that of the Italian and Sicilian Greeks, or what historians have rightly begun to call Western Greece.[2]

Before that, the submission of Taras and the Greeks of Italy to Rome was, in all probability, the fatal element for the fundamentals of Syracuse's power. Indeed, the turmoil and weakening caused to Syracuse and the other Sicilian Greeks after the end of Agathocles' regime are insufficient to justify and explain the evident shift of the balance of power between Syracuse and Carthage. Similar situations had appeared in earlier historical periods, too, without producing the critical weakening of the Sicilian Greeks against Carthage, as happened after Pyrrhus' departure. In tough times, such as the ones after the death of Dionysius the Elder and before the arrival of Timoleon, Syracuse and the Sicilian Greeks had always remained strong and maintained their status as Carthage's peer competitor.

Moreover, during Agathocles' African campaign, Carthage had barely managed to stay on foot just a few decades before, and Pyrrhus once more severely tested its domains and forces in Sicily. Nothing seems to explain the fact that only one decade later, when the First Punic War began in 264 BCE, Rome and Carthage would fight for the dominion over Sicily, with the Greeks almost in the role of extras. The former dominant power of Sicily, one of the two greatest powers of the Western Mediterranean for more than two centuries, Syracuse, had by then no independent claim and was downgraded from great power status. How did this happen? As already said, internal turmoil or the state of the Carthaginian force does not explain this dramatic and rapid overturn. There is another event whose importance has most likely been downplayed, just like the importance of the Italian Greeks for Hellenism in general. This event is the subordination of Taras and the Italian Greeks to Rome in 272 BCE and their entrance into the Roman Federation.

Greek Italy had always offered, it appears, a crucial strategic depth to Syracuse, which allowed it to maintain the balance of power against the Carthaginian Empire. Despite their rivalries and wars, the Greeks of Sicily and Italy were always an inner world, a common market in economic terms, and often a source of help for each other in case of threats coming from the outside of that inner world. The Sicilian and Italian Greeks had close commercial and cultural relations with the different peoples and tribes of the peninsula, sometimes even military alliances against other Greeks. Still, they always maintained a sense of community between them. We saw the decisive intervention of Syracuse against the Etruscans in the Battle of Cumae in 474 BCE and the several times the Italian Greeks sent troops to Sicily to support Syracuse during its wars with the Carthaginians.

After the capitulation of Taras in 272 BCE, the Italian Greeks integrated into the expanding Roman political, economic, and military system, ceasing the significant strategic depth they had objectively and consciously provided to Syracuse for centuries.

The Syracusans could not find other sources to cover this enormous vacuum. The result was a fast and critical weakening that brought a dramatic shift in the balance of power. Suddenly, the rival of Carthage in the Western Mediterranean was Rome and not Syracuse, which was reduced to the level of a secondary, local power.

The spark that would ignite the fire of conflict between the two great powers of the West provided the adventurous Mamertine regime of Messene. In 264 BCE, after a military defeat by the new tyrant of Syracuse, Hieron II, the Mamertines sought the help of Carthage. The Carthaginians rushed to assist the Mamertines, taking the opportunity to move against Syracuse again. However, when their forces entered Messene, they acted as if the city was now their vassal. Consequently, the Mamertines called on the now mighty Rome for help, this time against the Carthaginians.

For the Romans, the decision was complicated. The expansion of their dominance in mainland Italy was very recent, and their main concern was to stabilise it, while a conflict with the other great power in the region was risky. On the other hand, if Rome did not intervene, the complete domination of Carthage in Sicily was almost inevitable since the Syracusans probably no longer had the strength to oppose it. Such a development would mark a critical strengthening of Carthage and its influence in Mediterranean trade, limiting Rome's future possibilities and posing a direct threat to itself, as Sicily had always been directly linked to mainland Italy.

The Roman aristocracy remained very sceptical and divided as to what the answer should be, and consequently, the Senate referred the question to the popular assembly without taking any position. The citizens of Rome had no similar doubts but decided enthusiastically and unanimously in favour of intervention and war, seeing before them the considerable prospects of significant economic gains that would result from a victory in Sicily.[3]

Thus began the First Carthaginian War, which lasted twenty-three years and ended with the victory of Rome and the annexation to Roman territory of a large part of Sicily, but also Sardinia and Corsica. Carthage would then respond by annexing almost all of Spain and eventually invading Italy under the leadership of the famous general Hannibal Barca in 218 BCE. The Second Carthaginian War would begin with dramatic defeats for the Romans, but they would gradually tip the scales in their favour and eventually prevail by crushing Hannibal's army at Zama, in Africa, in 202 BCE under the leadership of Publius Cornelius Scipio, the so-called 'African'. At the war's end, Rome would emerge as the undisputed ruler of the Western Mediterranean, having also conquered the city of Syracuse, by then an ally of Carthage and Hannibal, in 212 BCE. That was Rome's decisive step towards the creation of the most famous empire in history.

The historical case of the Roman rise and dominance in a relatively short period in the Western Mediterranean, i.e. in a region of the world where for centuries two older great powers had been struggling for supremacy, is fascinating. From a geopolitical point of view, it is clear that the Carthaginians and the Western Greeks have mutually neutralised each other's potential and prospects to become the rulers of the Western Mediterranean. The fact that Carthage and Syracuse were nearby and in virtual direct contact contributed to locking them in a deadlocked, endless conflict that did not allow either of them to grow stronger to the extent that would put them in a position of strategic advantage over the other. Moreover, the rise of Roman power occurred in the shadow of Greco-Carthaginian rivalries and wars while Rome did not occupy the main stage of international politics and did not see other developed and organised societies with an extended sphere of influence turn against it until after it had already become the dominant power of much of mainland Italy.

However, equally or even more important for the historical development of the Western Mediterranean than the geopolitical dimension is that of the three protagonist ethnicities' internal institutional structure and political functioning. The analysis of the latter can even lead to conclusions not only of interpretative but also of theoretical and immediate practical political significance.

It is, therefore, clear that Syracuse and the other Greek cities of Sicily and Italy failed to achieve political stability and to establish institutions that would have restrained the divisive tendencies and internal antagonisms by channelling their energy and potential into choices that would have strengthened their position and role in the international arena. Permanent political instability and conflict were only temporarily overcome thanks to tyrannical regimes, which failed to evolve into long-term, sustainable, multi-dimensional institutional polities capable of maintaining social and political cohesion and leading to consolidation. On the contrary, Greek cities and their institutions have always remained at the mercy of conflicts between their various factions, and the consolidation achieved by some tyrannical leaders disintegrated and disappeared after the natural demise of these leaders.

The Carthaginian constitution was, on the contrary, very stable and functional through time. At the same time, there was no disintegration, but the various cities and possessions remained united under the leadership of Carthage. However, Carthaginian society and its empire in the Western Mediterranean did not develop institutional and cultural elements that would have allowed them to evolve into a more organic and dynamic whole. The heroic spirit and philosophical quest were fundamental moral and cultural components of the Greek world and were absent or had a minimal role in Carthaginian society. The latter was defined by its commercial and transactional function and mentality. It did not seek a heightened philosophical and scientific understanding of reality as the Greeks did, nor did it attempt to establish a deeper political identity and legal harmonisation within its territory as the Romans did.

The Carthaginian Empire was more like a 'company' whose unifying element was mainly the usefulness of mutual commercial and economic benefit, without ever developing stronger institutional and moral ties. A characteristic of this condition was that the tremendous economic and military potential of Carthage never led to the creation of a coherent, organised and stable military structure but always manifested itself in the ephemeral concentration of disconnected mercenary troops; the ideal of the active participation of all citizens in the military defence and promotion of the interests of the homeland was precisely absent from Carthaginian culture. Equally important is that while the Carthaginian possessions may not have been fragmented like those of the Greeks, neither did they form a fully coherent whole, as with Rome. The Carthaginians developed neither philosophical nor legal and political thought, but their activity and perception of things remained confined within the narrow limits of commercial reasoning.

Rome, for its part, increased its power far from the centres of international political development, drawing on the experiences of the older great powers and learning from them. The national temperament of the Romans was shaped by close contact with sophisticated Greek and Etruscan influence and by fierce conflicts with the hardy Italian and Gallic tribes. The Roman constitution was gradually shaped by the turbulent political evolution of Roman society and the observation of Greek political and legal concepts, resulting in a highly balanced system. Its structure contained checks and balances against the destructive tendency towards demagogy and mob rule that characterised democracies such as Athens and against the deadlocked stagnation and conservatism that characterised oligarchies such as Sparta and Carthage.

In Rome, combining an elected executive, popular assemblies with legislative power, and guidance from the aristocratic Senate preserved the city's cohesion. It did not allow internal divisions and contradictions to undermine its dynamics as a single political entity in the international arena, even though they were as severe and bloody as in the Greek cities. The Roman constitution was a superb blend of the best qualities of the previous aristocratic, oligarchic, and democratic Greek constitutions, a fact that was crucial to Rome's unprecedented historical success.

Finally, a decisive element of Rome's final victory in the ancient Mediterranean was the ability of the Romans to integrate the conquered peoples into the Roman political structure, unlike the classical Greek hegemonic powers and Carthage. From this fact, a crucial theoretical conclusion emerges, of fundamental importance also for contemporary attempts to create transnational and supranational political organisations: cultural penetration and economic interdependence are not sufficient for the constitution of powerful and enlarged political and social spaces but are of secondary importance to institutional robustness and harmonisation, which of course rather presuppose an unquestionable dominant central power.

The deepening and systematisation that the Romans carried out in the concept of law and justice proved to have a much more critical coherent function than culture and commerce, areas in which the Greeks and Carthaginians had already excelled. Neither cultural nor economic activity succeeded in uniting and pacifying the ancient Mediterranean, creating a single functional political entity. The focus on law and the effectiveness of political institutions succeeded.

Chapter 10

Hannibal and the Greeks

By the late third century BCE, a very strange and intriguing phenomenon unfolded in the Western Mediterranean: Greeks triumphed culturally, even as they receded politically and militarily from the regional stage. More precisely, the Greek culture solidified itself as the dominant culture and the standard of elegance and civilisation, while Western Greece politically failed to remain an independent great power and left the international and military stage to the Romans and the Carthaginians.

The Greek influence appeared in the fifth century BCE and in the fourth century BCE, Carthage itself brought Hellenisation to its domains, even in those places where a direct Greek influence was lacking. The transition from the Phoenician and Carthaginian to the Hellenised phase of Carthaginian culture is evident in the clothes, design, columns, and tombstones.[1] This development is even more remarkable considering that, at the same time, the Western Greeks – especially Syracuse – stood as the principal political and military adversaries of the Carthaginian Empire.

We can see an initial Greek influence on the coinage of the late fifth century in the Carthaginian part of Sicily. Apparently, Greek or Greek-influenced artisans expertly crafted and minted the coinage of Carthaginian towns in Sicily during the fifth and fourth centuries BCE. Between 430 and 405 BCE, Carthaginian coins were similar to those of Greek cities Akragas, Himera, and Selinus and the Elymian Segesta, which had been Hellenised in various ways. From the late fifth century BCE to the fourth and third centuries, Carthaginian coins began incorporating fresh Greek iconographic elements. I find it quite remarkable that the coins featured authentic Greek inscriptions rather than just imitating the Greek style. Panormos produced didrachms featuring a dog, the Segesta symbol, and a Syracusan nymph encircled by dolphins on the reverse side.

The inscriptions found were 'ΠΑΝΟΡΜΙΤΙΚΟΝ' or 'ΠΑΝΟΡΜΟΣ', i.e. Panormitan and Panormos in Greek, indicating that the Carthaginians of Panormos referred to their city by its Greek name in matters of commerce and currency.[2]

Archaeologists trace three phases of cultural evolution for the Phoenician settlements, and the evolution becomes particularly evident in Sardinia, where there are towns such as Sulcis, Nora, and Tharros, with much archaeological evidence. The first is the pre-Carthaginian Phoenician phase during the eighth and seventh centuries BCE, the second is the particularly Carthaginian phase during the sixth and fifth centuries BCE, and finally, there is the third phase with the rise of Greek cultural influence in the fourth century BCE and beyond.[3]

Sardinia is crucial in understanding the dynamics of cultural trends in the Mediterranean Sea in general, because there was not a Greek presence, at least organised and in relevant numbers, unlike in most of the other Mediterranean regions.[4] That means the cultural evolution archaeologists trace is an internal phenomenon of the Carthaginian society. Furthermore, it gives a glimpse of what was happening in Carthage, as the predominant influence on Sardinia was Carthage itself. Thus, the Greek transition registered in Sardinia came not from a direct Greek political influence but indirectly from Carthage. The Greek art and artisan style became fashionable in Carthage in the fourth century BCE, and Carthaginian artisans brought it to Sulcis, Nora, and Tharros in Sardinia and beyond.[5] Half of the ceramics found in the town of Nora had the Attic style. In Sulcis, the production of wall carvings adopted the Greek design entirely by the mid-fourth century BCE.[6] Tharros had been important for craft production since the seventh century BCE. The transformation of Tharros' ceramics production since the fourth century BCE is typical of the transition from Phoenician–Carthaginian lines to Greek style.[7]

Another essential fact is that Greek culture became dominant already by the mid-fourth century, that is, before Alexander the Great's conquest in the East and the rise of the Hellenistic era. The Hellenistic world created after Alexander in the East certainly enhanced Carthage's and, in general, the Western Mediterranean's cultural Hellenisation too, but it wasn't its cause, since Hellenisation was largely present before that.

Progressively, the autonomous characteristics of Punic art and design faded away as the impact of Hellenism was 'grandiose' in the entire Mediterranean. As Moscati notes, that's even more significant because it did not reach Sardinia directly but indirectly, through Carthage.[8] Thus, the power that had been the enemy of the Western Greeks for centuries became itself culturally Hellenised, to the point of exporting Greek features. It is imposing that something like that happened without any change in the essential balance of power in the Western Mediterranean and before Alexander's conquests.

It is hugely important that the decline of Punic culture and its replacement with Greek elements had nothing to do with a Greek conquest but came further from the centre of Punic culture itself.[9]

Moscati concludes that it was the cultural impact of Hellenism and the fading of cultural autonomy that really brought about the decline of Carthage as a civilisation. The fall to Rome and the destruction of Carthage was the political and military continuation and conclusion of the autonomous Phoenician Carthaginian culture's disintegration, which had long before occurred by assimilation into the Greek and Hellenistic one.[10] The Roman conquest did not erase Carthage as a culture but only as a state entity. The end of the Carthaginian culture had already happened before that.

To synthesise, Greek influences on Carthaginian culture appeared in the fifth century and became dominant in the fourth century BCE.[11] Then, the conquests of Alexander the Great further expanded Hellenisation everywhere, even in Asiatic regions it had not yet touched. Since the third century BCE, the Eastern Mediterranean was culturally united and homogenous[12] and Carthage's world was part of that cultural community. Between the late fourth century and the second centuries BCE, the most valued Carthaginian sanctuaries, the cult statues, and the votive dedications took the form of triumphant Hellenism.[13]

Moscati and the archaeological evidence underlines that the Roman victory in the Punic Wars in the late third century BCE and the rise of Rome as the dominant power in the West did not bring a new cultural transition. For example, there was no change after the Roman conquest of Sardinia in 238 BCE capable of cancelling the one that had occurred in the previous century with the cultural rise of Hellenism. The Roman conquest was politically epochal but culturally somewhat unimportant.[14]

Hellenised Rome Divorces from the Greeks

From its archaic era, Rome was in close contact with Magna Graecia – the Greek territories in Italy – and Roman society was familiar with the Greek language, not only among the upper classes. We saw the impact of the Italian Greeks in Rome's independence from the Etruscans and the efforts for a close alliance at the time of Alexander the Great and Alexander Molossus. Moreover, the cultural Greek influence was crucial in Roman history, since the dawn of the most precious cultural gift of the Romans to the world, which the Romans considered to be of Greek origin: the Roman law.[15] In fact, there is a vast historiographic and literary tradition both Greek and Latin that considers Rome as an indirect descendant, or in any case a relative of the Greek world, and we have seen a few parts of it in a previous chapter.

By the third century BCE, the Roman aristocracy and especially houses such as the Scipios wanted Rome to be part of the Italian Hellenism, which by then was not limited to the Greek cities of Italy but included in great part other Italian tribes, most of all the Etruscans and the Lucanians.[16] Giovanni Brizzi highlights that Rome not only embraced and consumed Greek literature but also assimilated norms, daily customs, and perhaps even the identity of a *polis hellenìs*, that is, Greek city-state. The Romans had finally pushed the Carthaginians back from Sicily and they were on the verge of pushing Gauls back from Italy. They felt and claimed they should be recognised as the leading power of a federation that would be the Western sentinel of Hellenism.[17] An Italian Hellenism led by Rome.

A new model was thus being born, adding another version to the various versions of Hellenism: apart from the Ionian, the Doric, or the Macedonian, now there was also a Syrian Hellenism, an Asian Hellenism, and many more, including, as we saw, even a Carthaginian Hellenism.[18] By then, over a century after Alexander the Great, Greek culture or cultural elements were transmitted, adopted, adapted, interpreted, reinterpreted, mixed, and conflated in the most diverse cultural and ethnic frames one could imagine, from the Iberian Peninsula to Bactria and India,[19] and now we know maybe even China.[20]

However, although Rome had been accepted at the feasts of Corinth by the late third century BCE, the Italian Greeks were not so favourable to that idea of Italian-Hellenism-led-by-Rome. First, they repeatedly rejected to connect with the top houses of the Roman nobility with marriages and to enter the Roman Senate along with the aristocracies of practically every other Italian tribe, such as the Latins, the Etruscans, the Campanians, the Sabines, the Aequi, the Volsci, and the Osci. The Greeks insisted on snubbing the Roman *Res publica*.

Nevertheless, the Romans knew how to be patient. Given their dominance over Italy and Sicily after the war with Pyrrhus and the First Punic War, they had every right to be confident that eventually the Western Greeks would integrate more warmly to the Roman political system. Instead, what eventually destroyed every prospect of a Hellenistic Rome and Italy as equal parts of the broader Hellenistic world was the choice of the Italian and Sicilian Greeks, along with the Macedonian king, Philip V, to ally themselves with Hannibal and Carthage during the Second Punic War. The Romans considered that choice treason, and their perception of the Greeks suffered a brutal transformation. This stance was unrelated to Greek culture, which the Romans, especially the elite but not exclusively, continued to cherish and adopt as their own culture and also export it for centuries – during the era of the Roman Empire, 'Hellenise' was synonymous with 'civilise'.[21] However, frustrated and disillusioned, the Romans of the late third century BCE saw their contemporaneous Greeks as just another rival nation, separating the Greek culture from the Greek states of their time.[22]

That also had consequences on the cultural level, however. The Romans of late third century and after promoted an idealised version of Athens and what we call the 'classical' era of the Greek civilisation, downplaying their contemporaneous 'Hellenistic' Greeks as a lesser, declined, not a pure version of Greek culture. The reason for that was not just resentment for the Italian Greeks but also the convenient need for anti-Macedonian and anti-Seleucid propaganda, as Macedonia and the Seleucid Empire were the next great powers Rome was about to clash with after the submission of Carthage.²³ On the contrary, Athens was an ally of Rome, and it had asked the Romans to intervene in mainland Greece against the Macedonians. Roman propaganda contributed enormously to the birth of the classicist ideal, which in great part continues to influence our way to think about antiquity and the ancient Greek culture. Only in later times, scholars have restored the Hellenistic era and its incredible achievements, particularly in natural sciences.²⁴

Back to the late third century BCE, the last straw for the Romans was Syracuse shifting its allegiance from pro-Roman to pro-Hannibal after the disastrous Roman defeat, or Hannibal's triumph, at the Battle of Cannae. The pro-Roman tyrant Hieron II died in 215 BCE, and his successor, Hieronymus, followed him just one year later. Then two Syracusan Carthaginians, Hippokrates and Epikydes, born and raised in Carthage but of Syracusan descent, managed to be elected as generals. They also convinced the people of Syracuse to drop the alliance with Rome. The Roman response would be tremendous and Syracuse as an independent state would cease to exist in 212 BCE, despite Archimedes' technological miracles used by the Syracusan defence forces against the Roman assault.

After the Hannibalic War, Rome's attitude towards the Italian and Sicilian Greeks changed drastically. Now the Romans saw them as subjects, not anymore as allies.²⁵ But how did Hannibal gain support of the Greeks, Carthage's traditional rivals?

Carthage's Military Reform and Hannibal's Greek Culture

As already said, Carthage began Hellenising intensely from the early fourth century BCE. Then, after the Battle of the River Crimissus in 341 BCE, or even earlier, the Carthaginians also made military reforms following the Greek military science and models. Initially, they couldn't rise above the level of simple imitation.²⁶ Nevertheless, around the end of the first Punic War, under the immense Roman military pressure and the growing influence of the broader cultural Hellenisation, there was a remarkable metamorphosis on military affairs, and the progress of Carthage in the art of war was extraordinary. In the new circumstances, following the events in the East with the rise of Hellenistic empires and the West with the rise of Rome, the North African metropolis decided to take military preparation and thought more seriously, and abandoned the tradition of relying almost exclusively on mercenaries.

The most crucial and enthusiastic supporters and promoters of both cultural Hellenisation and military reform were the Barcids, Hannibal's family.[27] The Barcids had a mixed Greek and Carthaginian culture and political approach, as indicated, among other elements, by the coinage attributed to them in Iberia.[28]

The protagonist of the military transformation for Carthage was a Greek mercenary, Xanthippus of Sparta.[29] Xanthippus reorganised the Carthaginian army and led it to victory in the battle against the legions of Marcus Atilius Regulus.[30] He also was the mentor of Hamilcar Barca. Hamilcar Barca read all the Greek military treatises of that time over and again – first, the writings of his mentor Xanthippus, and many others such as those of Eumenes, Ptolemeus Soter, Callisthenes, Proxenus, and Pyrrhus' memoirs. When Hamilcar had to find a teacher for his son Hannibal in the Iberian Peninsula, he chose and hired another famous Spartan of that time, the historian Sosylus. Sosylus was always beside Hannibal from then on, from Hannibal's youth in Spain to his epic war against Rome. He was also his official historiographer.[31] Another Greek tutor of Hannibal was Silenus from Kalè Actè in Sicily, who also followed him in his campaign.[32]

It is understood that Sosylus' books were favourable to Hannibal and the Carthaginians, and they would have given us their official version of the events if we had the chance to read them. Sosylus was not the only Greek historian with a pro-Carthaginian approach to the Punic Wars. Philinus of Akragas also had a similar stance, favourable to the Carthaginian side and anti-Roman, but unfortunately, his writings are lost as well. All we know about those two historians comes from brief references in later works. Fortunately, Polybius was a great historian, and although he literally stood by the Romans, as he was Scipio Aemilianus' advisor, he offered us an objective account and valuable insights into the geopolitical context of the conflict at that time. We can only despair for not having the pro-Carthaginian historians' books at our disposal, and we could be tempted to take it upon ourselves to fill the gap. However, that is risky, and can more easily offer examples of lousy scholarship where modern ideological biases are masquerading as interpretations of the past[33] than help us approach and understand historical reality.

Hannibal was deeply versed in Greek culture and education, and militarily, he was a disciple of Greek tacticians.[34] He became a master of strategy and stratagems, using many of these later against the Romans, who tended to hate him particularly for that reason because of their still archaic ethics. They initially condemned his attitude of deceiving and trapping the enemy, which they called *Punica perfidia* (Punic perfidy). In fact, what they despised was a rather Greek than Punic trait of Hannibal.[35]

As Giovanni Brizzi puts it, Xanthippus introduced the Hellenistic military techniques in Carthage, Hamilcar worked on establishing them in the Carthaginian army and developing them, and Hannibal was the one who perfected them. Hannibal emerged as the most illustrious representative of the Hellenistic military tradition, creating new schemes and solutions, innovating and transforming military science, as only an authentic genius can do.[36]

We can say it was a similar scheme to the one composed by Epaminondas, Philip, and Alexander in the previous century.

Hannibal as a Politician

The Barcids had developed an attitude of autonomy in negotiating with foreign powers and stipulating treaties that could frustrate the Carthaginian Senate, as with the one agreed with the Romans in Spain in 226 BCE. The Carthaginians should not pass east of the river Ebro and the Romans west of the river.

Hannibal's known admiration for Alexander the Great and his Greek education were undoubtedly essential factors in forming his political ideas. Nevertheless, their political project was more than just imitating the Hellenistic model, even though scholars parallelise them with Hellenistic rulers.[37] The Barcids pursued a decentralised policy that protected the Carthaginian interests in Iberia but also cultivated a certain autonomy that created a sort of Barcid Spain.[38] Carthage's Senate was not so happy about that, and there was always some tension between the Barcids' faction and the traditional Carthaginian oligarchy.

Hannibal's policy towards the Greeks of Italy and Sicily targeted to counter the Roman ideological frame. If the Romans had the ambition to become the Western leader and sentinel of Hellenism, Hannibal and Carthage presented themselves as the defenders and guarantors of Greek freedom against Roman imposition. Hannibal had the same attitude towards the other peoples of Italy besides the Greeks, prompting them to revolt against Rome and join his struggle for a free Italy in a free Mediterranean Sea.

Of course, we can see these patterns throughout history and in our own time when great powers clash and try to promote contrasting views of the international order. What makes the Roman–Carthaginian conflict particularly interesting on that matter is that the two Western great powers contested over an area culturally and economically dominated for centuries by a third part, which had ended in political and military decline. One could see an analogy with the Cold War and the US and USSR contesting over Europe. Still, our ancient case is even more intriguing because then the third part, i.e. the Sicilian and Italian Greeks, was integrated into the broader Greek world, which, conversely, was at the peak of its expansion and power. The Hellenistic Eastern Mediterranean and its profound pivot to central and even east Asia, with the Seleucid and Ptolemaic empires, Macedonia, and several other kingdoms, confederations, and city-states, continued to be the central stage of international politics for the entirety of the third century BCE, despite what was happening in the West between Carthage and Rome.

Hannibal declared that he had to come to Italy to restore the freedom of the peninsula's people – a freedom that the Romans had taken away. He liberated all the Italian non-Roman prisoners without demanding a ransom after the Battle of the Trebia. He aimed to attract the Italian tribes to his side and encourage them to rebel against Rome.[39] After the Battle of Trasimene, Hannibal did it again. He liberated the Italians without demanding a ransom, declaring that he was not in Italy to fight against the Italians but to fight against the Romans to liberate the Italians.[40] Hannibal and his entourage knew before the war started that the power of Rome was based upon the great resources of the Italian peninsula and the Roman control over its peoples and tribes, who were part of the Roman federation.

Hannibal's diplomatic activity became more intense after the Battle of Cannae when he entered with his army into the territory of Greek Italy, Magna Graecia.[41] Maria Intrieri points out that Hannibal's moves indicate something that hadn't been highlighted enough: that he acted following a complete plan. That plan was to get the Western Greeks to flank Carthage against Rome, presenting the Romans as the common enemies of Greeks and Carthaginians. That was a major diplomatic shift, since Rome and Carthage had been allies for a very long historical period, recognising the Greeks as a common rival, and during the First Punic War, the Greeks were on the Roman side. Now Hannibal was trying to make them pass to the Carthaginian side for the first time. Those shifts are nothing surprising as alliances change continuously following the balance of power and the need to counter emerging hegemonic powers and the common threats and enemies of the moment.[42]

The victories against the Romans in the north did not make the Italian allies of the Romans look more favourably towards Hannibal and the Carthaginian invading army, but he did find an important ally in the Greek world – the Macedonian king, Philip V. However, that alliance was only partial. Philip aimed to control Illyria, and to ally with Hannibal was useful at that point, but his ambitions were far greater and included Italy. Paradoxically, he also considered Hannibal and Carthage potential enemies. The speech of the Aetolian general Agelaus at the conference of Nafpaktos in 217 BCE is telling, as he prompted the Greeks to make peace between them and prepare to face whoever would win the war between Rome and Carthage. He did not doubt that the winner would later turn against the Greeks. Agelaus proposed Philip follow the war in Italy closely and intervene at the right time after establishing a stable peace among the Greeks.[43]

Ultimately, the pact between Philip and Hannibal after Cannae would recognise the Macedonian control of the Illyrian and the Carthaginian control in Italy. From Hannibal's point of view, the pact was the perfect message to the Italian Greeks. It helped him present himself as the defender of Hellenism, since he was not trying to conquer Italy but to liberate it in alliance with the Macedonian king. Thanks to this alliance, Hannibal could present himself as something similar with Alexander Molossus and Pyrrhus, although he had not received a call to intervention from Taras or another Greek city of Italy and Sicily as they had. Nevertheless, his approach towards the Western Greeks was similar to theirs, and like them, he was connected and an ally of the greatest power of mainland Greece, the homeland of Alexander the Great. After that, we can better understand Taras's choice to ally itself with Hannibal, abandoning Rome's federation after almost sixty years. Hannibal stipulated a pact that claimed the Carthaginians would liberate the city without imposing tributes or other obligations. Polybius describes the young Tarantines celebrating and calling the Carthaginians their friends who had come to help them regain their freedom.[44]

The worship of Hercules played a pivotal role in the Barcids' political agenda. Hercules was Hannibal's divine reference, and coins represented Hannibal as Hercules-Melqart. In addition, the statues representing Hannibal were clearly Hellenistic style. This is evidence that the Barcids intended to follow a model similar to the Alexandrian–Hellenistic one, reducing the Carthaginian oligarchy's power and integrating the ethnicities they conquered to a greater extent than Carthage had previously done.[45] In the end, Rome would be the one that completed the plan, after Julius Caesar and Augustus.

In 204 BCE, Hannibal dedicated a tablet written in both Punic and Greek at the sanctuary of Hera Lacinia in Croton, which narrated his accomplishments as a military commander.[46] Polybius writes that he saw and read the tablet with his own eyes, using it as his source to describe in precise detail the composition of the Carthaginian army.

Hannibal and Antiochus III

Under the leadership of Scipio, the Romans changed the fortunes of the Second Punic War despite the heavy defeats previously suffered by Hannibal and his troops. When Scipio landed in Africa, with a similar aim to that of Agathocles over a century earlier, the Carthaginian Senate called Hannibal back from Italy. The Battle of Zama in 202 BCE decided the outcome of the war. It was Hannibal's first defeat, although he likely had dominated the field tactically.[47] Carthage had to come to terms with Rome. Hannibal remained in the Carthaginian government but a pro-Roman fraction had the supervision of Carthaginian politics. In 195 BCE, Hannibal had to leave Carthage and he found refuge in the court of King Antiochus III, the ruler of the Seleucid Empire.

Antiochus thought Hannibal would be the best asset he could have as he prepared for his war against Rome, and vice versa, Hannibal knew that only the Seleucid power could now stand on equal terms with Rome. However, the great Carthaginian leader did not go along with Antiochus III's court. He also did not like the role of the advisor, thinking of him as an equal ally with still ambitions of his own.[48] But the worst part was that, as Hannibal came to understand, Antiochus, although conscious about the Roman threat, greatly underestimated its gravity and was delusional about the power of his own army, which he considered invincible and superior to the Roman legions. Since the Persian Wars, the phalanx had an aura of invincibility – even more so after the epochal success of Philip and Alexander's Macedonian type of phalanx. Then, during the late third century BCE, the Greek military theorists and tacticians had disproportionately lengthened the spears and thickened the ranks, thinking that this way, the phalanx was even more potent and destructive, and impossible to beat.[49]

Hannibal tried to convince Antiochus that his conviction was groundless and that Rome and its legions were far more dangerous opponents than he thought. Yet, he didn't achieve much, as the king's advisors bolstered his views, agreeing with him and trying to improve their status in his court by winning his favour instead of having a critical approach that might actually help him and the empire. Not surprisingly, the relations between Hannibal and most of Antiochus' Greek advisors were not ideal. Hannibal had cordial relations only with a Rhodian exile, Polyxenidas. On the contrary, others, such as Filon and Eubulides from Chalcis, Mnasilochus from Acarnania, and Thoas from Aetolia, were arrogant, so full of themselves and their alleged cultural superiority.[50]

Hannibal persevered and talked a lot with Antiochus. He explained why the phalanx could meet severe challenges and dangers if it fought against the Roman legions. The phalanx was terrifying in a frontal attack on a flat battlefield, but it was cumbersome and inflexible. The legions' formation, which consisted of clusters capable of moving autonomously in various directions with flexibility, had the advantage on rough terrain. In any case, they could also make quick manoeuvres and hit the phalanx's flanks or back.

At the same time, by the late third and early second century BCE, the Hellenistic armies had remarkably transformed the function of the Macedonian phalanx compared to how it was during the times of Philip and Alexander. In Alexander's army, the phalanx had an essentially defensive role, acting as a moving wall that supported the cavalry's attacks and definitively crushed the enemy. The basic tactical scheme was like a hammer and anvil, with the cavalry being the hammer and the phalanx being the anvil. The enemy's assaults were destined to crumble on the phalanx, while Alexander's heavy cavalry gave mortal blows to their formation, and the phalanx moved forward, flattening the disorganised enemy army like a steamroller.[51] It seems that this quality of the phalanx was far too evocative, and the Greek military theorists and tacticians of a century later forgot about the crucial role of the cavalry, focusing on the phalanx and thinking that by making it even bigger and stronger, they would have resolved everything.[52]

Facts would prove Hannibal right during the Roman–Seleucid war (192–188 BCE), whose verdict was the establishment of Rome as the dominant power of that time. Before that, and beyond the tactical military aspect, Hannibal had also proposed a strategic political plan to Antiochus to confront Rome. Hannibal proposed the formation of a colossal coalition between the Seleucid Empire, Macedonia, Aetolia, and as many more Greek states as possible, plus Carthage, for a massive war against the rising superpower of Rome; he knew better than anyone else that it had become enormous and that the Hellenistic world should unite and create a compact front if they were to beat it.[53]

Antiochus was not so sure about Hannibal's plan, but he agreed to try. Hannibal sent to Carthage one of his loyal collaborators with the mission to contact his supporters in the city and prepare with them a revolt that would have seized power in Carthage when the time was right. The man Hannibal sent to Carthage on that mission was a perfect example of the cultural and political situation of the moment. He was a Phoenician from Tyre, with the Greek name Ariston, completely Hellenised and integrated into the Greek world, as was the Phoenician metropolis itself, some 140 years after Alexander's Macedonians had conquered it.

Indeed, Ariston met the faction leaders who supported the Barcids and Hannibal and had a series of conversations about the plan. Despite the highly hostile political climate, the faction was still numerous. However, the authorities, dominated by the pro-Roman regime, came to know about Ariston's presence and moves. They called him for an audience to explain why he visited the city, and after his not-so-satisfying explanations, they appointed a trial for the next day. At the same time, the pro-Roman factions immediately informed the Romans about the suspect and his hidden moves and contacts.

Ariston panicked, fearing that he would be arrested and condemned, so he left Carthage secretly in the middle of the night. Before he left, he dropped a note with a message from Hannibal to the Carthaginian citizens, which had been prepared just in case Ariston had to abort the mission. Hannibal prompted his compatriots to reject submission to Rome and join his patriotic plan for revolt against it and alliance with the Hellenistic world. He thought his plan was the only way to save Carthage and allow it to regain its dignity. Antiochus and the assimilation to the Greek culture should not preoccupy the Carthaginians since it was an inevitable and already ongoing process. Moreover, the Phoenician metropolis of Tyre was proof that Carthage and its specific cultural traits and traditions could also find a place inside the multidimensional and diverse Hellenic cultural universe, with autonomy, prosperity, and privileges.[54]

However, the plan to make Carthage revolt against Rome and join the Greeks failed. Ariston was a merchant and obviously not a cold-blooded, experienced secret agent to act in a clandestine fashion, and furthermore, the message he left couldn't reach many Carthaginian citizens. Probably, the authorities intercepted it and prevented its circulation. The Romans were quick to react, too, as they sent a delegation that comprised Publius Cornelius Scipio, Caius Cornelius Cethegus, and Marcus Minucius Rufus to Carthage to ensure everything was under control. For his part, Antiochus abandoned the idea of the great coalition, thinking he would beat the Romans by his own. He even invaded mainland Greece, while Philip V and Macedonia had opportunistically come close to Rome despite their wars a few years before.

Falling short of winning back his homeland and passing his grand strategy agenda through, Hannibal had to settle with the role of Antiochus' official and advisor. After the Seleucid defeat, he lived his last years as a fugitive, from Armenia to Crete and ending up in Bithynia, where he died in 183 BCE. His exact cause of death remains uncertain, but the most dramatic and widely recounted version is that he took his own life to evade Roman capture, as the consul Titus Quinctius Flamininus approached with a contingent, demanding the Bithynian king, Prusias, to hand Hannibal over.[55]

Fifteen years later, Macedonia surrendered to Rome after the Battle of Pydna, and finally, in 146 BCE Carthage was destroyed by the legions of Scipio Aemilianus, under the gaze of Polybius. That same year, the Romans also brought Corinth to the ground, after defeating the Achaean League at the Battle of Corinth. The era of Roman imperial dominion had officially begun.

According to Livy and Appian,[56] Scipio and Hannibal met for the second time in their lives, after their first meeting before the Battle of Zama. This happened in Ephesus, in 194 BC, when Hannibal was a guest of Antiochus, and Scipio visited the city as member of a Roman embassy to the Seleucid Empire. Scipio asked Hannibal who he thought was the greatest commander of all history. Hannibal responded that the best was Alexander the Great. Then Scipio asked him whom he would have as second, and Hannibal said Pyrrhus. Scipio went on, asking about the third best, and Hannibal appointed himself. Scipio smiled and asked Hannibal what he would then be if he hadn't lost to him at Zama. Hannibal said that had he won at Zama, he would be even better than Alexander.

This legendary dialogue between two iconic figures of ancient history would certainly be made in Greek, because not only was it the international language of the time, but most importantly, because Hannibal and Scipio represented two aristocratic houses known for adopting and promoting Hellenisation, and they had both received a high-level Greek education. Alexander and the rise of the Hellenistic era had certainly played a role in that, but for the great nations of the West, which were not parts of the Hellenistic world, that process had begun way back in time, and the basic promoters of it were the Greeks of Sicily, Italy, Gaul, Iberia, and Africa – the Western Greeks. The contribution of the Western Greeks, such as of those of the Asia Minor or the Black Sea, to what we call ancient Greek civilisation, was immense. However, it is often overlooked and underestimated. Not only is this unfair, but most importantly, it misrepresents the essence of Greek culture and its origins.

For example, think about this: Greek philosophy, that is, the most valuable product of ancient Greek civilisation, the systematic rational study and thought on the world, reality, and life, was born not in mainland Greece, but in the eastern and western columns of the Greek world, namely in Asia Minor and Italy. Athens emerged as the philosophical powerhouse and the term philosophy came to be identified with Athens and its schools, such as the Platonic Academy, Stoicism, Epicureanism, and more. Yet, the initial philosophical schools were those of the Ionians and Eleatics. This is not to downplay classical Athens – which is anyway impossible to do – but to propose a wider perspective on how we should study and interpret ancient Greek culture, and most of all, the sources of science, rationalism, high aesthetics, and art. We are going to see more on that in the concluding chapter of this book.

Epilogue

In his seminal book *Why the West Rules – For Now* (2010), Ian Morris argues that the Western core of the human population remained mainly at the eastern end of the Mediterranean from 11,000 BCE to about 1400 CE. During all those millennia, the Western core of humanity lay in the geographical area between the modern states of Iraq, Egypt and Greece, except for the era of the original Roman Empire, when the core also included Italy.[1] The Greek and Phoenician colonisation of the early and mid-first millennium BCE thus expanded the main Western core further westwards. Similarly, another landmark study, Jared Diamond's *Guns, Germs, and Steel* (1997), demonstrates that the same area was the cradle of agriculture and crucial innovations for the subsequent history of Mediterranean civilisations. More recent genetic research suggests that the Bronze Age Minoan, Aegean, and Mycenaean populations shared a predominantly common genetic heritage with Western Anatolia and an influence from the Caucasus region. The Mycenaeans additionally possessed a northern steppe genetic influence.[2]

We can therefore say that Greek and Phoenician colonisation was the last wave of migration towards the sparsely populated lands of the western basin of the Mediterranean Sea from the flourishing human cores of the Fertile Crescent and broader Anatolia and Caucasus regions' initial western expansion in the Eastern Mediterranean and Aegean coasts. The Greek and Phoenician colonisation is the most thoroughly documented and recognised because it happened in historical times, when numbers of human populations were big enough to establish consistent new towns and cities, and historiography was appearing. Before that, we had movements and the founding of towns covered by the fog of myths, or no mentions at all, as *Homo sapiens* moved towards the western capes of the Eurasian supercontinent.

The Greek and Phoenician colonisation expanded human cores towards mostly virgin or sparsely populated territories containing no advanced civilisations, similar to how the Chinese colonised East Asia.[3] This illustrates the difference between the Greek and Phoenician colonisation and the Arab and Mongol–Turkic conquests and European colonialism that followed. The distinction lay not in the moral standards of the archaic Greeks and Phoenicians but in concrete data on world population and civilisational development.

We know there were a few hundred thousand people in Italy. The fact that the Greeks founded so many cities, and that they needed to do so, confirms they were much more numerous than the populations of other regions. Moreover, the populations of the Greek cities far exceeded those of inland Sicily and, presumably, inland Italy, even during the time of the significant events we have talked about. Why didn't the Greeks expand inland? Why did they stay on the coasts instead?

We can answer that question if we consider the world population's total numbers, estimated from 50 million to 150–200 million people around the whole of planet Earth from the beginning to the end of the historical period we are discussing in this book.[4] The Greeks and humans in general were too few in number to be able to control all those landmasses, or to need them in the first place. The Greeks met their agricultural needs by limited penetration inland and added resources from fishing and commerce thanks to the extensive control of the seas. When their numbers grew, and they would have liked to expand further inland in Italy or Gaul, so too grew the numbers of people indigenous to those areas. Sited on the coasts, the Greeks were at a strategic disadvantage, as the population inland became a heavy burden that applied more pressure.

The centuries-long conflict between Greeks and Phoenicians/Carthaginians in the Western Mediterranean was crucial in not turning the Mediterranean entirely Greek or Phoenician. This rivalry consumed enormous potential, resources, armies, and fleets. The Western core of the human population did not expand westwards in the form of a single ethnicity, but two – Greek and Phoenician – and that was crucial for the formation of Western history as we know it. The two ethnicities blocked each other's imperial destiny and indirectly allowed indigenous tribes to grow and become more numerous and powerful over time.

Eventually, the city that united the potential of the Italian peninsula and the entire Mediterranean was, unsurprisingly, as close as possible to the Greek world without actually being Greek, and from early times, was also connected to the Carthaginian second pole of power in the Mediterranean. Rome further maintained and promoted Greek culture's centrality to the ancient Mediterranean world. It destroyed Carthage, but the enormity of the Roman historical success secured Hannibal's everlasting fame as the man who had made Rome tremble more than anyone else ever had.

Notes

Chapter 1: The Phoenician Colonisation and the Rise of Carthage
1. Justin, XVIII.
2. Moscati 1994.
3. Moscati 1994, pp. 56–61.
4. Ibid., pp. 62–3.
5. Ibid. p. 71.
6. Ibid. p. 135.
7. Braudel, p. 294.
8. Rainey, pp. 77–80.
9. Manfredi, p. 72; Rainey, p. 109; p. 143.
10. Moscati 1994, p. 141.
11. Thucydides, VI, 2, 6.
12. Bagnall, p. 13.
13. According to Aristotle, they were 104, *Politics*, 1272b, 30.
14. Aristotle, *Politics*, II, 1273a, 5–10.
15. Ibid., II, 1273b, 25.
16. Ibid., II, 1272b, 25–30.
17. Brizzi 2002, p. 58.
18. Bagnall, pp. 11–12.
19. Isocrates, 'To Nicocles', 24.
20. Brizzi 2002, p. 59; Bagnall, pp. 8–10.
21. Bagnall, p.9.

Chapter 2: The Greek Colonisation and the First Conflicts
1. Strabo V, 247–248; Manfredi, pp. 34–5.
2. Manfredi, pp. 25–6.
3. Dommelen 2012.
4. Morakis 2011.
5. Baslez, p. 83.
6. Shepherd 2009.
7. Dommelen 2012.
8. Boardman, John, 'Aspects of "Colonization"', 2001.

9. Snodgrass 1988.
10. Baslez, p. 78.
11. Manfredi, *Greci*, p. 54.
12. Manfredi, p. 186.
13. Justin, XLIII, 41.2; Kleiner 1973.
14. Diodorus, IV, 29.
15. Baslez, p. 180.
16. Herodotus, I, 162–167.
17. Diodorus, V, 1.
18. Ferrugia, pp. 51–5.
19. Manfredi 2015, p. 88.
20. Manfredi 2015, p. 88.
21. Strabo III, 2.13.
22. Livy, I, 34; Strabo, I, 22; Dionysius of Halicarnassus, *Roman Antiquities*, III, 46.5.
23. Tacitus, *Annals*, XI, 14.4; Dionysius, III, 46.2–5; Cicero, *De Republica II*, 19.34.
24. Diodorus, V, 93; Pausania, 10, 11, 3.
25. Justin, XV, III, 7.
26. Sallustius, LXIX, 1–2; Manfredi, pp. 193–4.
27. Herodotus, I, 166.
28. Casson, pp. 74–9.
29. Manfredi, pp. 130–4.
30. Polybius, 3, 22.7; Serrati 2006.
31. Braccesi-Raviola, 2008, pp. 55–64.
32. Thucydides, VI, 17.
33. Carter 1993.
34. Manfredi, p. 68; pp. 57–8.
35. Aristotle, *Politics*, IV, 1295b.
36. Ibid., pp. 79–82.
37. Homer, *Odyssey*, XV, 415–84.
38. Herodotus, IV, 196.

Chapter 3: The Rise of Syracuse and the Battle of Himera
1. Herodotus, VII, 154.3; Braccesi, p. 112.
2. Ibid., VII, 155.1.
3. Ibid., VII, 155.2.
4. Herodotus, VII, 156.1
5. Burns, Alfred 1974.
6. Herodotus, VII, 156.2.
7. Ibid., VII, 158–61.
8. Braccesi 2003, p. 129.

9. Polybius, III, 22.1–3.
10. Aristotle, *Politics*, 3, 1280a.
11. Herodotus, VII, 159.
12. Herodotus, VII, 165.
13. Kay 2016; Manning-Morris 2005; Scheidel-von Reden 2002; Finley 1973.
14. Herodotus, VII, 167.1.
15. Dionysius of Halicarnassus, *Roman Antiquities*, VII.
16. For convenience, I use the modern terms 'Sicilians' and 'Italians', although they should not be confused with modern identities. The ancient Greek terms would sound like '*Siciliotes*' and '*Italiotes*' and were strictly geographical, identifying the Greeks who lived in those regions.
17. Diodorus, XI, 51.
18. Pindar, *Pythian*, I, 140.
19. Herodotus, III, 136.
20. Ibid., VII, 170.
21. Diodorus, XI, 53.

Chapter 4: The Second Major Carthaginian Attack in Sicily
1. Aristotle, V, 1312b; Robinson 2000. ('Democracy in Syracuse, 466-412 B.C.')
2. Robinson 2000.
3. Diodorus, XII, 30.
4. Ibid., XII, 8.
5. Drokalos 2022.
6. Thucydides, III, 86.
7. Ibid., IV, 58.
8. Ibid., IV, 59–64.
9. Hanson, p. 229.
10. Diodorus, XIII, 43–44.
11. Xenophon, Hellenica, I, 1.37; Diodorus XIII, 54.5.
12. Hoyos, p. 57.
13. Diodorus, XIII, 54.
14. Ibid., XIII, 56.2.
15. Morris A.E.J., p. 53.
16. Diodorus, XIII, 56.5–8.
17. Ibid., XIII, 58.3.
18. Ibid., XIII, 59.
19. Ibid., XIII, 60.
20. Ibid., XIII, 60.6–7.
21. Ibid., XIII, 61.4–5.
22. Ibid., XIII, 62.4.

23. Ibid., XIII, 111.4.
24. Ibid., XIII, 62.6.
25. Ibid., XIII, 63.1.
26. Ibid., XIII, 63.4.
27. Ibid., XIII, 75.2.
28. Ibid., XIII, 75.5.
29. Ibid., XIII, 80.1–2.
30. Xenophon I, 5.15; Diodorus, XIII, 80.5.
31. Diodorus, XIII, 80.6.
32. Ibid., XIII, 84.3.
33. Ibid., XIII, 90.3.
34. Burns 1974.
35. Diodorus., XIII, 85.1.
36. Ibid., XIII, 85.3–4.
37. Ibid., XIII, 85.5.
38. Ibid., XIII, 86.1.
39. Ibid., XIII, 86.3.
40. Ibid., XIII, 86.4.
41. Ibid., XIII, 87.1.
42. Ibid., XIII, 87.2.
43. Ibid., XIII, 87.4–5.
44. Ibid., XIII, 88.
45. Ibid., XIII, 88.3–5.
46. Ibid., XIII, 88.5.
47. Ibid., XIII, 90.
48. Ibid., XIII, 90.4.
49. Ibid., XIII, 90.1–3.
50. Meritt 1940.
51. Hoyos, p. 60.
52. Diodorus, XIII, 91.2.
53. Ibid., XIII, 91.4.
54. Ibid., XIII, 92.3–7.
55. Ibid., XIII, 93–95.
56. Plutarch, 'Alexander', 8, 3.
57. Diodorus, XIII, 108.2.
58. Ibid., XIII, 109.1–2.
59. Ibid., XIII, 109.4.
60. Ibid., XIII, 110.7.
61. Ibid., XIII, 111.3.
62. Ibid., XIII, 112.

63. Ibid., XIII, 112.3–4.
64. Ibid., XIII, 113.3.
65. Ibid., XIII, 114.
66. Ibid., XIII, 114.2.

Chapter 5: Dionysius I of Syracuse against Carthage
1. Ibid., XIV, 1.7.
2. Ibid., XIV, 1.5.
3. Ibid., XIV, 8–9.
4. Ibid., XIV, 9.8.
5. Ibid., XIV, 14.1–2.
6. Ibid., XIV, 41.1–3.
7. Ibid., XIV, 42.5.
8. Ibid., XIV, 42.1.
9. Ibid., XIV, 45.
10. Ibid., XIV, 44.3.
11. Ibid., XIV, 45.5.
12. Ibid., XIV, 46.
13. Ibid., XIV, 47.2.
14. Ibid., XIV, 47.4–6.
15. Ibid., XIV, 48.2.
16. Plutarch, 'Dion'.
17. Diodorus., XIV, 48.1.
18. Ibid., XIV, 49.
19. Ibid., XIV, 50.1.
20. Polyaenus, *Stratagems* 5.2.6.
21. Diodorus, XIV, 50.4.
22. Ibid., XIV, 51.
23. Ibid., XIV, 53.1.
24. Ibid., XIV, 53.2.
25. Ibid., XIV, 53.4.
26. Protolongo 2014.
27. Diodorus., XIV, 54.2.
28. Ibid., XIV, 54.4-5.
29. Ibid., XIV, 54.2-3.
30. Ibid., XIV, 55.4-5.
31. Ibid., XIV, 58.3.
32. Ibid., XIV, 59.3.
33. Ibid., XIV, 60.6-7.
34. Ibid., XIV, 61.

35. Ibid., XIV, 63.1.
36. Ibid., XIV, 62.1.
37. Ibid., XIV, 64.2.
38. Ibid., XIV, 69.4.
39. Ibid., XIV, 70
40. Ibid., XIV, 71.
41. Ibid., XIV, 72.
42. Ibid., XIV, 72.
43. Ibid., XIV, 72.3.
44. Ibid., XIV, 72.
45. Ibid., XIV, 73.
46. Ibid., XIV, 74.2-3.
47. Ibid., XIV, 75.4.
48. Justin, 19, 3.1-11, Diodorus XIV, 76.3.
49. Diodorus, XIV, 75.6.
50. Ibid., XIV, 77.
51. Ibid., XIV, 78.
52. Ibid., XIV, 95.
53. Ibid., XIV, 90.3-4.
54. Ibid., XIV, 95.4.
55. Ibid., XIV, 96.
56. Ibid., XIV, 95.2-3.
57. Ibid., XIV, 13.1.
58. Dzino 2014.
59. Diodorus., XIV, 91.1.
60. Ibid., XIV, 100.2-4.
61. Ibid., XIV, 102.2-3.
62. Ibid., XIV, 100.3.
63. Ibid., XIV, 104.
64. Ibid., XIV, 100.5.
65. Dionysius of Halicarnassus 20, 7.3.
66. Diodorus., XIV, 100.6.
67. Sorg, 2020.
68. Livy, 24, 3, 8.
69. Diodorus., XIV, 114-116.
70. Ibid., XIV, 111.1-3.
71. Diogenes Laertius, III, 18.
72. Diodorus, XV, 7.
73. In Plato's seventh letter, whose authenticity is contested by some scholars, Plato or the unknown author writes that Dionysius erroneously thought he knew philosophy already too well, making him an inadequate learner (341b).

74. Ferrugia, p. 168.
75. Diodorus, XV, 14.2.
76. Ferrugia, p. 168.
77. Diodorus, XV, 14.3.
78. Strabo, V, 2.8.
79. Diodorus, XV, 7.3–4.
80. Diodorus, XV, 15.1–3.
81. Polyaenus, 6, 16.1; Diodorus, XV, 16.1–2.
82. Diodorus, XV, 16.
83. Ibid., XV, 17.5.
84. Strabo, VI, 1.4; VI, 1.10.
85. Xenophon, Hellenica, VII, 20.
86. Diodorus, V, 11.
87. Ibid., XV, 15.73.
88. Tusa 1982.
89. Jenkins 1977.
90. Ferrugia, 171–172.
91. Justin, 20, 5.11–13.
92. Hoyos, p. 89; Justin, 21, 4.1.
93. Diodorus, XV, 73.3.
94. Ibid., XV, 73.4–5.
95. Ibid., XV, 74.

Chapter 6: Liberator Timoleon and the Battle of the Crimissus
1. Ferrugia, pp. 179–80.
2. Lysias, 'Olympiacus', 33.3; Plutarch, 'Timoleon', I. 1–2.
3. Occhipinti 2016.
4. Diodorus, XVI, 65.
5. Ibid., XVI, 66.1.
6. Justin, 21.4.1–8ff.
7. Diodorus, XVI, 67.2.
8. Ibid., XVI, 68.3–4.
9. Pratolongo 2014.
10. Diodorus, XVI, 68.9–10.
11. Ibid., XVI, 70.1.
12. Ibid., XVI, 73.
13. Ibid.
14. Ibid., XVI, 73.3.
15. Ibid., XVI, 78–79.
16. Ibid., XVI, 79.3–5.
17. Ibid., XVI, 80.

18. Ibid., XVI, 80.4–5.
19. Ibid., XVI, 82.3.
20. Diodorus, XVI, 90.
21. Strabo, VI, 3.4.280.
22. Manfredi, p. 215.
23. Justin, XII, 2.12.
24. Ibid., XII, 2.; Livy, VIII, 3.17; 3.24.
25. Braccesi-Raviola, 2008, p. 165.
26. Drokalos 2020.

Chapter 7: Agathocles and the Greek Attack on Carthage
1. Diodorus, XIX, 4.6.
2. Justin XXII.1.
3. Ibid., XXII, 12.
4. Diodorus, XIX, 5.1.
5. Ibid., XIX, 5.3–4.
6. Justin, XXII, 2.5.
7. Ibid., XXII, 2.12.
8. Diodorus, XIX, 8.1–2.
9. Ibid., XIX, 71.
10. Ibid., XIX, 71.7.
11. Justin, XXII, 3.
12. Ibid., XIX, 102.6.
13. Ibid., XIX, 103.4.
14. Ibid., XIX, 103–104.
15. Justin, XXII, 4.
16. Diodorus, XX, 4.1.
17. Polybius, V, 3.4; Justin, XXII, 4.
18. Diodorus, XX, 5.5.
19. Frontinus, I, 12.9.
20. Diodorus, XX, 5.1.
21. Strabo, XVII, 3.16. 400 stadiums from Pantelleria.
22. Justin, XXII, 5.
23. Diodorus, XX, 7.
24. Ibid., XX, 4.1.
25. Ibid., XX, 8.1–9.
26. Ibid., XX, 10.5.
27. Ibid., XX, 11.1.
28. Ibid., XX, 12.1.
29. Ibid., XX, 12.7.

30. Justin, XXII, 6.6; Diodorus, XX. 13.1.
31. Diodorus, XX, 14.1
32. Ibid, XX, 14.
33. Ferrugia, p. 215.
34. Diodorus, XX, 29.4.
35. Ibid., XX, 29.6.
36. Ibid., XX, 31.1.
37. Paretti 1959.
38. Diodorus, XX. 33.1.
39. Justin, XXII, 8.
40. Diodorus, XX, 34.1–6.
41. Ibid., XX, 8.1.
42. Ibid., XX, 38.5.
43. Ibid., XX, 39.5.
44. Justin, XXII, 7.4.
45. Diodorus, XX., 40.1–2.
46. Ibid., XX, 41.
47. Polyaenus V, 3.4.
48. Diodorus, XX, 43.1.
49. Ibid., XX, 44.6.
50. Diodorus, XX., 93; XX, 48.1–3.
51. Marcus Vitruvius Pollio, *De Architectura*, X, 13.
52. Appian, *African Wars*, 122.
53. Diodorus, XX, 56.2.
54. Ibid., XX, 57.2.
55. Ibid., XX., 59.4.
56. Ibid., XX., 60.6–7.
57. Ibid., XX. 61.1.
58. Plautus, *Mostellaria*, 775–777.
59. Diodorus, XX, 61.5–6.
60. Ibid., XX, 62.2–5.
61. Ibid., XX. 62.5.
62. Diodorus, XX, 64.2–3.
63. Ibid., XX, 65.1.
64. Ibid., XX. 65.2.
65. Ibid., XX. 66.1–3.
66. Ibid., XX, 67. 1–4.
67. Ibid., XX, 68.4.
68. Ibid., XX, 69.3.
69. Ibid., XX, 69.5.

70. Diodorus, XX, 71.1–5.
71. Justin, XXII, 8.
72. Diodorus, XX, 72.1.
73. Ibid., XX, 79.5.
74. Polyaenus, V, 3.2.
75. Diodorus, XXI, 3; XXI, 4; XXI, 8, XXI, 15.
76. Justin, XXIII, 2.

Chapter 8: The Campaign of Pyrrhus
1. Plutarch, 'Pyrrhus', XIII, 2.
2. Ibid., XV, 1.
3. Ibid, XVI, 2.
4. Ibid., XVI, 3.
5. Ibid., XVII, 4.
6. Ibid., XVIII, 19.
7. Ibid., XXI, 5–10.
8. Polybius, III, 25.3–5.
9. Ibid., XXII, 2.
10. Plutarch., IX, 1.
11. Ibid., XXIII, 4.
12. Pausania, I, 12.5.
13. Plutarch, XXII, 4.
14. Diodorus, XXII, 10.2.
15. Plutarch, XXII, 4; Diodorus, XXII, 10.2–3.
16. Diodorus, XXII, 10.5–7.
17. Caruso 2003.
18. Plutarch, XXIII, 4–5.
19. Ibid., XXIII, 5.
20. Ibid., XXXIV, 2–3.

Chapter 9: The Rise of Rome
1. Manfredi, p. 186.
2. See *Conflict and Competition: Agon in Western Greece': Selected Essays from the 2019 Symposium on the Heritage of Western Greece*, 2020.
3. Drokalos 2015.

Chapter 10: Hannibal and the Greeks
1. Moscati 1993, pp. 21–2.
2. Morón 2017.
3. Moscati 1993, p. 20.

4. Ridgway 2006.
5. Moscati 1993, p. 25.
6. Ibid., p. 29.
7. Ibid., p. 27.
8. Ibid., p. 26.
9. Ibid., p. 156.
10. Ibid., p. 157.
11. Ibid., p. 32.
12. Carpentier-Lebrun, pp. 75–6.
13. Bernardini 2006.
14. Moscati 1993, p. 29; pp. 154–5.
15. Dalla, p. 30; Sommariva, pp. 125–6.
16. Brizzi 2010, p. 20.
17. Grimal, p. 87; Brizzi 2010, p. 21.
18. Brizzi 2010, p. 20.
19. Stoneman 2021.
20. *The Guardian*, 12 October 2016.
21. Veyne, p. 163; Rassias, p. 131.
22. Brizzi 2010, pp. 21–2; Grimal, pp. 90–1.
23. Canfora, p. 52; Grimal, p. 91.
24. Russo 2003. Moreover, the Hellenistic era's philosophical schools, Stoicism, Epicureanism, and Skepticism, became increasingly influential in recent times.
25. Serrati 2020.
26. Brizzi 2002, p. 58.
27. Ibid., p. 60
28. Fariselli 2006.
29. Ibid., p. 61.
30. Polybius, I, 32–35.
31. Brizzi 2002, p. 62.
32. Intrieri 2008.
33. Like in Miles 2011.
34. Grimal, p. 90.
35. Brizzi 2006.
36. Brizzi 2002, p. 69.
37. Ibid.
38. Fariselli 2006.
39. Polybius, III, 77.6–7.
40. Ibid., III, 85.4.
41. Intrieri 2008.
42. Waltz 1979; Walt 1987.

43. Polybius, 5, 104.7–8.
44. Polybius, VIII, 31.2.
45. Fariselli 2006.
46. Polybius, III, 33.17–18; III, 56.54.
47. Brizzi 2010.
48. Ibid., p. 255.
49. Ibid., p. 259.
50. Ibid., p. 258.
51. Drokalos 2020, pp. 74–8.
52. Brizzi 2010, p. 260.
53. Ibid., pp. 263–4.
54. Brizzi 2010, pp. 264–5.
55. Livy, 39.51; Cornelius Nepo, Hannibal, 12.5.
56. Livy, 35.14; Appian, Syrian Wars, 2.10.

Epilogue
1. Morris, I. 2010, p. 159.
2. Clemente et al., 2021; Lazaridis et al., 2017.
3. Morris, I. 2010.
4. McEvedy & Jones 1978; United States Census Bureau.

Bibliography

Aristotle. *Politics*, University of Chicago Press, 2013.
Astour, Michael C. 'Ancient Greek Civilization in Southern Italy', *Journal of Aesthetic Education*, vol. 19, no. 1, 1985, pp. 23–37.
Bagnall, Nigel. *The Punic Wars*. Pimlico, London, 1999 (1st ed., 1990).
Baslez, Marie-Françoise. *Political History of the Ancient Greek World*, Εκδόσεις Πατάκη, Athens, 2013 (1994). [Greek edition]
Bassanelli Sommariva, Gisella. *Lezioni di storia del diritto romano*, Edizioni Nautilus, Bologna, 2003.
Becking, Bob. 'Mercenaries or Merchants? On the Role of Phoenicians at Elephantine in the Achaemenid Period', *Die Welt Des Orients*, vol. 47, no. 2, 2017, pp. 186–97.
Benson, Frank Sherman. 'Ancient Greek Coins: V. Syracuse, Sicily', *American Journal of Numismatics (1897–1924)*, vol. 35, no. 4, 1901, pp. 93–102.
Berlin, Andrea M. 'From Monarchy to Markets: The Phoenicians in Hellenistic Palestine', *Bulletin of the American Schools of Oriental Research*, no. 306, 1997, pp. 75–88.
Bernardini, Paolo. 'La Sardegna tra Cartagine e Roma: Tradizioni Puniche e Ellenizzazione', *Pallas*, no. 70, 2006, pp. 71–104.
Boardman, John. 'Aspects of "Colonization"', *Bulletin of the American Schools of Oriental Research*, no. 322, 2001, pp. 33–42.
Braccesi, Lorenzo & Raviola, Flavio. 'La Magna Grecia', *Il Mulino*, Bologna, 2008.
Braccesi, Lorenzo. *I Greci delle Periferie. Dal Danubio all'Atlantico*, Editori Laterza, Bari, 2003.
Braudel, Fernand. *The Memories of the Mediterranean*, Εκδόσεις Λιβάνη, Athens, 2000. [Greek edition]
Brizzi, Giovanni. 'Carthage et Rome: Quelles Prises de Contact Avec l'Hellénisme?', *Pallas*, no. 70, 2006, pp. 231–43.
Brizzi, Giovanni. 'Il Guerriero, l'Oplita, il Legionario. Gli eserciti nel mondo classico', *Il Mulino*, Bologna, 2002.
Brizzi, Giovanni. *Scipione e Annibale. La guerra per salvare Roma*, Editori Laterza, Bari, 2010.
Brown, Shelby. 'Perspectives on Phoenician Art', *The Biblical Archaeologist*, vol. 55, no. 1, 1992, pp. 6–24.
Burns, Alfred. 'Ancient Greek Water Supply and City Planning: A Study of Syracuse and Acragas', *Technology and Culture*, vol. 15, no. 3, 1974, pp. 389–412.
Carpentier, Jean & Lebrun, François (directed by). *History of the Mediterranean*, Εκδόσεις Πατάκη, Athens, 2009 (1998).
Canfora, Luciano. *Il mondo di Atene*, Editori Laterza, Bari, 2011.
Caruso, Enrico. *Lilibeo-Marsala: le fortificazioni puniche e medievali*, Atti di Quartet Giornata Internazionale di Studi sull'area Elima, Pisa, 2003, pp. 173-226.
Casson, Lionel. *The Ancient Mariners* (2nd ed.), Princeton University Press, New Jersey, 1991.
Clemente, F., Unterlander, M., Dolgova, O. et al. 'The genomic history of the Aegean palatial civilizations', *Cell* 184, 2565–2586 (2021).

Collective. *The Cambridge History of Greek and Roman Warfare*, Cambridge University Press, 2007.
Collective. *The Cambridge History of Greek and Roman Political Thought*, Cambridge University Press, 2006.
Collective, *I Greci in Occidente*, Bompiani, Milan, 1996.
Chiat, Marilyn Joyce Segal. *Phoenician Cities*, Handbook of Synagogue Architecture, Brown Judaic Studies, 2020, pp. 13–18.
Choksy, Jamsheed K. 'Ancient Religions', *Iranian Studies*, vol. 31, no. 3/4, 1998, pp. 661–79.
Church, Alfred J. & Gilman, Arthur. *Carthage or The Empire of Africa*, Alpha Editions, Breinigsville, 2019 (1888).
Cline, Eric H. *1177 B.C.: The Year Civilization Collapsed*, Princeton University Press, New Jersey, 2014.
Dalla, Danilo. *Introduzione a un corso romanistico*, Giappichelli, Torino, 1997.
Dalla, Danilo & Lambertini, Renzo. *Istituzioni di Diritto Romano*, Giappichelli, Torino, 2001.
Diamond, Jared. *Guns, Germs, and Steel: The Fate of Human Societies*, W.W. Norton, New York, 1997.
Diodorus Siculus. *Library of History* (10 volumes), Loeb Classical Library, Harvard University Press, 1933.
Diogenes Laertius. *Lives of Eminent Philosophers*, Cambridge University Press, 2017.
Drokalos, Sotirios F. *Greeks against Carthaginians. The relentless conflict for dominance in the Western Mediterranean*, Gnomon Publishing, Athens, 2017. [Greek edition]
Drokalos, Sotirios F. 'The Greco-Carthaginian Wars', in *On the shores of the Mediterranean Sea: Greece and Tunisia*, Hellenic National Defense General Staff, Athens, 2023, pp. 91–104.
Drokalos, Sotirios F. *Alessandro Magno e pensiero strategico moderno*, Edizioni Saecula, Zermeghedo, 2020.
Drokalos, Sotirios F. *Imperialismo romano: scelta di élite o di popolo? Espansione romana e reoria delle relazioni internazionali*, Edizioni Saecula, Zermeghedo, 2015.
Eshel, Tzilla, et al. 'Lead Isotopes in Silver Reveal Earliest Phoenician Quest for Metals in the West Mediterranean', *Proceedings of the National Academy of Sciences of the United States of America*, vol. 116, no. 13, 2019, pp. 6007–12.
Evangeliou, Christos C. 'Plato and Sicilian Power Politics: Between Dion and Dionysius II', *Plato at Syracuse: Essays on Plato in Western Greece with a New Translation of the Seventh Letter by Jonah Radding*, edited by Heather L. Reid & Mark Ralkowski, vol. 5, Parnassos Press – Fonte Aretusa, 2019, pp. 187–200.
Faust, Avraham & Ehud Weiss. 'Judah, Philistia, and the Mediterranean World: Reconstructing the Economic System of the Seventh Century B.C.E.', *Bulletin of the American Schools of Oriental Research*, no. 338, 2005, pp. 71–92.
Fariselli, Anna Chiara. 'Il Progetto Politico Dei Barcidi', *Pallas*, no. 70, 2006, pp. 105–22.
Ferruggia, Aldo. *Le Guerre Senza Nome. L'epico scontro tra Greci e Cartaginesi*. Neos Edizioni, Rivoli (Torino), 2015.
Frangié-Joly, Dina. 'Perfumes, Aromatics, and Purple Dye: Phoenician Trade and Production in the Greco-Roman Period', *Journal of Eastern Mediterranean Archaeology & Heritage Studies*, vol. 4, no. 1, 2016, pp. 36–56.
Fraser, P.M. 'Greek-Phoenician Bilingual Inscriptions from Rhodes', *The Annual of the British School at Athens*, vol. 65, 1970, pp. 31–6.
Frediani, Andrea. *Le Grandi Battaglie dell'Antica Grecia*, Newton Compton Editori, Rome, 2011 (2005).
Frediani, Andrea. *Le Grandi Battaglie tra Greci e Romani*, Newton Compton Editori, Rome, 2012.

Finley, Moses. *L'economia degli antichi e dei moderni*, Editori Laterza, Bari, 2008.
Grethlein, Jonas. 'The Manifold Uses of the Epic Past: The Embassy Scene in Herodotus 7.153–63', *The American Journal of Philology*, vol. 127, no. 4, 2006, pp. 485–509.
Grimal, Pierre. *Il secolo degli Scipioni. Roma e l'ellenismo al tempo delle guerre puniche*, Paideia Editrice, Brescia, 1981 (1975).
Gschnitzer, Fritz. *Storia Sociale dell'Antica Grecia*, Il Mulino, Bologna, 1988 (1981).
Hencken, Hugh. 'Syracuse, Etruria and the North: Some Comparisons', *American Journal of Archaeology*, vol. 62, no. 3, 1958, pp. 259–72.
Hoyos, Dexter. *Carthage's other wars. Carthaginian warfare outside the 'Punic Wars' against Rome*, Pen & Sword, Yorkshire–Philadelphia, 2019.
Ierardi, Michael. 'The Tetradrachms of Agathocles of Syracuse: A Preliminary Study', *American Journal of Numismatics* (1989-), vol. 7/8, 1995, pp. 1–73.
Jenkins, G. Kenneth. 'Coins of Punic Sicily', *Swiss Numismatic Review*, 56, 1977, pp. 5–69.
Justin. *Epitome of Pompeius Trogus* (2 volumes), Loeb Classical Library, Harvard University Press, 2024.
Kay, Philip. *Rome's economic revolution*, Oxford University Press, 2016.
Kennedy, Maev, 'Ancient Greeks "may have inspired China's Terracotta Army"', *The Guardian*, 12 October 2016, https://www.theguardian.com/science/2016/oct/12/ancient-greeks-may-have-inspired-china-terracotta-army-sculptors-ancient-dna
Kleiner, Fred S. 'Gallia Graeca, Gallia Romana and the Introduction of Classical Sculpture in Gaul', *American Journal of Archaeology*, vol. 77, no. 4, 1973, pp. 379–90.
Lazaridis, I., Mittnik, A., Patterson, N. et al. 'Genetic origins of the Minoans and Mycenaeans', *Nature* 548, 214–218 (2017).
Lee, Ian. 'Entella: The Silver Coinage of the Campanian Mercenaries and the Site of the First Carthaginian Mint 410–409 BC', *The Numismatic Chronicle* (1966-), vol. 160, 2000, pp. 1–66.
Littman, R.J. 'The Plague at Syracuse: 396 BC', *Mnemosyne*, vol. 37, no. 1/2, 1984, pp. 110–16.
Livy, Titus. *Ab Urbe condita* (4 volumes), Penguin Classics, London, 2002.
López-Ruiz, Carolina. 'Gargoris and Habis: A Tartessic Myth of Ancient Iberia and the Traces of Phoenician Euhemerism', *Phoenix*, vol. 71, no. 3/4, 2017, pp. 265–87.
Manfredi, Valerio M. *I Greci d'Occidente*. Mondadori, Milan, 1996.
Manfredi, Valerio M. *Mare Greco. Eroi ed esploratori nel Mediterraneo antico*, Mondadori, Milano, 2015 (1992).
Manning, J.G. & Morris, Ian (eds.). *The Ancient Economy. Evidence and Models*, Stanford University Press, 2005.
Markoe, Glenn. 'The Emergence of Orientalizing in Greek Art: Some Observations on the Interchange between Greeks and Phoenicians in the Eighth and Seventh Centuries B.C.', *Bulletin of the American Schools of Oriental Research*, no. 301, 1996, pp. 47–67.
McEvedy, Colin & Jones, Richard. *Atlas of World Population History*, Penguin Books, Harmondsworth, 1978.
Meritt, Benjamin D. 'Athens and Carthage', *Harvard Studies in Classical Philology*, vol. 51, 1940, pp. 247–53.
Miles, Richard, *Carthage Must be Destroyed*, Penguin Books, London, 2011.
Morakis, Andreas. 'Thucydides and the Character of Greek Colonisation in Sicily', *The Classical Quarterly*, vol. 61, no. 2, 2011, pp. 460–92.
Morón, José Miguel Puebla. 'Imitation Game?: The First Mintings of Punic Sicily', *The Many Faces of Mimesis: Selected Essays from the 2017 Symposium on the Hellenic Heritage of Western Greece*, edited by Heather L. Reid & Jeremy C. DeLong, vol. 3, Parnassos Press – Fonte Aretusa, 2018, pp. 357–67.

Morris, Ian. *Why the West Rules – for now: The patterns of history and what they reveal about the future*, Profile Books, London, 2010.
Morris, A.E.J. *History of Urban Form: Before the Industrial Revolution*, Routledge, New York, 2013 (1994).
Moscati, Sabatino. *Il tramonto di Cartagine*, Società Editrice Internazionale, Torino, 1993.
Moscati, Sabatino. *Introduzione alle Guerre Puniche. Origine e Sviluppo dell'Impero di Cartagine*, Società Editrice Internazionale, Torino, 1994.
Motta, Rosa Maria. 'Myths, Coins, and Semiotics: Arethusa and Persephone on the Coins of Syracuse', *Philosopher Kings and Tragic Heroes: Essays on Images and Ideas from Western Greece*, edited by Heather L. Reid & Davide Tanasi, vol. 1, Parnassos Press – Fonte Aretusa, 2016, pp. 371–86.
Musti, Domenico. *Storia Greca. Linee di sviluppo dall'età micenea all'età romana*, Editori Laterza, Bari, 2011 (1989).
Occhipinti, Egidia. 'Greek or Barbarian? Plutarch's Portrait of the Syracusan Dēmos in the Life of Dion', *Acta Classica*, vol. 59, 2016, pp. 137–56.
Oost, Stewart Irvin. 'The Tyrant Kings of Syracuse', *Classical Philology*, vol. 71, no. 3, 1976, pp. 224–36.
Osek, Ewa. 'Ritual Imitation During the Thesmophoria at Syracuse: Timaeus of Tauromenium's History of Sicily', *The Many Faces of Mimesis: Selected Essays from the 2017 Symposium on the Hellenic Heritage of Western Greece*, edited by Heather L. Reid & Jeremy C. DeLong, vol. 3, Parnassos Press – Fonte Aretusa, 2018, pp. 279–92.
Paretti, Luigi. *Sicilia Antica*, Edizioni Palumbo, Palermo, 1959
Plato. *The Platonic Epistles: Translated with Introduction and Notes by J. Harward*, Cambridge University Press, New York, 2014 (1932).
Plutarch. *Parallel Lives, The Complete 48 biographies*, Royal Classics, Vancouver, 2021.
Polyaenus. *Stratagems of war*, Translated from the Original Greek, by R. Shepherd, F.R.S, Gale Ecco, 2018.
Polybius. *The Histories*, Oxford University Press, 2010.
Poma, Gabriella. *Le Istituzioni Politiche della Grecia in Età Classica*, Il Mulino, Bologna, 2003.
Poma, Gabriella. *Le Istituzioni Politiche del Mondo Romano*, Il Mulino, Bologna, 2009 (2002).
Rainey, Sean. *The Nature of Carthaginian Imperial Activity: Trade, Settlement, Conquest, and Rule* (PhD Thesis), University of Canterbury, 2004.
Pratolongo, Valeria. 'The Greeks and the Indigenous Populations of Eastern Sicily in the Classical Era', *Mediterranean Archaeology*, vol. 27, 2014, pp. 85–90.
Rassias, Vlasis G. *Hellenization. The contact between Hellenism and Judaism from the time of Alexander to Late Antiquity*, Ανοιχτή Πόλη, Athens, 2014.
Ridgway, David. 'Early Greek Imports in Sardinia, Greek Colonisation', *An Account of Greek Colonies and Other Settlements Overseas*, Volume One, Brill, Leiden, 2006.
Robinson, Eric. 'Democracy in Syracuse, 466–412 B.C.', *Harvard Studies in Classical Philology*, vol. 100, 2000, pp. 189–205.
Rostovtzeff, Michael I. 'The Hellenistic World and Its Economic Development', *The American Historical Review*, vol. 41, no. 2, 1936, pp. 231–52.
Russo, Lucio. *La rivoluzione dimenticata. Il pensiero scientifico greco e la scienza moderna*, Feltrinelli, Milano, 2003 (1996).
Sanders, L.J. 'Diodorus Siculus and Dionysius I of Syracuse', *Historia: Zeitschrift Für Alte Geschichte*, vol. 30, no. 4, 1981, pp. 394–411.
Sanders, Lionel J. 'Dionysius I of Syracuse and the Origins of the Ruler Cult in the Greek World', *Historia: Zeitschrift Für Alte Geschichte*, vol. 40, no. 3, 1991, pp. 275–87.

Scheidel, Walter & Von Reden, Sitta (eds.). *The Ancient Economy*, Routledge, New York, 2002.

Schmitz, Philip C. 'The Phoenician Text from the Etruscan Sanctuary at Pyrgi', *Journal of the American Oriental Society*, vol. 115, no. 4, 1995, pp. 559–75.

Schneider, Marion Theresa. 'Success Against All Odds, Failure Against All Logic: Plutarch on Dion, Timoleon, and the Liberation of Sicily', *Plato at Syracuse: Essays on Plato in Western Greece with a New Translation of the Seventh Letter by Jonah Radding*, edited by Heather L. Reid & Mark Ralkowski, vol. 5, Parnassos Press – Fonte Aretusa, 2019, pp. 105–26.

Semmler, María Eugenia Aubet & Bierling, Marilyn R. 'Notes on the Economy of the Phoenician Settlements in Southern Spain', *The Phoenicians in Spain: An Archaeological Review of the Eighth-Sixth Centuries B.C.E. – A Collection of Articles Translated from Spanish*, edited by Seymour Gitin, Penn State University Press, 2002, pp. 79–96.

Serrati, John. 'A Syracusan Private Altar and the Development of Ruler-Cult in Hellenistic Sicily', *Historia: Zeitschrift Für Alte Geschichte*, vol. 57, no. 1, 2008, pp. 80–91.

Serrati, John. Agōn Sikelia: 'The Hannibalic War and the (Re)Organization of Roman Sicily', *Conflict and Competition: Agon in Western Greece: Selected Essays from the 2019 Symposium on the Heritage of Western Greece*, edited by John Serrati et al., vol. 5, Parnassos Press – Fonte Aretusa, 2020, pp. 67–92.

Serrati, John. 'Neptune's Altars: The Treaties between Rome and Carthaga (509–226 B.C.)', *The Classical Quarterly*, vol. 56, no. 1, 2006, pp. 113–34.

Shepherd, Gillian. 'Greek "Colonisation" in Sicily and the West. Some Problems of Evidence and Interpretation Twenty-Five Years On', *Pallas*, no. 79, 2009, pp. 15–25.

Sieben, Karen. 'Plato and Diogenes in Syracuse', *Plato at Syracuse: Essays on Plato in Western Greece with a New Translation of the Seventh Letter by Jonah Radding*, edited by Heather L. Reid & Mark Ralkowski, vol. 5, Parnassos Press – Fonte Aretusa, 2019, pp. 233–46.

Sorg, Tim. 'Syracuse, City of Unwilling Immigrants: A Comparative Approach to Competitive Advantage', *Conflict and Competition: Agon in Western Greece: Selected Essays from the 2019 Symposium on the Heritage of Western Greece*, edited by Tim Sorg et al., vol. 5, Parnassos Press – Fonte Aretusa, 2020, pp. 49–66.

Stager, Jennifer M.S. 'Let No One Wonder at This Image: A Phoenician Funerary Stele in Athens', *Hesperia: The Journal of the American School of Classical Studies at Athens*, vol. 74, no. 3, 2005, pp. 427–49.

Strabo. *The Geography of Strabo* (translated by Duane W. Roller), Cambridge University Press, 2014.

Sulimani, Iris. 'Mimēsis in Diodorus Siculus: The Role of History and Sicilian Role Models', *The Many Faces of Mimesis: Selected Essays from the 2017 Symposium on the Hellenic Heritage of Western Greece*, edited by Heather L. Reid & Jeremy C. DeLong, vol. 3, Parnassos Press – Fonte Aretusa, 2018, pp. 201–14.

Thatcher, Mark. 'Syracusan Identity between Tyranny and Democracy', *Bulletin of the Institute of Classical Studies*, vol. 55, no. 2, 2012, pp. 73–90.

Treumann-Watkins, Brigette. 'Phoenicians in Spain', *The Biblical Archaeologist*, vol. 55, no. 1, 1992, pp. 29–35.

Tusa, V. 'I Cartaginesi in Sicilia all'epoca dei due Dionisi. I Cartaginesi nella Sicilia occidentale', *Kokalos*, 1982–1983, 28–29, pp. 131–49.

United States Census Bureau. 'Historical estimates of world population', https://www.census.gov/data/tables/time-series/demo/international-programs/historical-est-worldpop.html.

Urbanus, Jason. 'Masters of the Ancient Mediterranean', *Archaeology*, vol. 69, no. 3, 2016, pp. 38–43.

Urquhart, Lela M. 'Competing Traditions in the Historiography of Ancient Greek Colonization in Italy', *Journal of the History of Ideas*, vol. 75, no. 1, 2014, pp. 23–44.

van Dommelen, Peter. 'Colonialism and Migration in the Ancient Mediterranean', *Annual Review of Anthropology*, vol. 41, 2012, pp. 393–409.
Veyne, Paul. *L'Impero Greco-Romano*, Rizzoli, Milano, 2007.
Walbank, Michael B. 'Athens, Carthage and Tyre (IG Ii2 342+)', *Zeitschrift Für Papyrologie Und Epigraphik*, vol. 59, 1985, pp. 107–11.
Walt, Stephen M. *The Origins of Alliances*, Cornell University Press, 1990.
Waltz, Kenneth N. *Theory of International Politics*, Addison-Wesley, Reading, 1979.
Winter, F.E. 'The Chronology of the Euryalos Fortress at Syracuse', *American Journal of Archaeology*, vol. 67, no. 4, 1963, pp. 363–87.
Wonder, John W. 'The Italiote League: South Italian Alliances of the Fifth and Fourth Centuries BC', *Classical Antiquity*, vol. 31, no. 1, 2012, pp. 128–51.
Xenophon. *A History of My Times* (Hellenica), Penguin Classics, London, 1979.

Index

Abacaenum, 77, 105
Abdera, 5
Abolus (stream), 99
Academy (Platonic), 83, 163
Acarnania, 159
Acestorides, 104
Achaean League, 162
Acheron, 101
Achradina, 70, 95
Acrotatus, 105
Adranon, 94
Adria, 78, 80
Adriatic (Sea), 15, 78–9, 83–4, 91, 129, 132
Aegean (Sea), 38, 39, 52, 164
Aegospotami, 65
Aequi, 152
Aetolia, 159, 160
Africa, xvi, 3, 16, 17, 18, 19, 52, 75, 86, 87, 101, 109–11, 114, 116, 118, 121–5, 127–8, 130, 141, 144, 158, 163
Agamemnon, 28
Agathocles, 103–31, 135
Agelaus, 157
Agrigento, 6, 24
Agylla, 15
Agyris, 77
Aigos Rivers (Aegospotami), 65
Akragantines, 35–6, 47, 50–1, 105, 116, 122
Akragas, 6, 13, 22, 24–6, 30–2, 35–6, 38, 41, 42, 44, 46–51, 52–3, 55, 58, 99, 105–108, 122–3, 125, 136, 148, 154
Alalia, 14–15, 17–18, 34
Alcetas, 87
Alcibiades, 20, 40
Alexander (III, the Great), 32, 55, 78, 83, 100–102, 113, 120, 122, 124, 132, 140, 149, 150, 151, 155, 158–63

Alexander Molossus, 100–102, 133, 151, 158
Alexandrian Empire, 102, 133
Alykans, 68
Alykes, 65, 67, 137
Alykos River, 87, 99
Anapo River, 70
Anatolia, 164
Anaxilaus, 25–7, 30, 33
Ancona, 78
Antalcidas, 83
Antander, 109, 128
Antiochus III, 158–62
Antipater, 124
Apollo, 15, 55, 59
Appian, 162
Apulia, 134
Arcadian, 25
Archagathus, 112, 117–18, 122–4, 127, 130
Archidamus, 100
Archimedes, 22, 153
Archytas, 91, 100
Ariccia, 34
Aristomache, 63
Ariston, 161
Aristotle, 7, 21, 28, 76, 100–102
Armenia, 162
Arruns Tarquinius, 16
Asculum, 134
Asia, 2, 101–102, 156, 165
Asia Minor, xvi, 14, 16, 26, 83, 163
Assyrian Empire, 1
Assyrians, 2
Astarte, 28
Athena, 51, 112
Athenians, 19, 20, 27, 38, 40–1, 52, 62, 71, 83
Athens, 21, 22, 25, 27, 37–40, 52, 61, 83–4, 90, 146, 152–3, 163

Attica, 39
Augustus, 158
Azona, 137

Baal, 32, 114
Babylon, 113
Babylonians, 2, 3
Bactria, 152
Balearic Islands, 3, 4, 9, 108
Barcids, 154–6, 158, 161
Beneventum, 140
Bithynia, 162
Bizerte, 122
Bomilcar, 112–13, 115, 121
Braccesi Lorenzo, 28
Brizzi Giovanni, 151, 155
Bruttians, 101, 131, 133
Bruttium, 76

Cádiz, 3
Caius Cornelius Cethegus, 162
Callisthenes, 154
Cambyses II, 18
Campania, 33–4, 135
Campanians, 41, 45, 57, 62, 152
Cannae, 153, 157
Cape Bon, 3, 110
Cape Lilybaeum, 96
Caria, 16
Carthage, 1–9, 17–19, 23, 25, 26, 28–33,
    39–42, 44, 46–7, 51–2, 59, 61, 63–8, 70,
    75–6, 78, 84–93, 95–6, 102–12, 114–15,
    118, 120–31, 134–5, 137–9, 141–50,
    152–62, 166
Carthaginians, xv, 1–3, 8–10, 13, 15–19,
    23, 27–8, 30–3, 35, 41, 43–52, 55–60,
    62, 64–78, 85–90, 93, 95–9, 103–10,
    112–21, 123–30, 134–7, 139, 141–3,
    145–9, 151, 153–5, 157–8, 161, 165
Cassander, 129
Catania, 41, 42, 62, 69, 70, 94–5, 99
Catanzaro, 87
Caulonia, 80–2
Caulonians, 82
Cefalù, 123
Celts, 125
Centoripa, 123
Cephalus, 22

Cere, 15
Chalcis, 159
China, 152
Chinese, 165
Cinyps (river), 18
Cnidus, 16
Corax, 37
Corfu, 129
Corinth, 152, 162
Corinthians, 75, 92
Corsica, 3, 14–19, 85, 144
Crete, 162, 164–5
Crimissus, 91, 96–7, 103, 106, 153
Cronium, 86
Croton, 13, 18, 22, 79–82, 87, 129, 158
Crotonians, 19
Cumae, 13, 33–5, 56
Cumaens, 34–5
Cyane, 72
Cyllyrians (Killirioi), 24
Cyprus, 13
Cyrenaica, 18, 120
Cyrene, 17–18, 120
Cyreneans, 17–18
Cyrus II, 14

Danube, xvi
Daphnaeus, 48, 50–1, 53, 55
Dascon, 70, 72–3
Deinarchus, 96
Deinomenids, 37–8, 56
Delphi, 11–12, 15, 32, 35, 96
    Oracle of, 11, 15, 96
Demaratus, 16
Demaretus, 96
Demeter, 32, 70–1, 75, 110
Demetrius, 121, 129
Demophilus, 122
Dexippus, 47, 54
Diamond Jared, 164
Dikaiopolis, 128
Dinocrates, 107, 123, 128–9
Diocles, 43, 45
Diodorus, 36, 47, 63, 71–4, 88, 96–8,
    109–10, 114, 126
Dion, 91–2
Dionysius I (the Elder), 52–9, 61–92, 94,
    104, 105, 129, 131, 136, 142
Dionysius II, 91–4

Dionysus, 90
Dorians, 17
Dorieus, 18–19, 27–8
Doris, 63

Ebro, 155
Ebusus (Ibiza), 4
Ecnomus, 108
Egypt, 15, 18, 120, 130, 164
Elba, 85
Elea, 18, 22
Eleatics, 163
Elleporus, 80–1
Elymians, 5, 16, 19, 38–9, 59
Empedocles, 22, 46
Emporion, 14, 85
Enna, 77, 116
Entella, 65, 67, 88, 93, 96–7
Epaminondas, 155
Ephesus, 162
Epicureanism, 163
Epikydes, 153
Epipolae, 93
Epirus, 78, 87, 100–101, 132–4, 136–8, 140
Erbessus, 116
Eshmuniaton (Suniatus), 89
Etna, 59, 61–2, 69
Etruria, 15–16, 34, 108
Etruscans, 15–16, 18–19, 33–5, 85, 124–5, 143, 151–2
Eubulides, 159
Eumachus, 123
Eumenes, 154
Europe, 3, 14, 141, 156
Euryalus, 62, 115–16

Falarion, 108
Felsina (Bologna), 15
Fertile Crescent, 164
Filon, 159
Finley Moses, 30
Flamininus Titus Quinctius, 162
France, 14
Frontinus, 110

Gadeira, 3–5
Galeria, 107
Gamoroi, 24

Gaugamela, 101, 113
Gaul, xvi, 14, 18, 163, 165
Gauls, 9, 14, 78, 82, 151
Gela, 6, 13, 24, 25, 26, 30, 33, 38, 39, 41, 47, 51–8, 99, 105, 106, 108, 116, 122, 125
Geloans, 55–7
Gelon, 24–8, 30–3, 35, 37, 48, 56, 61, 70, 82, 104
Gibraltar, 3
Gisco, 40
Greece, 10, 14, 22, 25, 27–8, 32–3, 35–6, 38–9, 61, 82–3, 87, 100, 124, 135, 140, 142, 148, 153, 158, 162–4
  Western, 32, 83, 142, 148
Greeks, xv, xvi, 1, 4–6, 9–11, 13–18, 20–3, 26–8, 30–1, 33–8, 41, 43–53, 56–7, 59, 60, 62–71, 75–6, 78–81, 83–4, 86, 94–8, 100–102, 106, 108, 112–16, 118–20, 122–6, 128, 130–1, 133–9, 141–3, 146–8, 150–3, 156–8, 161, 163, 165
  Italian, 35, 56–7, 63, 68, 78–81, 95, 101, 131, 141, 143, 151–2, 156–7
  Sicilian, 22, 30, 38, 46, 56–7, 64, 67, 70, 76, 94, 100, 115, 118, 134, 136–8, 142, 152–3
  Western, xvi, 20, 23, 102, 131, 141, 145, 148, 150, 152, 157–8, 163

Hamilcar (4th century BCE), 103–106, 108, 114–16, 154–5
Hamilcar Mago (5th century BCE), 30, 32, 40, 44
Hannibal Barca, 140, 144, 148, 152–63, 166
Hannibal Mago, 40–7
Hanno, 89–90, 92–3, 112–13
Helepolis, 121
Hellenism, 35, 91, 102, 143, 150–2, 156, 158
Heloris, 80–1
Helorus, 24
Helots, 24
Hera Lacinia, 158
Heraclea Minoa, 31, 101, 106, 123, 133, 137
Heraclides, 127
Herbessos, 61
Hercules, 3, 158

Hermocrates, 39, 44–5, 53, 55
Herodotus, 23, 27–8
Hicetas, 92–5, 99
Hieron, 25, 33, 35–7, 56
Hieron II, 143, 153
Hieronymus, 153
Himera, 13, 19, 24, 26, 29–33, 35, 37–40, 42–5, 47, 48, 51, 53, 56, 58, 64, 70, 77, 106, 148
Himerians, 66
Himilco, 45–6, 48–53, 58, 59, 62, 65–9, 70, 74, 75
Himilco Mago, 86
Hippo, 99
Hippo Diarrhytus (Bizerte), 122
Hippocrates, 24, 26
Hippokrates, 153
Hipponians, 82
Hipponio, 82
Homer, 23

Iberia/Iberian Peninsula, 3–5, 14–17, 19, 29, 152, 154–5, 163
Iberians, 41, 45, 47, 57, 64
Ilithyia, 85
Illyria, 157
India, 152
Ionia, 14
Ionians, 64, 163
Iraq, 164
Ischia, 11
Isocrates, 9
Italians, 48–9, 156
Italics, 133
Italy, xvi, 13–16, 18, 22–3, 25–6, 33, 35, 38, 46, 48, 51, 53–4, 63, 70, 77–9, 82–5, 87, 91, 95, 100–102, 107, 129–33, 135–7, 139–45, 151–2, 156–9, 163–5

Julius, 158

Kamarina, 24–5, 38–9, 58–9, 116, 122
Kephaloídion (Cefalù), 123
Killirioi, 24
Kore, 75

Lars Porsenna, 34
Latins, 34, 131, 152

Latium, 33–4, 134
Lenaia, 90
Leontini, 38, 41–2, 62, 76, 92, 99, 116, 122
Leptines, 67–9, 71–2, 79, 85–6, 122
Libya, 9, 17–18, 64, 108
Libyans, 18, 41, 45, 47, 71, 77, 87, 93, 125–6
Ligurians, 14
Lilybaeum, 16, 88–9, 96, 98, 137–8
Lion, 14
Lisbon, 16
Livy, 162
Lixus, 3
Locri, 38, 63, 76, 80, 82, 91–2, 135, 139
Locrians, 81
Locris, 13
Lucanians, 78–9, 100–101, 131, 133, 151
Lucius Tarquinius Priscus, 16
Lysander, 65
Lysias, 22

Macedonia, 78, 83, 100, 129, 152, 156, 160, 162
Macedonians, 32, 153, 161
Magna Graecia, 151, 157
Mago (admiral), 69–70, 77, 83
Mago (345 BCE), 93, 95
Mago (3rd century BCE), 134–5
Mago II, 86
Magonids, 89
Malaca (Malaga), 5
Malchus, 17
Mamercus, 94, 99
Mamertines, 135–6, 139, 143
Marcus Atilius Regulus, 154
Marcus Minucius Rufus, 162
Massalia, 14–15, 17–18, 34, 85, 141
Massalians, 17
Mediterranean (Sea), xv, xvi, 2, 3, 4, 5, 12–14, 22, 24, 39, 46, 82, 84–5, 118, 147, 149, 150, 156, 164–6
    Eastern, xv, 150, 156, 164
    Western, xv, 1–6, 9, 11, 13–14, 17, 23, 25, 35, 85, 87, 100–102, 120–1, 131–2, 141–5, 148, 150, 165
Medma, 76
Megalopolis, 111
Megara, 13, 36

Megara Hyblaea, 13, 31
Melqart, 114, 158
Menaenum, 77
Messapians, 35, 100, 101, 133
Messene, 6, 26, 30, 38, 61, 63, 68–9, 76–7, 80, 99, 105–107, 135–6, 139, 143
Messenians, 26, 68–9
Metapontium, 13
Milazzo (Mylae), 105
Milesians, 26
Mnasilochus, 159
Morgantina, 39, 77
Morris, Ian, 164
Moscati, 150
Motya, 6, 16, 31, 41, 43, 45, 50, 63–8
Motyans, 65
Mycenaeans, 16, 164
Mylae (Milazzo), 105

Nafpaktos, 157
Naples (Bay), 11
Naucratis, 15
Naxos, 24, 38, 41–2, 62, 69
Neapolis, 1
Nicias, 38, 40
Nora, 149
Numidia, 9, 120, 123
Numidians, 45, 93, 118–19

Odysseus, 16
Olbia, 14
Olympia, 32, 35
Olympiaeum, 70, 74
Olympias, 101
Ophellas, 120–1
Ortygia, 61–2, 70, 93–4, 128, 136

Palermo (Panormos), 6
Pandosia, 101
Panhellenic, 67
Panormos, 6, 148–9
Panormus, 29, 45, 50, 64–5, 68, 86, 129, 137
Parmenides, 22
Parmenion, 124
Pasiphilus, 107, 129
Peloponnese, 26, 39, 54, 95
Peloponnesians, 18–19, 76
Pentapolis, 17

Pentathlos, 16
Pericles, 22, 38, 40
Persephone, 32, 70, 110
Persia, 28
Persian Empire, xv, 9, 78, 83, 101
Persians, 18, 26–7, 35, 83
Peucetians, 35, 101
Pharacidas, 70–2
Philinus, 154
Philip II, 78, 83, 155, 159–60
Philip V, 152, 157, 162
Philistus, 55, 62, 79, 84–5
Phocaeans, 14
Phoenicia, xv, 1, 2, 5, 8, 12
Phoenicians, xv, xvi, 1–6, 9, 11, 13–16, 20, 23, 34, 98, 165
Pillars of Hercules (Gibraltar), 3
Pithecusa, 11
Plato, 83–4, 91
Platonism, 83
Plautus Titus Maccius, 124
Plemmyrium, 70, 74
Plutarch, 92, 96, 134
Polichni, 70, 73
Polybius, 19, 28, 114, 154, 158, 162
Polyxenidas, 159
Pompeius Trogus, 14
Portugal, 16
Poseidon, 98
Poseidonia, 13
Priscus, 16
Proxenus, 154
Prusias, 162
Ptolemaic Egypt, 120
Ptolemaic Empire, 120
Ptolemeus, 154
Ptolemies, 120
Ptolemy Keraunos, 135
Publius Decius Mus, 134
Publius Valerius Laevinus, 133
Pydna, 162
Pyrgi, 28, 85
Pyrrhus, 131–42, 152, 154, 158, 162
Pythagoras, 22

Rhegians, 81
Rhegio, 13, 18, 25–6, 30, 33, 38, 61, 63, 77, 79, 81, 83, 93, 104, 135, 139
Rhodes, 16

Roman Empire, 152, 164
Roman Federation, 141, 143, 157
Roman Republic, 34
Romans, 19, 32, 34, 44, 101, 131, 133–5, 139, 141–2, 144, 146–8, 151–8, 161–2
Rome, xv, 6, 8, 12, 16, 19, 25, 28, 34, 82, 84, 101–102, 125, 131–5, 137, 140–7, 150–4, 156–62, 166

Sabines, 152
Salamis, 32
Samians, 26
Samnites, 101, 125, 131
Samnium, 132, 134
Santorini (Thera), 17
Sardinia, 3, 14–15, 17, 29, 70, 77, 85, 144, 149–50
Sardinians, 77, 87
Scipio (Publius Cornelius), 140, 144, 158, 162–3
Scipio Aemilianus, 154, 162
Scipios, 151
Segesta, 16, 38, 40–1, 65, 67–8, 97, 127–8, 137, 148
Segestians, 128
Seleucid Empire, 152, 159–60, 162
Seleucids, 120
Selinunteans, 16, 31, 40–1, 66
Selinus, 13, 16, 30–1, 38, 40–5, 53, 58, 62, 64, 86–8, 106, 123, 137, 148
Senate (Carthaginian), 6–9, 40, 46, 64, 86, 106, 114, 155, 158
Senate (Roman), 132, 134, 144, 147, 152
Sennacherib, 2
Sicani, 5, 19, 42, 59, 65, 68, 96
Sicels, 38, 42, 67, 77, 94, 96, 116
Sicilians, 5, 39, 48–9, 116, 131, 138–9
Sicily, 4–6, 13, 16–22, 24–7, 29–33, 35, 37–41, 44–8, 50–4, 58–60, 62–5, 67–8, 70, 75–8, 82–96, 98–100, 103, 105, 106, 108–10, 114–16, 120–3, 125–31, 134–9, 141–5, 148, 151–2, 154, 156, 158, 163
Siculi, 5
Sidon, 1
Solunto, 65
Solus, 6, 65, 77
Sosistratus, 136, 139
Sosylus, 154

Spain, xvi, 3–5, 144, 154–5
Spanish, 9
Sparta, 18, 24, 38–9, 61, 68, 76, 83, 87, 100, 105, 140, 146, 154
Spartans, 27–8, 38, 83, 87, 100, 105
Spina, 15
Stoicism, 163
Strabo, 16, 100
Sulcis, 149
Suniatus (Eshmuniaton), 89
Sybaris, 13, 18
Syracusans, 24, 28, 31, 36–8, 40–2, 46, 48–50, 52–4, 56, 62–3, 68, 71, 73–4, 79, 82, 85–6, 92, 100, 107–108, 111–12, 114–16, 119, 123, 126–7, 131, 136, 138, 143–4
Syracuse, 6, 13, 20, 22, 24–7, 29–32, 35–41, 43–5, 47–8, 50–6, 58–9, 61–5, 67–71, 73–5, 77–85, 87–96, 98–9, 103–11, 114–17, 119, 121, 123–5, 127–32, 134–6, 139, 142–5, 148, 153

Taormina (Tauromenio), 93, 107, 136
Tarantines, 35, 100–102, 105, 131–4, 158
Taras, 25, 35, 91, 100, 102, 105, 131–3, 139, 141–3, 158
Tarquinia, 15
Tauromenio (Taormina), 107
Tellias, 51
Terillus, 26
Tharros, 149
Thearides, 80
Thebes, 83, 87
Theonon, 136, 139
Thermae Himerenses, 106, 123
Thermae Selinuntinae, 86
Theron, 24, 26, 30–1, 35, 48
Thoas, 159
Thrasius, 96–7
Thrasybulus, 37
Thrasydeus, 35–6
Thucydides, 20
Thurians, 79, 131
Thurii, 78–9, 82, 95, 131–2
Timaeus, 1, 47
Timoleon, 91–100, 103–105, 142
Tisias, 37
Trasimene, 156

Trebia, 156
Trogus, 14, 101
Tunis, 9, 111, 118, 124
Tyndaris, 76, 94
Tyre, 1–4, 55, 114, 161
Tyrrhenian (Sea), 15–17, 34–5, 83, 85, 87–8, 91, 141

US, 156
USSR, 156
Ustica, 88
Utica, 3, 6, 109, 121–2
Uticans, 121

Venice, 78
Volsci, 152

Xanthippus, 154–5
Xenodocus, 125
Xenophanes, 22
Xenophon, 113
Xerxes, 27

Zama, 144
Zancle (Messene), 13, 24–6
Zeno, 22

Dear Reader,

We hope you have enjoyed this book, but why not share your views on social media? You can also follow our pages to see more about our other products: facebook.com/penandswordbooks or follow us on X @penswordbooks

You can also view our products at www.pen-and-sword.co.uk (UK and ROW) or www.penandswordbooks.com (North America).

To keep up to date with our latest releases and online catalogues, please sign up to our newsletter at: www.pen-and-sword.co.uk/newsletter

If you would like a printed catalogue with our latest books, then please email: enquiries@pen-and-sword.co.uk or telephone: 01226 734555 (UK and ROW) or email: uspen-and-sword@casematepublishers.com or telephone: (610) 853-9131 (North America).

We respect your privacy and we will only use personal information to send you information about our products.

Thank you!